Children of Perdition

Melungeons
and the Struggle
of Mixed America

D1127964

MERCER
UNIVERSITY PRESS

Endowed by
TOM WATSON BROWN
and
THE WATSON-BROWN FOUNDATION, INC.

Children of Perdition

Melungeons
and the Struggle
of Mixed America

by
Tim Hashaw

Mercer University Press
Macon, Georgia

ISBN 0-88146-074-5   MUP/P340

Children of Perdition.
Melungeons and the Struggle of Mixed America.
Copyright ©2006
Mercer University Press, Macon, Georgia USA
All rights reserved
Printed in the United States of America
First edition, March 2006
First paperback edition, April 2007

The paper used in this publication meets the minimum requirements
of American National Standard for Information Sciences—
Permanence of Paper for Printed Library Materials,
ANSI Z39.48-1984. ∞

Library of Congress Cataloging-in-Publication Data

Hashaw, Tim, 1954-
Children of perdition : Melungeons and the struggle of mixed America
    / Tim Hashaw. — 1st ed.
    p. cm.
Includes bibliographical references and index.
ISBN-13: 978-0-88146-013-1 (hardback : alk. paper)
ISBN-10: 0-88146-013-3 (hardback : alk. paper)
ISBN-0-88146-074-5 (paperback : alk. paper)
1. Melungeons — History. 2. Melungeons — Race identity. 3. Melun-
geons — Genealogy. 4. Racism — United States — History. 5. United
States — Race relations — History. I. Title.
E184.M44H37 2006
973'.040509073--dc22   2006001474

Contents

Publisher's Note

Children of Perdition is in the series "The Melungeons: History, Culture, Ethnicity, & Literature." N. Brent Kennedy, founder of the Melungeon Research Committee, is founding editor of this series. Brent routinely proposes and/or approves monographs to be included in the Melungeon series. Originally he approved this monograph for inclusion in the series. However, during the process of preparing the manuscript for publication, Brent was struck down by a massive stroke and as we go to pages is still in serious condition and unable to read proof or write his usual editor's foreword. Hence we go to press without the series editor's reading of the press pages and without his foreword.

All of us at Mercer University Press and all those associated with the Melungeon series wish for Brent a speedy and full recovery and look forward to his sterling advice and consent in this ongoing series.

* * * * *

Preface

Melungeons have been a source of mystery and curiosity for Americans for almost 200 years and that interest is reflected in a long list of books, studies, bulletins, articles, and, recently, television documentaries.

What does this book then offer on the subject? Much of the attention in the past has focused on sensational theories of Melungeon origins, ignoring evidence that the Melungeon "mystery" was a diversion to conceal African ancestry during slavery and Jim Crow. The "origin myth" was to the Melungeon seeking full American citizenship what the Underground Railroad was to the slave seeking freedom.

There is no intent here to debunk. Rather, myths are interpreted to reveal the struggle of mixed Americans through four centuries of apartheid. This is not a general history of the Melungeons and related communities but a history of how Americans have traditionally reacted to race mixing as documented in the struggles of historic mixed communities.

Melungeons are uniquely qualified to chronicle the development of the country's views on race and mixing. At least two Melungeon ancestors were among the "20 and odd" Africans delivered to Jamestown, Virginia in 1619 by a pirate ship called the *White Lion*, sixteen months before the *Mayflower* arrived with the Pilgrims at Plymouth Bay Colony. One of these Africans was a woman named Margaret Cornish who voluntarily began a relationship with a gentleman named Robert Sweet—son of a member of the Virginia Burgesses—and who produced three mixed children by him. In 1639 the Virginia court required that Sweet do penance in public. Margaret was publicly whipped. Prior to this incident Margaret Cornish had given birth to two sons by a black man named John Gowen. The families of Gowen, Sweet, and Cornish were founders of many mixed communities that survive today. Gowen (aka Gowan, Goins, Goings) is the most common surname among Melungeons and other mixed communities.

The earliest American laws and views on "mixing" mostly were formed in context with these mixed "malungu" communities in the old colonial region of British North America—mixed communities which continue to thrive around the early power centers of American government such as Philadelphia, New York, and Washington.

Melungeon history details how American race attitudes evolved from the very first English-speaking generation of the early 1600s, and why we react to race mixing as we do today.

Part one

Melungia

Chapter 1

A Mysterious People

The biologists may have seemed out of place at the Appalachian folk gathering, but they had been invited to come up from the University of Virginia to report on a two-year DNA investigation into an early American mystery—a people of unknown origin called "Melungeons."

Melungeons have lived in the mountains so long that no one remembers where they came from. Early accounts said the first Melungeons were "dark-skinned devils with blue eyes." Shunned by black folks and white folks alike, they were tricksters, "children of perdition"—the unholy off-spring of the devil and a Cherokee woman in Tennessee—rowdy hellions so mean they drove ole Scratch back to hell and his lawful wife.

Curious about their true origin, more than 100 Melungeons offered DNA samples to the university. After months of lab work, the biologists were ready to reveal their findings. Hundreds gathered in Kingsport, Tennessee to learn if the biologists could confirm wild tales that they descended from Portuguese pirates, the lost colony of Roanoke, King Arthur, or Templar knights. Reporters crossed the mountains hoping to report the old Melungeon mystery was finally solved and the AP wire service waited to flash the news nationwide.

But when the biologists stood to speak, they stunned their audience: Melungeon DNA, they reported, appeared identical to that of their non-Melungeon neighbors. This was puzzling. Why then had early Melungeons been banned from voting, from attending white schools and white churches? Why the tales of winged, six-fingered Melungeon ogres swooping down to carry off disobedient children? Why the folklore of a "Briga-doon-like" village lost in the mountains with bewitching Melungeon beauties and flint-eyed men with guns as long as garden hoes guarding lost silver mines "long before the white man came?"

It was a mystery twenty-first-century science said it could not solve. But biologists did confirm one rumor about Melungeons: mitochondrial DNA showed that Melungeon women long ago were overwhelmingly

Northern European in ethnicity. This supported a description of Melungeon ancestors in 1730 as "free Negroes with white wives."[1]

---

[1]Several Melungeon ancestors named Gibson, and others, all black men with white wives, moved in a group from Tidewater Virginia to North Carolina in 1730. Local whites became alarmed and notified members of the South Carolina legislature. "They came to the attention of the South Carolina Commons House of Assembly in 1731 when a member announced in chamber that several 'free colored men with their white wives' had immigrated from Virginia with the intention of settling on the Santee River." Winthrop D. Jordan, *White over Black: American Attitudes toward the Negro, 1550–1812* (Chapel Hill: University of North Carolina Press, 1968) 171.

Governor Robert Johnson of South Carolina summoned Gideon Gibson and his family to explain their presence there and after meeting them reported, "I have in Consideration of his Wifes being a white woman and several White women Capable of working and being Serviceable in the Country permitted him to Settle in this Country." Box 2, bundle: S.C., Minutes of House of Burgesses (1730–1735), 9, Parish Transcripts, N.Y. Hist. Soc., cited by Jordan, *White over Black*, 172.

Paul Heinegg, *Free African Americans of North Carolina, Virginia, and South Carolina from the Colonial Period to about 1820*, 4th and rev. ed. (Baltimore: Genealogical Publishing Co. & Clearfield Co., 2001): see under "Gibson."

Similarly, the related Ashworths who moved from the Carolinas to Texas in the early 1800s, were resented by their white neighbors for having white wives. In the 1890s, in Tennessee, Will Allen Dromgoole also observed white Melungeon women nursing black babies. Earlier, in 1849, an anonymous writer had noted the first Melungeons in Hancock County:

> These intermixed with the Indians, and subsequently their descendants (after the first advances of the whites into this part of the state) with the negroes and the whites, thus forming the present race of Melungens [*sic*]. They are tall, straight, well-formed people, of a dark copper color, with Circassian features, but wooly heads and other similar appendages of our negro.

Anonymous, "The Melungens [*sic*]," *Littell's Living Age* 20/254 (31 March 1849): 618-19, quotation from 618. (*Living Age* apparently reprinted this "article" [or letter to the editor?] from the *Knoxville Register* of 6 September 1848.)

Interview in *O Jornal* (newspaper of record for the Portuguese-American community in the Northeast of the United States) with Dr. Kevin Jones, a biologist at the University of Virginia's College at Wise: "About 100 hair samples were studied for mitochondrial, or maternal, DNA, and about 30 samples of cheek cells were taken to study the Y-chromosome, or male, DNA." The technology available to Jones allowed him to study only the mitochondrial DNA samples; the Y-chromosome samples were sent to University College in London, England, for study. While the Melungeons are predominantly European in their genetic backgrounds, they are indeed triracial. "There appears to be a small percentage of both Native American and African-American sequences in there, too," Jones stated. "Although they are certainly both in the minority. They're both in there in about equal levels of representation as well. . . . With regard to the male lineage's investigated, the Y chromosome data also suggests a multiracial origin, including Sub-Saharan African and European components." "Melungeon DNA tests raise more questions" <ojornal.com/engl/Pages/7-24-02/

Was it true then? Had black men married white women in the heart of the American South during the harshest period of slavery? Unfortunately, mitochondrial DNA does not reveal the race of the male ancestor. The women were white, but who were their husbands? Having cracked open the door to the mystery, the biologists left the Melungeons to recover a lost chapter of American history.

Melungeons Discovered

First recorded in Southern Appalachia 200 years ago, the existence of Melungeons was not widely known outside eastern Tennessee until a woman set out to find them in 1889. This budding Knoxville writer with the unusual masculine name of Will Allen Dromgoole had heard ghost stories of flying Melungeon ogres as a child, but when she heard the name again as an adult she was astonished that the fantasy characters of her childhood might be real. Dromgoole immediately began questioning state historians. Some flatly dismissed Melungeons as myth. Others said they knew of Melungeons but warned that they were a violent renegade race of ridge raiders and begged her to arm herself if she planned to go among them.[2]

After months of interviews, Dromgoole had nothing else to go on. Then one day while visiting the state capitol, she overheard a senator describe a colleague as "tricky as a Malungeon."

Asked she, "Senator, what is a Malungeon?"

Said he, "A dirty Indian sneak."

He pointed her to another senator. She went at once and again asked, "Senator, what is a Malungeon?"

The second senator answered, "A Portuguese nigger."[3]

---

art4.htm>.

While those tested were triracial, mostly European, with a lesser percentage of African and American Indian DNA, a small number of participants tested had additional DNA similar to an Indian-African group, and a few others were completely anomalous. "Among the Y chromosomes, a few were completely inexplicable. When Jones searched a database of European populations at University College London, the samples matched none of the 4,500 entries. . . . " Kathleen McGowan, "Where Do We Really Come From?" *Discover* 24/5 (May 2003).

[2]Will Allen Dromgoole, "Land of the Malungeons," *Nashville Sunday American*, 31 August 1890, 10; see also Dromgoole, "The Malungeons," *The Arena* 3/3 (March 1891): 470-79.

[3]Dromgoole, "Land of the Malungeons."

Two different answers from two Tennessee legislators only heightened the mystery.

One thing however was clear—Melungeons did not represent anything positive to these white men and they were not alone in their disdain. The children of black slaves loathed the Melungeon and relegated him to the basement of Southern society as

> the most pathetic figure in North Carolina prior to the Civil War. Hedged about with social and legal restrictions, he ever remained an anomaly in the social and political life of the State. The origin of this class of people may be attributed to many sources . . . cohabitation of white women and negro men, intermarriage of blacks and whites, manumission, military service in the Revolution, and immigration from adjoining States. . . . The group still bears the appellation "old issue" and are heartily detested by the well-to-do Negroes in the adjoining counties.[4]

At the time Will Allen Dromgoole knew nothing of tales of white women and black men. In the late 1800s, such a scandal was horrible to imagine, much less to speak of in mixed company. She was only aware of a curious rumor that Melungeons were descendants of some forgotten lost colony, perhaps Portuguese, perhaps pre-Columbian.

Dromgoole persisted and eventually narrowed the search by locating a legislator whose district included some Melungeon communities. At first, he was hardly more helpful than previous sources: "And into the House of Representatives I went, fast upon the lost trail of the forgotten Malungeons." She asked, "please tell me what is a Malungeon?"

"A Malungeon," said he, "isn't a nigger, and he isn't an Indian, and he isn't a white man. God only knows what he is. I should call him a Democrat, only he always votes the Republican ticket."[5]

But then he added something she did not know: the Melungeons still haunted the wild regions of the Clinch Mountains—or simply "the Clinch"—where moonshine and feuds had simmered for ages, where four state borders converged and disappeared among nameless ridges and valleys to create an infamous no-man's-land called "Melungia."[6]

---

[4]Rosser Howard Taylor, *The Free Negro in North Carolina* (Chapel Hill: University of North Carolina, 1920).

[5]Dromgoole, "The Malungeons."

[6]Dromgoole, "Land of the Malungeons."

With a location at last, this single, white, newspaper reporter Will Allen Dromgoole hired a guide and an artist and set out on an adventure to the Clinch and a place ironically known as Newman's Ridge. Melungia would be forever changed by her visit.

Hunter's Trail

The bits and pieces Dromgoole had picked up promised an exciting story. Some said Melungeons were living in the Clinch before whites arrived in Eastern Tennessee, before Daniel Boone, perhaps even before Columbus.

As a matter of record, however, the occasion that brought Melungeons to Appalachia was the French and Indian War of 1754–1763.[7] This conflict pitted Britain and her American colonies against the French for control of lands between Appalachia and the Mississippi, and ended when France and Spain traded territory to Britain.[8]

Land-hungry American colonists east of Appalachia were packing to move to the new territory when King George III of England abruptly announced a scheme known as the "Proclamation of 1763." The mass migration halted in its tracks.[9] George proclaimed that lands west of the Appalachian range were exclusive hunting grounds for Indians living there. The king retained exclusive rights to the territory. Americans would voice their complaint in the Declaration of Independence a few years later.[10]

King George fenced colonists between the Appalachian range and the Atlantic coast, an area stretching from Maine to Florida, and as wide as the present state of Virginia. British soldiers burned homes in the new territory and escorted settlers out at bayonet point.[11]

However, hunters, traders, and some land speculators ignored the royal proclamation and continued crossing the mountains in small parties to explore the rugged region. With the exception of these small exploratory

---

[7]John M. Murrin, "French and Indian War (1754–1763)," *Encyclopedia of American History* (Guilford CT: Dushkin Publishing Group, 1973).

[8]Murrin, "French and Indian War."

[9]Samuel Eliot Morison, *Sources and Documents Illustrating the American Revolution, 1764–1788 and the Formation of the Federal Constitution*, 2nd ed. (New York: Oxford University Press, 1965).

[10]Bernard Bailyn, *The Ideological Origins of the American Revolution* (Cambridge MA: Harvard University Press, 1992).

[11]Alan Rogers, *Empire and Liberty: American Resistance to British Authority* (Berkeley: University of California Press, 1974).

parties, few settlers dared to follow; not only because of King George's proclamation, but because wagons could not cross the terrain. That was about to change. While trading with Shawnee Indians in present-day Kentucky, Long Hunter John Findley heard of a gap through the rugged Appalachians.[12] He told Daniel Boone of North Carolina about the passage.[13] In 1769, following an ancient buffalo trace known as the Hunter's Trail, Boone, Findley, and James Mooney set out to explore the Cumberland Gap and the nearby ridges of the Clinch. The Boone journal:

> On the first day of May, 1769, started from Boone's on the Head of Yadkin . . . course westwardly . . . across the valley to Moccasin Gap in the Clinch Mountain . . . continued westwardly crossing Walden's Ridge and Powell Mountain into Powell's Valley, then down the Valley leaving Cumberland Mount but a little to their right, so on to Cumberland Gap.[14]

This was the region later known as Melungia, but in 1769 it was completely empty.[15] Boone's expedition recorded absolutely no one living there at the time—no Indians, no Melungeons. The tameness of the deer convinced them that very few Cherokees even hunted there. In 1769, the Clinch was ghostly silent.

That stillness did not last. Daniel Boone spread the word about Cumberland Gap, and westward migration began as the last muskets were fired at Yorktown. In 1780, the first settlers from North Carolina and Virginia began clearing homesteads at Walden's Ridge, Moccasin Gap, and Powell Mountain around the Clinch. And among the first Easterners through Cumberland were the mysterious settlers of color known as the Melungeons. Lewis Jarvis who knew the first Melungeons, said, "I have given their stations and stops on their way as they emigrated to this country with white people. When Daniel Boone was here hunting 1763–1767, these Melungeons were not here."[16]

---

[12]Lyman C. Draper, *The Life of Daniel Boone*, ed. Ted Franklin Belue (Mechanicsburg PA: Stackpole Books, September 1998).

[13]Emory L. Hamilton, "The Long Hunter," *The Mountain Empire Genealogical Quarterly* (Spring 1984).

[14]Daniel Bryan, "The Life of Daniel Boone," Draper manuscript. See also Draper, *The Life of Daniel Boone*, 208-11.

[15]Emory L. Hamilton, "The Boone Trail," *Historical Sketches of Southwest Virginia*, Historical Society of Southwest Virginia (December 1978) online: <http://www.rootsweb.com/~vawise2/sketches/HSpubl70.html>.

[16]Plecker-Moore letters, August 1942, Tennessee State Library and Archives, Research

Although Daniel Boone found no Melungeons living on the Clinch in the 1760s, he knew Melungeons. He knew them back east in North Carolina. One was his friend Jordan Gibson.[17] However, Gibson was no mysterious pre-Columbian "lost colonist." In 1770 Gibson was a duly recorded British subject and Carolina farmer who accompanied Daniel and his brother Squire Boone on several Appalachian expeditions.[18] In fact, Gibson's son Jim later lived in Daniel Boone's home in Kentucky and in Missouri.[19]

Because Melungeons were among the first to pass through the Cumberland Gap they claimed the first available land around the Gap where Dromgoole found their descendants a century later. Late-eighteenth-century land documents identify Melungeons as Revolution-era pioneering patriots from old colonial America, not as lost colonists.

The Name

Melungeons did not come to Southern Appalachia in a single group or as a tribe of Indians as Lewis Jarvis declared. They came from different parts of Virginia and the Carolinas in the early days of the United States over a period of about thirty years.

How did they come to America? Their ancestors suddenly appeared in Tidewater Virginia nearly two centuries earlier. Thomas Goin for example, was one of the first Melungeons in the Appalachians in the 1780s. His ancestor John Gowen arrived in old Jamestown on a mysterious pirate ship in 1619—one year before the *Mayflower*.

Thomas Goin was a patriot "of color," a veteran of the American Revolution when his claim was recorded in Hawkins County, Tennessee in 1788.[20] Others followed and five years later while surveying the frontier,

---

Department, 403 Seventh Avenue North, Nashville TN.

[17]Heinegg, *Free African Americans of North Carolina, Virginia, and South Carolina.* See also "Map of Davie County, N. Carolina Showing Original Land Grants, Map by Andrew Lagle, 1976, Deed Research by Pink Tatum," subsection of "Daniel Boone. The Extraordinary Life of a Common Man," and online at <http://www.mpcps.org/boone.misc/yadkin-main.shtml>. See also "Census of 1830 Records 331 FPC In Hawkins County, Tennessee," compiled by Phillip Edwin Roberts, *Gowen Research Foundation Newsletter* (April 1997).

[18]Alexander Gregg, *History of the Old Cheraws* (New York: Richardson and Co., 1867).

[19]Gregg, *History of the Old Cheraws.*

[20]Thomas Goin was a private in the militia company of Capt. Turner Bynum of Greensville County, North Carolina. See: "Roll of Captain Bynum's Company of Militia,

Tennessee's first governor, John Sevier, spent the night with a Melungeon family on Black Water Creek in Hawkins County.[21]

In 1810 the name "Melungeon" was used when Jacob Mooney drove Tennessee cattle to the Ozarks:

> The four men who had come with Mooney were men of mystery, referred to by old-timers who knew of them as 'Lungeons. They were neither Negro nor Indian and in later years Jacob Mooney was ostracized for living with these "foreigners." By the time he moved to Arkansas for good, his former slaves and the 'Lungeon men had died and most of their families had moved west with the Indians.[22]

Mooney may have been related to the James Mooney who explored the Cumberland Gap with Boone.[23]

Three years later, another reference to Melungeons was recorded at an early frontier church near Fort Blackmore in Scott County, Virginia. The minutes of the Stony Creek Baptist Church for September 26, 1813, noted that a white church member, Sook Kitchen, complained when another sister, Susanna Stallard, said she "harbored them Melungins."[24]

The minutes did not elaborate on the implied iniquity of harboring Melungeons. Curiously, four years earlier the tolerant church approved of blacks testifying against whites in court.[25] Why then their singular antagonism against "them Melungins?"

At the time, some Melungeons moved to Black Water, nearby on the Tennessee-Virginia border.[26] Some were kicked out of the Stony Creek church. Reuben Gibson and others were ousted for "persevering wicked-

---

7th of April, 1781," ed. Judge Walter Clark, *Abstract of the Army Accounts of the North Carolina Line, State Records of North Carolina*, vol. 17 (1781–1785), pub. 1899. See also Carol Anne Ledford, "Elijah Goin Goes to Court with Slanderer in Claiborne County, Tennessee," *Gowen Research Foundation Newsletter* 2/10 (June 1991).

[21]"Sevier Family Papers, 1790-1822," McClung Museum, Tennessee State Library Archives.

[22]*Centennial History*, published by Baxter County, Arkansas, 1972.

[23]Hamilton, "The Boone Trail."

[24]C. S. Everett, "Melungeon History and Myth," *Appalachian Journal* (Summer 1999).

[25]"Stony Creek Baptist Church Minute Books, 1801–1814," Fort Blackmore, Scott County, Virginia, copied by Emory L. Hamilton, August 1966, Wise, Virginia, archives of the Southwest Virginia Historical Society, Clinch Valley College, Wise, Virginia, and Virginia State Library, Richmond, Virginia.

[26]Everett, "Melungeon History and Myth."

ness" and moved to Black Water.[27] By 1815, only a few Melungeons were still members of Stony Creek church. Blacks remained on the roll.

The Blood Quantum

The next scene occurred when the Tennessee State Legislature met in 1834 and adopted an old colonial law forbidding certain civil rights to people with more than one-quarter mixed blood.[28] Other states set it at the same level or higher. Generally, the blood quantum of 1834 defined people with more than one-quarter African or Indian ancestry, as "persons of color" with drastically reduced rights. The 1834 law apparently included Melungeons with people of color and decades later Will Allen Dromgoole claimed that Melungeons were specifically mentioned.[29]

Not coincidentally, Melungeons made news during the election campaign that followed the adoption of the one-quarter law. On October 7, 1840, in the *Jonesborough Whig and Independent*, Tennessee newspaperman William "Parson" Brownlow waged a blistering attack against a certain "Malungeon."[30] Brownlow, though antislavery, believed Democrats were insulting whites by endorsing a certain Melungeon to campaign for the party. Brownlow called the Melungeon a "half Indian/half Negro from Washington City" and in the blustery style of the time described his adversary as an "impudent Malungeon, a scoundrel who is half Negro and half Indian," and, "an impudent Free Negro." In the October 28 edition of the *Whig*, Brownlow howled that

---

[27]September 22, 1804 entry, "Stony Creek Baptist Church Minute Books, 1801–1814."

[28]Joshua W. Caldwell, *Studies in the Constitutional History of Tennessee*, 2nd ed. (Cincinnati: Robert Clarke Co., 1907).

[29]Virginia Easley DeMarce, "The Melungeons," *National Genealogy Society Quarterly* 84/2 (June 1996): "In Tennessee, state law limited the term ["persons of color"] to those whose parent or grandparent was a full-blooded Indian or Negro (i.e., descent to the third degree). North Carolina's law extended it to 'all Negroes, Indians, and mulattos . . . to the fourth generation, inclusive' (i.e., individuals with one-eighth-degree Negro or Indian ancestry). The laws of the 1830s did not affect families who were legally white, they did not change anyone's classification, and they did not mandate anyone to be legally nonwhite once they passed the point that had been defined in the 1700s." See also Jack Goins, "History of the Melungeons," <www.geocities.com/ourmelungeons/history.html> (posted 2003).

[30]William G. Brownlow, "Impudent Melungeon," *Jonesboro* (Tennessee) *Whig and Independent*, 7 October 1840.

a half Negro and half Indian has been speaking to the citizens of Sullivan on the subject of politics! This surely is a great insult and ought not to be tolerated . . . we have seen and heard the vile scamp. And he was put up by the Democratic party, and by that party sustained, and now apologized for, on the ground of his having some Indian blood.

A week later the *Whig* referred to the Melungeon as an "infamous and dissipated Mulatto" and a "kinky headed villain."

This early editorial said nothing about fantastic lost colonies. Brownlow's point was that it was scandalous for a Melungeon to lecture whites on politics since these people he described as half-breeds were barred from voting in 1834.

However, less than a decade later the *Jonesborough Whig*'s opinion of Melungeons was challenged by a rival newspaper. In 1848 a reporter for the *Knoxville Register* visited a "Melungen" village at Black Water Creek in Hancock County, Tennessee.[31] The anonymous reporter described these Melungeons as hiding from the outside world, strategically remote and "situated in a narrow gorge, scarcely half a mile wide, between Powell's Mountain and the Copper Ridge . . . almost inaccessible."

The *Register* reporter noted a startling change in the status of Melungeons in 1848. "They are privileged voters in the state in which they live and thus, you will perceive, are accredited citizens of the commonwealth." Melungeons suddenly could vote in 1848 after being denied in 1834 and after Brownlow's challenge in 1840. How? Why? The answers were implied when the *Register* reporter added a bolt out of the blue: "A great many years ago, these mountains were settled by a society of Portuguese Adventurer."

Melungeons did not have Portuguese names. They did not speak Portuguese and in fact were described as speaking an old "Elizabethan" style of English. Genealogy reveals no Portuguese ancestors and the University of Virginia found no DNA trace of Portuguese. Melungeons certainly had not appeared in the mountains "a great many years ago," because the first generation of Appalachian Melungeons was still alive in 1848.

---

[31]Anonymous, "The Melungens [*sic*]," reprinted from the *Knoxville Register*, 6 September 1848 (which probably had reprinted it from the *Louisville Examiner*, 1847?), in *Littell's Living Age* 254 (31 March 1849): 618-19. *Living Age*, however, prefaces their reprint as follows: "[We are sorry to have lost the name of the Southern paper from which this is taken.]" (p. 618).

Between 1840 and 1848 Brownlow's "half-breed Melungeons" and Jarvis's "Indian tribe" had disappeared.[32] In their place was a colony of "Portuguese adventurers" who came to the mountains "long before the white man" and married Indian women to produce dark-skinned, blue-eyed Melungeons. Newspapers as far away as New York were intrigued.

Birth of a Mystery

Why did the story change? The *Register* article linked the "Portuguese" story to voting.[33] In a trial that began two years earlier—on January 25, 1846—a Hancock County court had just ruled that Melungeons could vote.[34] Eight Melungeons had been charged with illegally voting in the August 7, 1845 election. Six of the men were Collinses and the other two were Zachariah Minor and his brother Lewis Minor. The charge was based on the 1834 Tennessee law: "Not a free white man 21 year of age and thus not being a citizen of the United States and a citizen of the said county where he voted."

One chronicler explained the background: Melungeons were "held by the whites to be a mixed race with at least a modicum of Negroes blood, and there is at least one instance on record in which the matter was brought before the courts. It was before the Civil War—during the period of slavery, that the rights of a number of people in this group to vote was questioned." Brought before the court, "the question was decided by an examination of the feet. One was found sufficiently flat-footed to deprive him of the right of suffrage. The other four or five were judged to possess enough white blood to be allowed to vote. Col. John Netherland, a prominent local lawyer, defended them."[35]

At the time of the "Hancock County Eight" trial, a national debate over slavery had come to full boil. Rival newspapers, scholars, ministers, and politicians lined up on opposing sides. Scientists also demanded to be heard and the loudest was a botanist who popularized a controversial race theory. Dr. Samuel Morton, a proslavery advocate, published *Crania Americana* in 1839 and *Crania Ægyptiaca* in 1844 in which he introduced the theory

---

[32]L. M. Jarvis, interviewed in *Hancock County Times* (Sneedville TN), 17 April 1903.

[33]"The Melungens," *Littell's Living Age*.

[34]Goins, "History of the Melungeons."

[35]Swan Burnett, "Notes on the Melungeons," read before the Society of American Anthropologists on 5 February 1889, and published in *American Anthropology* 2/21 (October 1889): 347-49.

of polygenism, a theory that mixed black and white couples produced sterile offspring. Some Harvard University scholars endorsed the sterility theory and slaveholders began quoting Morton in opposition to abolition. So in the early 1840s, just before Melungeons became "Portuguese," racism had begun feeding on a new fear: mixing, once a social disgrace, was suddenly also biological suicide! This new fear left Melungeons facing slow extinction. A small community needs outside marriage to avoid inbreeding, and illegal mixing had gone on for decades. Suddenly even sympathetic whites were fearing their own racial extinction.

But a clever attorney was able to turn a sow's ear into a silk purse in the Hancock Eight trial by using Morton's 1844 book, *Crania Ægyptiaca*. To prove "they were not negroes, the beautiful hands and feet of some of the race were examined, and the marked difference between them and the negroes decided the question in their favor."[36] The attorney for the Melungeons argued they could not be half black because they did not show physical degeneration. The court's verdict came just in time to be picked up by the visiting reporter from Knoxville who wrote that Melungeons had "enough white blood" to vote.[37]

Creative Lawyers

Parson Brownlow's claim that Melungeons were half-breeds was overruled, at least in one court, by the new legend of the lost Portuguese colony.[38] Brownlow had mentioned a "Mr. Netherland" as an ally of the Melungeons in 1840. The attorney for the Hancock County Eight in 1846 was Col. John Netherland.[39] However, it is likely that Netherland did not invent the Portuguese defense. According to Edward Price who researched the Melungeons for the University of California at Berkeley, "the persistent rumor that they are of Portuguese descent seems to be without foundation; the Melungeons themselves may have started it to counter the hints of Negro blood."[40]

---

[36]Will T. Hale, *The Melungeons of East Tennessee* (Chicago: Lewis Publishing Co, 1913), photocopied from Will T. Hale and Dixon Lanier Merritt, *A History of Tennessee and Tennesseans: The Leaders and Representative Men in Commerce, Industry, and Modern Activities*, 8 vols. (Chicago, New York: Lewis Publishing Co., 1913).

[37]Anonymous, "The Melungens [*sic*]," *Littell's Living Age*. (See n. 31.)

[38]Burnett, "Notes on Melungeons."

[39]Hale, *The Melungeons of East Tennessee*.

[40]Edward T. Price, "The Melungeons: A Mixed-Blood Strain of the Southern Appala-

In fact, Melungeons also used other ethnic claims. In 1872, Chatta-nooga attorney Lewis Shepherd represented a Melungeon child for an inheritance worth $100,000.[41] Betsy Bolton had been born to the white heir of a Virginia plantation and his Melungeon wife. The wife died giving birth and the white father, overcome with grief, was confined to an asylum. The mother and cousins of Betsy's wealthy white father had bitterly opposed his marriage to the Melungeon. While he was in an asylum they sued to dis-inherit his mixed daughter claiming Melungeons had African ancestry, and because the law forbade mixed marriage Betsy was illegitimate and not a legal heir.

Attorney Shepherd argued in court that Melungeons were not "Negro" but descendants of ancient Phoenicians. Surprisingly, the court agreed with Shepherd and he won the case.[42]

Social Stigma

Just before the Civil War, Elijah Goin, great grandson of old Revolutionary War patriot Thomas Goin of Hawkins County was forced to use the Portu-guese defense. His daughter Polly married a white man named William Mayes in Claiborne County but the groom's family resented the marriage:

> Sterling Mayes, brother to the groom, took exception to the marriage, and one week later was telling everyone that his brother had married a mulatto and that the whole Goin family was mulattos and negroes. Sterling even instructed his children to taunt the Goin children with the mulatto label. By July, the whole county had heard the accusations.
>
> Sterling had gone so far as to make up a little song about blacks and mulattos which he sang to the tune of *Old Dan Tucker*, a popular jig tune of the day. In September, Sterling sang his doggerel verses in church. He made his rhymes fit the hymns that were being sung at the camp meeting, an evangelistic meeting held outdoors in a tent. Several rows of worshipers heard the caustic mulatto slurs drowning out the gospel words.
>
> That was the last straw, Elijah Goin filed suit in Circuit Court for slander against Sterling Mayes on Sept. 15, 1853. The charges were

---

chians," *Geographical Review* (April 1951).

[41]Lewis Shepherd, "Romantic Account of the Celebrated 'Melungeon' Case," *Watson's Magazine* 17/1 (May 1913): 34-40. See also Lewis Shepherd, *Personal Memoirs of Lewis Shepherd, L.L.M. March 7, 1915* (Chattanooga TN, 1915). ("Shepherd" sometimes appears in the literature as "Shepard" or "Sheppard.")

[42]Shepherd, "Romantic Account of the Celebrated 'Melungeon' Case."

damaging to Elijah Goin who was a schoolteacher and active in community affairs. He had once been elected as constable.[43]

In another case in 1858, Jacob F. Perkins filed a slander lawsuit in Johnson County, Tennessee against a business partner who had called him a "Negro." Some witnesses claimed Perkins was black and others swore he was Portuguese. Records revealed that his white neighbors shortly before the Civil War were arguing that Melungeons could not reproduce, that they had no souls and that it should not be against the law to kill them.[44] Although the wealthy Perkins family associated with the likes of Tennessee Secretary of State Landon Carter, the court ruled against them.

Lincoln Frees a Melungeon

For Melungeons, the Portuguese myth was an escape just as the Underground Railroad was for slaves. Young attorney Abraham Lincoln played the Portuguese card for a Melungeon client:

> As the result of a family dispute over William Dungey's marriage to Joseph Spencer's sister, Spencer claimed that his brother-in-law "Black Bill" was a Negro. Because Illinois denied free blacks the right to settle in the state, Dungey faced losing his marriage, property, and right to stay in Illinois. Lincoln filed suit against Spencer for slander and during the trial managed to not only demolish his opponent's reputation and the credibility of his witnesses, but to win the case for his client while using clever word play against the opposing attorney.[45]

Lincoln argued, "My client is not a Negro, though it is a crime to be a Negro—no crime to be born with a black skin. . . . His skin may not be as white as ours, but I say he is not a Negro, though he may be a Moore."

---

[43]Carol Ledford, "Elijah Goin Sues Slanderer in Claiborne County, TN," *Gowen Research Foundation Newsletter* 2/10 (June 1991).

[44]"The Perkins File," in the T. A. R. Nelson Papers, Calvin M. McClung Collection, East Tennessee Historical Center, Knox County, Tennessee. See also Pamela R. Cresswell, "Perkins vs White," <TNjctcuzins.com/pam/perkins/>. See "Jacob F. PERKINS vs. John R. WHITE," T. A. R. Nelson Papers at the Calvin M. McClung Historical Collection.

[45]Virginia Easley DeMarce, *Gowen Research Foundation Newsletter* (April 1994), citing Janet Key, *American Bar Association Journal*, "Papers of Abraham Lincoln," Illinois Historic Preservation Agency, Springfield, 1992. See also <papersofabrahamlincoln.org/Briefs/briefs23>.

"Mr. Lincoln," interrupted Judge Davis, scarcely able to restrain a smile, "you mean a Moor, not Moore."

"Well, your Honor, Moor, not C. H. Moore," replied Mr. Lincoln, with a sweep of his long arm toward the table where Moore sat. "I say my client may be a Moor, but he is not a Negro."

Melungeons in southern Tennessee used the Portuguese defense again when their right to attend white schools in Rhea County was "established in a lawsuit of the 1890s when a Melungeon ancestry was shown not to be Negro."[46]

In 1885 an attorney for Melungeons and Lumbees of North and South Carolina appealed to the Assembly when children were banned from white schools.[47] Sen. Hamilton McMillan amazingly claimed they came from Raleigh's 1587 Roanoke colony: "The chroniclers who keep the tradition of the tribe speak of themselves as Malungeons."[48] The state built special schools for the children.[49] The legends served their purposes.

The year Will Allen Dromgoole discovered the Clinch—1889—marked a somber event for the world. Adolf Hitler was born that year. Myths would be tested in the twentieth century—not only those of the Melungeons, but those of the races who claimed superiority over them.

[46]Raymond Evans, "The Graysville Melungeons: A Triracial People in Lower East Tennessee," *Tennessee Anthropologist* 4/1 (1979).

[47]Gerald M. Sider, *Lumbee Indian Histories: Race, Ethnicity, and Indian Identity in the Southern United States* (Cambridge UK and New York: Cambridge University Press, 1993).

[48]Hamilton McMillan, *Sir Walter Raleigh's Lost Colony* (Raleigh NC: privately printed, 1907); idem, *The Croatans*, North Carolina Booklet 10 (1911); Stephen B. Weeks, "The Lost Colony of Roanoke: Its Fate and Survival," *Papers American Historical Association* 5 (1891); idem, "Raleigh's Settlements on Roanoke Island, A Historical Survival," *Magazine of American History* 25 (1891). See also Saundra Keyes Ivey, "Oral, Printed, and Popular Culture Traditions Related to the Melungeons of Hancock County, Tennessee" (Ph.D. diss., Indiana University, 1976), quoting Stephen B. Weeks, "The Lost Colony of Roanoke: Its Fate and Survival," *Papers of the American Historical Association* 5/4 (1891). See also George E. Butler, *The Croatan Indians of Sampson County, North Carolina. Their Origin and Racial Status. A Plea for Separate Schools* (Durham NC: Seeman Printery, 1916), North Carolina Collection, University of N.C. at Chapel Hill.

[49]Tim Funk, "Dole is dramatic shift from Helms," *Charlotte Observer*, Sunday 8 June 2003.

Chapter 2

The First Mixed Generation

Surprisingly, the fantastic Melungeon story about pirates and Portuguese and of arriving before the *Mayflower* was partly true, although some details were changed and omitted.

Jamestown, Virginia, 1607 — Capt. John Smith plants Britain's first successful colony in North America. Seven years later, in the Jamestown church, the first "legal" mixed marriage unites tobacco planter John Rolfe and a baptized Pocahontas, daughter of Indian Chief Powhatan.

Amid famine, sickness, and Indian attacks, Virginia manages to produce one valuable export—tobacco. But the colony can't attract migrant workers from Britain because of the high frontier mortality rate. So, in 1616, the Virginia Company holding the colony's charter sends Pocahontas and Rolfe to England as publicity to encourage migration. Pocahontas becomes ill and dies in London in 1617, leaving a mixed infant child, Thomas Rolfe.

August 1619 — Two years after Pocahontas's death, a mystery ship appears in the Chesapeake Bay with Africans to trade. This is the very first African Middle Passage to English-speaking North America. Jamestown is where the roots of the American Melungeons start, sixteen months before the *Mayflower* drops anchor at Cape Cod. The first African odyssey had begun in 1618 in the season when armies go forth to war. An ambitious Portuguese general stationed in Luanda on the coast of Angola in West Africa launched a campaign into the interior against a kingdom called Ndongo. The Portuguese army consisted of several hundred European soldiers and cavalry, but its most powerful weapons were three companies of ruthless cannibalistic Imbangala (or Mbangala) mercenaries.

The powerful kingdom of Ndongo encompassed the misty heights of the Malange Plateau in central Angola.[1] On the throne sat the untested

---

[1]Thornton, John, "The African Experience of the '20 and Odd Negroes' Arriving in Virginia in 1619," *William and Mary Quarterly* 55/3 (1998).

young Mbundu Bantu ruler, Ngola Mbandi, brother of the warrior queen, Nzinga. Rebel *sobas*, or chieftains, had recently assassinated the prince's father, and the Ngola had not yet brought them to heel.

The Portuguese took timely advantage of Ndongo's civil war. Crossing the Kwanza River, Gen. Luis Mendes de Vasconcelos launched his Imbangala mercenaries. One by one the Ngola's warrior chieftains were defeated until at last the Portuguese army surrounded the royal city of Kabasa. The city fell in late 1618 and Ngola Mbandi fled, leaving subjects and several wives and children to be captured—or eaten.

The victorious Portuguese marched thousands of prisoners to the coast, and in May 1619 a Portuguese frigate, the *St. John the Baptist*, sailed from the castle prison at Luanda with 400 Ndongo shackled men, women, and children. Capt. Mendes de Acuna, hoped to sell his captives as slaves to the silver mines of Mexico. However, the voyage to Vera Cruz was interrupted. Two pirate ships, the *White Lion* and the *Treasurer*, working in consort, were lurking off the tip of the Yucatán Peninsula when they spotted the *Baptist*'s sails and gave chase. On July 15, 1619, in the Bay of Campeche, the pirates disabled the slaver's main mast and boarded her. Finding no gold, the two pirates divided sixty of the healthiest Ndongo captives between them and sailed away from the smoking Portuguese slaver.[2]

Five weeks later John Rolfe reports the arrival in Chesapeake Bay of a corsair with a cargo of Africans to trade.[3] Taking Virginia planter

---

[2]Tim Hashaw, "Malungu," "African Origin of American Melungeons," *Appalachian Quarterly* 6/3 (September 2001) and 6/4 (December 2001). See also Engel Sluiter, "New Light on the '20 and Odd Negroes' Arriving in Virginia in 1619," *William and Mary Quarterly* 54/2 (1997). See also Peter Coldham, *English Adventurers and Emigrants, 1609–1660* (Baltimore: Genealogical Publishing Co., 1984) 182.

[3]"XCIV. John Rolfe. A Letter to Sir Edwin Sandys. January 1619/20," in *The Records of the Virginia Company of London, 1607–1626*, 4 vols., ed. Susan M. Kingsbury (Washington DC: G.P.O., 1906–1935) 3:241-48; quotation on 243 [*sic*]:

About the latter end of August, a Dutch man of Warr of the burden of a 160 tuñes [tons] arrived at Point-Comfort, the Comando[rs] name Capt Jope, his Pilott for the West Indies one Mr Marmaduke an Englishman. They mett w[th] the Trēr [Treasurer] in the West Indyes, and determyned to hold consort shipp hetherward, but in their passage lost one the other. He brought not any thing but 20. and odd Negroes, w[ch] [which] the Governo[r] and Cape Marchant bought for victualle (whereof he was in greate need as he p[re]tended) at the best and easyest rate they could. He hadd a lardge and ample Com[~]yssion from his Excellency to range and to take purchase in the West Indyes.

Three or 4. daies after the Trēr arrived. At his arriuall he sent word p[r]esently to the Gou[9]no[r] to know his pleasure, who wrote to him, and did request myself Leiften[a]nte

William Evans and the captain of the militia, Rolfe goes out to meet the *White Lion*. Her captain is John Colyn Jope of Plymouth, fresh from capturing the Portuguese slaver, the *Baptist*. Jope trades "20 and odd" Africans. The men, women, and children who step onto the pier at Jamestown have been handpicked from the Angola Ndongo captives taken by the two pirates.

Two of the Africans that day were noted in a later Jamestown census as "John" and "Margaret." John was hired as the servant of the planter William Evans who went with Rolfe to meet the pirates. He became John Gowen. Margaret was enslaved by a neighboring planter, Robert Sheppard; she would become Margaret Cornish.[4]

The English planters at Jamestown at first regarded Africans as indentured servants on the same par with English servants freed after three to seven years. In this way John Gowen obtained his freedom. He had a son by Margaret Cornish in 1635, but she remained a slave on the next plantation, and when John Gowen prepared to move and start his own farm, neither she nor the child could go with him. This episode would be critical to the birth of the Melungeon people, and the legend of the children of perdition.

Peace and Mr Ewens to goe downe to him, to desyre [2^a] him to come vp to James Cytie [City]. But before we gott downe he hadd sett saile and was gone out of the Bay. The occasion hereof happened by the unfriendly dealing of the Inhabitants of Keqnoughton, for he was in greate want of victualle, wherewth they would not relieve him nor his Company vpon any termes.

[4]John Gowen's surname has been variously transcribed as Graweere, Grasheare, Grasher, and Geaween. The case for Gowen as the name for John Graweere is based on the various surname spellings of his supposed son, Michael Gowen, also transcribed as Milhill Gowree. See endnote section for "Gowen" in Paul Heinegg, *Free African Americans of North Carolina, Virginia, and South Carolina*. Heinegg writes: "The name Mihill Gowen appears like Mihill Gowree in the 1668 patent, but the 11 September 1717 inquisition refers to the same land as belonging to Mihil Goen/Michael Gowen." See above "Michael Gowen" in Gowen section of Heinegg. Regarding the debated transcription of the name John Graweere as John Geaween, see "Patents Issued during the Regal Government," as documented in the *William and Mary Quarterly Historical Magazine* 9/3 (1901): 139-44. See also Library of Virginia microfilm reel #113: "Surry Deeds, Wills &c (1652–1673)" and the *Newsletter of the Surry County, Virginia Historical Society and Museum* for September 2003. See also McIlwaine, *Minutes of the Council*, 477. For the counterargument, see Jack Goins, "Our Melungeons: John Graweere or Geaween," online, <http://www.geocities.com/ourmelungeons/johngraweere.html>.

In 1848, to escape racial prejudice, the Melungeons altered the story. Their ancestors became "Portuguese pirates." Some truth was there: Angola *was* a colony of Portugal so their ancestors *were* Portuguese, not ethnic Portuguese, but Angolan subjects of Portugal.

Before Slavery

A unique mix of events, circumstances, and customs at the beginning of English-speaking North America, 1619–1690, created and then isolated an anomaly later called a "mystery." Simply put, during these few decades some blacks began on equal footing with white indentured servants even as other blacks were held as permanent slaves. When black men, fortunate to be indentured rather than enslaved, completed their contracts, they moved to the frontier to establish their farms. There were fewer black women than black men, and black women tended to be held as slaves rather than as servants, creating an inequity in marriage partners. England was new to Africa in the 1600s, so English people, at first, did not despise blacks. Free black men in Virginia married white women and Indian women because these women were free to leave plantations, unlike many black women. Their children were the Melungeons. Within twenty years of arriving in Virginia, these first free blacks went from planting the fields of their masters to hiring white servants to gather their own increase. And some married the white daughters of planters.

Virginia had no law against such mixed marriages at first. But tolerance didn't last. Planters prospered just as the British African slave trade began in 1660–1670. The number of black slaves swelled. By the late 1600s, surrounded by African slaves and fearing uprisings, Virginians restricted the rights of free blacks because some of them led slave rebellions. Free black communities shrank as fewer blacks were freed. The view of whites regarding Africans changed. In 1732, Virginia ended a right held by free people of color for a century—the right to a fair trial. The law said that "negros, mulattos, and Indians . . . are people of such base and corrupt natures, that the credit of their testimony cannot be certainly depended upon."[5]

---

[5]William W. Hening, ed., *The Statutes at Large; Being a Collection of All the Laws of Virginia, from the First Session of the Legislature in the Year 1619*, 13 vols. (1819–1823; facsimile repr.: Charlottesville VA: University Press of Virginia, 1969) 4:326, 327.

Mixed Marriage Outlawed

In 1616, John Rolfe brought his baptized Algonquian bride, Indian Princess Pocahontas, to England. Receiving them at court, King James and his courtiers were appalled, but not because of race mixing: "The silly bigot on the British throne was angry because one of his subjects had dared to marry a lady of royal blood."[6] In Britain and in British America at that time, class and religious differences mattered more than race. A century later, this had changed.

Legally recognized with Rolfe and Pocahontas, mixed marriage would not be banned until 1691, allowing only one "legal" mixed generation to be born. The ban was passed to prevent "that abominable mixture and spurious issue which hereafter may encrease [*sic*] in this dominion as well as by negroes, mulattoes, and Indians intermarrying with English, or other white women, as by their unlawfull accompanying with one another."[7]

Between 1614 and 1691 the state church had blessed many mixed marriages. In 1681 a black man, Little Robin, was wed to Elizabeth Shorter, a white woman, by Rev. Nicholas Geulick. The couple had three daughters in St. Mary's County, Maryland. A Catholic priest united a black servant named Dick in holy matrimony to a white woman named Mary Fisher.[8]

Racism began in the wealthy, scholarly, aristocrat-conscious planter class and, because the social taboo developed at the top, working-class white women in seventeenth- and eighteenth-century America were not averse to marrying black men for many years. One colonial gentleman, Edward Long, wrote in horror that in America, "the lower class of women in England, are remarkably fond of the blacks, for reasons too brutal to mention."[9]

The legislated punishment for mixing was banishment, whipping, fines, and forced servitude. Even preachers who officiated mixed marriages were punished. In 1725, Rev. John Cotton was indicted for uniting a "Molatto man to a white woman." In 1726, in North Carolina, Rev. John Blacknall

---

[6]Benson John Lossing, *Our Country: A Household History for all Readers, from the Discovery of American to the Present Time*, 3 vols. (New York; H. J. Johnson, 1877–1880).

[7]Hening, ed., *The Statutes at Large* 3:86-87.

[8]Heinegg, *Free African Americans of North Carolina, Virginia, and South Carolina*.

[9]Lerone Bennett, *Before the Mayflower, a History of Black America*, 7th ed. (Chicago: Johnson Pub. Co., 2003).

was fined fifty pounds for joining in matrimony Matthew Thomas Spencer and Martha Paule, a mulatto.

Refused the protection of sanctioned marriage, mixed couples were hauled into court on morals-related charges. The man sometimes disappeared, leaving the woman holding the child alone. Often the woman refused to name the father and bore the punishment alone. This created problems. Courts became saddled with single-parent mixed children dependent upon county welfare. So, legislators imposed more severe penalties hoping to send a message. Fatherless mixed children were indentured for up to thirty years and their unwed white mothers were jailed, whipped, pilloried, and essentially enslaved for life.

Alice Miles was a white indentured servant convicted of "fornication with a Negro." The York County court ordered she be whipped "till her backe be bloody." After 1720 in Northampton County, Virginia, Tamar Smith had to serve half a year in prison and pay a ten-pound fine for marrying Maj. Hitchens, a black man. In 1728 in Maryland, Mary Welch admitted she had given birth to a mulatto child. The court added seven years to her original servitude to Thomas Harwood and her two-month old son Henry was bound to Harwood for thirty-one years. (At the time, life expectancy was less than forty years.) Mary Wise, servant of a man named Wells admitted in 1732 to having a mixed child in Prince George County. The court sold her nine-week-old daughter Becky into thirty-one years of servitude. In Delaware, in 1704, Mary Plowman was charged with giving birth to a child by a black man named Frank. The court gave her twenty-one lashes and added several years to her indenture. Her mulatto daughter Rose was bound until the age of twenty-one.

In 1703, in Kent County, Delaware, seventeen-year-old Eleanor Price admitted to "Fornication with a Negro Man named Peter." She received twenty-one lashes and an extended period of eighteen months servitude. Her daughter was bound out until the age of twenty-one. In Accomack County, Virginia, in 1721, Ann Shepard, a "Christian white woman," had a child by Henry Jackson. Ann was sold for a five-year term. In 1716, Elizabeth Bartlett was ordered to pay 1,200 pounds of tobacco to her mistress Mary Bailey for eloping with the mistress's African servant, James. Sarah Dawson, a white servant, endured twenty-one lashes in 1784 for having a child by her master's servant, Peter Beckett.

In Lancaster County, Virginia, in 1703, Elizabeth Bell ran away from her master and was lashed twenty times at the county whipping post. A year later she was indentured to another master during which time she had a child by a black man. Five years were added to her term. Alice Bryan confessed to bearing a "bastard Molattoe Child" by a "Negro man Called Jack." An extra two years of servitude and thirty-nine lashes was her punishment. Her mulatto son Peter was bound out for thirty-one years and her daughter Elizabeth for eighteen years.

Lovers rebelled. George Ivie, a Melungeon ancestor, and others, petitioned the Council of Virginia on May 11, 1699 for the repeal of the Act against English people marrying "Negroes, Indians or Mulattos."[10] The petition was rejected. On August 16, 1705, a mulatto named John Bunch and a white woman named Sarah Slayden appealed to Virginia to permit them to be married after being refused by the Blisland Parish minister. The Council countered that the "intent of the Law [is] to prevent Negroes and White Persons intermarrying." "Bunch" is a Melungeon name.

Ann Wall was found guilty of "keeping company with a Negro under pretense of marriage." Elizabeth County bound her for five years, sold her children for thirty-one years, and warned "if ye said Ann Wall after she is free from her said master doe at any time presume to come into this county, she shall be banished to ye Island of Barbadoes."[11]

Some colonies relented. Pennsylvania for one repealed the ban during the American Revolution. Thomas Branagan visited Philadelphia in 1805: "There are many, very many blacks who begin to feel themselves consequential will not be satisfied unless they get white women for wives, and are likewise exceedingly impertinent to white people."[12]

Newspapers ran notices of black and white servants running away together. In the Southern journal *American Weekly Mercury* in 1720: "Runaway in April last from Richard Tilghman, of Queen Anne County in Maryland, a mulatto slave, named Richard Molson, of middle stature, about forty years old, he is in company with a white woman who is supposed now goes for his wife." And in the *Pennsylvania Gazette* of June 1, 1746: "Runaway from the subscriber the second of last month, at the town of Potomac, Frederick County, Maryland, a mulatto servant named Isaac Cromwell, runaway at the same time, an English servant woman named Ann Greene."[13]

The ban on mixed marriage was frequently ignored until the Nat Turner revolt:

---

[10]Bennett, *Before the Mayflower*.

[11]Heinegg, *Free African Americans of North Carolina, Virginia, and South Carolina*.

[12]Thomas Branagan, in Philadelphia in 1805, cited by Bennett, *Before the Mayflower*.

[13]Bennett, *Before the Mayflower*.

White servant women ignored the law and continued to have children by
Negro fathers through the late 17th century and late into the 18th century.
The records indicate that the primary source of the increase in the free
African American population for this period was the unions of free blacks
and free whites. Many observers assumed when they saw mulattos that
they were produced from white slave owners and their female slaves.[14]

Some complained the penalties to be extreme. In 1692, Thomas
Plummer of Anne Arundel County, Maryland asked the governor to dismiss
"unparalleled and unheard of extraordinary and unusull excessive fines" of
6,000 pounds levied by the Calvert County, Maryland court. His daughter
had a child after "unfortunately having too much familiarity and commerce
with a certain Negro man [and] was supposed by him to have a child."[15]

Lovers sought innovative ways to evade the ban. In 1807 in Kentucky,
John Levy Going, a descendant of seventeenth-century John Gowen and
Margaret Cornish of Virginia, attempted to marry a white woman in
Livingston County and was denied by the local justice because of his
African ancestry. They left but returned a few days later. The white woman
swore that she had "Negro blood" in her. John Levy Going had cut a vein
before returning and she drank some of his blood.[16]

The reverse was rumored in the 1857 Melungeon lawsuit *Perkins v.
White*. When Jacob F. Perkins sued his neighbor John R. White for saying
he was a "Negro," he called county constable John J. Wilson, age seventy,
to testify. Apparently Perkins had been accused of drinking some of his
white wife's blood in order to claim he had white blood. Wilson testified
that "Some of Jock's neighbors called him a negro. They called themselves
Portuguese. Never heard of them drinking wive's blood."[17]

Sociologist Brewton Berry reported that a black settler named
Benjamin Gould and his white wife, Elizabeth Adams, originally established Gouldtown, New Jersey. Elizabeth was the granddaughter of John

---

[14]Heinegg, *Free African Americans of North Carolina, Virginia, and South Carolina*.

[15]Letitia Woods Brown, *Free Negroes in the District of Columbia, 1790–1846*, The
Urban Life in America series (New York: Oxford University Press, 1972).

[16]Anna Going Friedman, Jaymie Friedman Frederick, and Helen Bonnie Moore, "Going
Family Futily Criss-Crossed America to Escape Racial Discrimination," *Gowen Research
Foundation Electronic Newsletter* 3/3 (March 2000) online at <http://bz.llano.net/gowen/
electronic_newsletter/el2003.htm>.

[17]*Perkins v. White*, Perkins File in the T. A. R. Nelson Papers in the Calvin M.
McClung Collection.

Fenwick, who came to Delaware in 1675. The rich planter Fenwick warned his granddaughter that he would disown her and leave her penniless "unless the Lord open her eyes to see the abominable transgression against Him, me, and her good father, by giving her true repentance and forsaking that Black which hath been the ruin of her."[18] There was no repentance, the family multiplied, prospered, and mixed towns were born.

Insolence raged. In 1708 the Virginia court ruled that William Driggus fathered a child by a white woman, Mary Winslow, and ordered William be given twenty-five lashes for telling the justices that "they had no more to do with said Woman than his Arse."[19]

The ban had a long-lasting impact on Melungeon custom. The *Knoxville Register*'s "Melungen" article of 1848 said Melungeons came to Tennessee to be free

> from the restraints and drawbacks imposed on them by any form of government. They uprooted all conventional forms of society and lived in a delightful Utopia of their own creation, trampling on the marriage relation. . . . Husband and wife separate at pleasure, without meeting with any reproach or disgrace from their friends and want of chastity on the part of the females is no bar to their marrying.[20]

Will Allen Dromgoole disapprovingly wrote:

> By marriage I mean to say (in their own language) they "took up together," having no set form of marriage service. After the forming of Hancock County old Mullins and Collins were forced to marry their wives according to the laws of the land, but all had children and grandchildren before they were lawfully married.[21]

One reader noted that black slaves also despised mixing, calling Melungeons "negroes who had married Indians and their children. Negroes

---

[18]Brewton Berry, *Almost White: A Provocative Study of America's Mixed-Blood Minorities* (New York: Macmillan, 1963; 2nd ptg. 1967).

[19]Joseph Douglas Deal, *Race and Class in Colonial Virginia: Indians, Englishmen, and Africans on the Eastern Shore during the Seventeenth Century* (revision of the author's dissertation), Studies in African American History and Culture series (New York: Garland, 1993).

[20]Anonymous, "The Melungens" [*sic*], *Knoxville Register*, 6 September 1848. Reprinted in *Littell's Living Age* 20/254 (31 March 1849): 618-19.

[21]Will Allen Dromgoole, "The Malungeon Tree and Its Four Branches," *The Arena* 3/6 (Boston, June 1891): 745-51.

belonging to quality folks would not associate with Malungeons. Most of the Negroes held these Malungeons in great contempt. They were always insulted if called a Malungeon."[22] Henry Price observed:

> The available early marriage records for Hawkins County indicates that marriages among the people of Newman's Ridge prior to the 1820s were either performed out of Hawkins County, the records thereof were lost or destroyed, or perhaps were common-law marriages entered into without the usual formalities required by statute. The marriage records for the period beginning after 1870 reveal the Melungeon girls had little difficulty finding husbands—both from their own kind as well as among the neighboring white settlers. The men, on the other hand, had less luck in finding wives outside the clan.[23]

Dromgoole thought Melungeons "exceedingly immoral," because of their attitude on legal vows. In fact, Melungeons of the nineteenth century were copying their ancestors' responses to the ban when they settled into common-law marriage.

In 1705, the Assembly first defined "mulatto" and that definition, cast in the bias of that time, colors the perception of race mixing that Americans have even today.[24]

Early Communities of Color

It begins with John Gowen, one of the original Angolans who arrived in Jamestown in 1619. He became free and had a child by Margaret Cornish in 1635. Because she was a slave, their child Mihill Gowen, was the property of her owner Robert Sheppard. John Gowen, just starting out as a lower-class freeman could not buy her freedom. So about five years later the slave Margaret fell in love with a white gentleman named Robert Sweat (aka Sweet) and bore a mulatto child out of wedlock. On October 17, 1640, the Virginia Assembly censured Sweat and Margaret Cornish for fornica-

---

[22]"C.H." in a letter to *The Daily American* (Lawrence MA), 14 September 1891, in response to Dromgoole.

[23]Henry R. Price, *Melungeons: The Vanishing Colony of Newman's Ridge*, originally a paper presented at the spring meeting of the American Studies Association of Kentucky and Tennessee, Tennessee Technological University, Cookeville TN, 25-26 March 1966 (Sneedville TN: Hancock County Drama Association, 1971).

[24]Hening, ed., *The Statutes at Large* 3:250-51, 252.

tion. She was whipped and Sweat, son of a Virginia legislator, appeared at church in a white gown as penance.[25]

By this time John Gowen had enough money to buy his son's freedom from Margaret's master.[26] Because she was in love with Sweat, he did not buy Margaret's freedom. Seeking an education for his son, John indentured Mihill to planter Christopher Stafford, to be freed at the age of twenty-one. While a servant in the Stafford household, Mihill Gowen had a child by a black slave with the Kimbundu name of Pallassa (aka Prossa). When freed, Mihill was allowed to take his son, but not the black mother of the child.[27]

As a free black man Mihill Gowen purchased several acres in James City County, began planting tobacco, and then took a free white woman for his wife.[28]

Through the 1620s and 1630s, the earliest African Americans like the Gowens, labored as servants alongside indentured Europeans and American Indians on the plantations of wealthy planters named Robins, Custis, Littleton, Jordan, Pott, Caulfield, Hawley, Charlton, Scarburgh, Shepard, Evans, Kendall, Vaughn, and Andrews.[29] From 1619 to 1630 they were concentrated in the Virginia counties of Northampton, Surry, York, James City, Charles City, and Elizabeth City. After they served their terms of indenture, in the 1640s, they started buying land near the plantations on which they had toiled. As free people they sought mates who were also free and because free black women were rare, free African men frequently married white or Indian women.

The Kimbundu-speaking Angolans had a name for fellow Angolans taken to America: *malungu*, "those from the same homeland who came on the same ship."[30] It is the earliest word to mean "African American." In time, *malungu* became "Melungeon."

---

[25]H. R. McIlwaine, ed., *Minutes of the Council and General Court of Colonial Virginia*, 477; see also Hening, ed., *The Statutes at Large* 1:552.

[26]McIlwaine, ed., *Minutes of the Council and General Court of Colonial Virginia*, 477.

[27]October 25, 1657—The Manumission of Mihill Gowen, York County Deeds, Orders, and Wills (3) 16, 26 January 1657/8.

[28]York County, Virginia Wills, Deeds, and Orders; and Evans, "The Graysville Melungeons," *Tennessee Anthropologist* 4/1 (1979).

[29]Deal, *Race and Class in Colonial Virginia: Indians, Englishmen, and Africans on the Eastern Shore during the Seventeenth Century.*

[30]Robert W. Slenes, *Malungu, Ngoma Vem!: Africa encoberta e descoberta no Brasil* (Luanda, Angola: Museu Nacional da Escravatura, I.N.P.C., Ministério da Cultura, 1995).

After serving their indentures, the earliest free *malungu* clans acquired land and settled on King's Creek on the Eastern Shore. Before the 1640s, another free group appeared on Cherrystone Creek in Northampton County, Virginia. At the same time, a third Tidewater *malungu* community was developing around the free Johnson family on Pungoteague Creek. The Johnson plantation was named "Angola." The Angolan-American Emanuel Driggers of King's Creek knew and did business with the Angolan-American Anthony Johnson of the Pungoteague.[31] The Driggers (aka Driggus) in Accomack County on the Eastern Shore knew the mixed families of Gowen, Cornish, and Sweat on the Virginia mainland, all before 1670. Before 1700, their families intermarried, adopted each other's children, purchased each other from slavery and traded cattle.

A fourth important *malungu* community was in the lands of Delaware's Nanticoke Indians near a hamlet still named "Angola" and a larger region still today called "Angola Neck." Another *malungu* community centered around the families of John Gowen and John Pedro in Lancaster County, Virginia.

These free Tidewater families of color began appearing in colonial Virginia records over several decades in the 1600s and many of these names are carried by Melungeons today.

[1620s and earlier]: Carter, Cornish, Dale/Dial, Driggers, Gowen/Goins, Johnson, Longo, Mongom/Mongon, Payne

[1630s] Cane, Davis, George, Hartman, Sisco, Tann, Wansey

[1640s] Archer, Kersey, Mozingo, Webb

[1650s] Cuttillo, Jacobs, James

[1660s] Beckett, Bell, Charity, Cumbo, Evans, Francis, Guy, Harris, Jones, Land(r)um, Lovina/Leviner, Moore, Nickens, Powell, Shorter, Tate, Warrick/Warwick

[1670s] Anderson, Atkins, Barton, Boarman, Bowser, Brown, Bunch, Buss, Butcher, Butler, Carney, Case, Church, Combess, Combs, Consellor, Day, Farrell, Fountain, Game, Gibson, Gregory, Grimes, Grinnage, Hobson, Howell, Jeffries, Lee, Manuel, Morris, Mullakin, Nelson, Osborne, Pendarvis, Quander, Redman, Reed, Rhoads, Rustin, Skipper, Sparrow, Stephens, Stinger, Swann, Waters, Wilson

[1680s] Artis, Booth, Britt, Brooks, Bryant, Burkett, Cambridge, Cassidy, Collins, Copes, Cox, Dogan, Donathan, Forten/Fortune, Gwinn,

---

[31]Deal, *Race and Class in Colonial Virginia.*

Hilliard, Hubbard, Impey, Ivey, Jackson, MacDonald, MacGee, Mahoney, Mallory, Okey, Oliver, Penny, Plowman, Press/Priss, Price, Proctor, Robins, Salmons/Sammons, Shoecraft, Walden, Walker, Wiggins, Wilkens, Williams

[1690s] Annis, Banneker, Bazmore, Beddo, Bond, Cannedy/Kennedy, Chambers, Conner, Cuffee, Dawson, Durham, Ford, Gannon, Gates, Graham, Hall, Harrison, Hawkins, Heath, Holt, Horner, Knight, Lansford, Lewis, Malavery, Nichols, Norman, Oxendine, Plummer, Pratt, Prichard, Rawlinson, Ray, Ridley, Roberts, Russell, Sample, Savoy, Shaw, Smith, Stewart, Taylor, Thompson, Toney, Turner, Weaver, Welsh, Whistler, Willis, Young.[32]

At the height of Nazi Germany in the 1930s–1940s, the state of Virginia published a blacklist alerting officials to Melungeons "now attempting to pass as white." The blacklist included many of these surnames of the original seventeenth-century Tidewater *malungu* families.

---

[32]Heinegg, *Free African Americans of North Carolina, Virginia, and South Carolina.*

Chapter 3

Revolutionary Struggles

In the 1960s, as bitter civil rights battles raged, a sociologist named Brewton Berry traveled through the part of the U.S. that made up old colonial America (the region between the Atlantic coast and the Appalachian mountains). He was intrigued by certain villages and communities; small anomalous islands of mysterious people with obscure roots shrouded in the legends and myths of colonial America. Among them were the so-called Melungeons of Appalachia, the Pea Ridge community in Kentucky, and the Guineas in West Virginia. Virginia had the Ramps in Wise County, the 'Brown People' of Rockbridge County, and the Free Issues of Amherst County. North Carolina had Lumbees, Smilings, the Laster Tribe, the 'Portuguese' and the Persons County People.

A Smithsonian Institution study in 1947 indicated kinship between these and certain Native American (Indian) groups, revealed by shared surnames from seventeenth-century *malungu* groups. The report by William Gilbert entitled *Surviving Indian Groups of the Eastern United States*, presented to the Board of Regents of the Smithsonian Institution in 1948, stated:

> These families are found in more than one group and this would point to a possibility of some degree of intermarriage between them at various times in the past. The Croatans (Lumbees) for example, share names with the Cubans, Issues, Melungeons, Brass Ankles, Cajuns and Nanticokes (Indians). Not only do such nearby groups as the Nanticokes and Moors share names, but we find such sharing rather remote from each other, as for example, Cajans and Moors, Brass Ankles and Nanticokes, or Melungeons and Brass Ankles.

Between 1619 and 1660, during the colony's tolerance for mixed marriages and indentured Africans, the Tidewater plantations depended on pirates to bring them Africans before England established slave-trading companies based in Africa. The West Indies Company records show these English and Dutch privateers between 1619 and 1660 stole Africans, not from Africa, but from Spanish and Portuguese slave ships sailing from Angola to the Americas. The *malungu* arrived in Tidewater Virginia culturally and linguistically cohesive. When Bristol and London slave companies began moving captives directly from Africa in the 1670s, the planters ceased depending on random pirate raids. New large-scale slave operations after 1680 increased black numbers from hundreds to many thousands. Around 1700, the colonies came to view lifelong slavery as the proper condition for blacks. This growing intolerance isolated the earlier free *malungu* generation and they became a people apart. The Kimbundu word *malungu* does not mean "African" but rather "African American," and that is how they viewed themselves. Even after taking white wives and Indian wives, their freeborn descendants centuries later continued to live in distinct separate *malungu* communities.

Pressures—prejudice and the search for affordable land—pushed the free *malungu* clans away from the plantations ringing the Chesapeake and out into the frontier. In 1723, Virginia passed a law forbidding free people of color from bearing arms.[1] The American dream was to own a farm. Not long after the Virginia gun-control law was enacted, a free Virginian of color named Gideon Gibson Sr., led several free *malungu* families from Virginia to North Carolina.[2] Gibson acquired thousands of acres and became a successful farmer. In 1728 he married the white daughter of wealthy gentleman planter William Brown.[3] Gideon and Mary Brown Gibson's family were allied with other early *malungu* families in Chowan County including those named Bunch, Chavis, Driggers, and Sweat.[4]

Eventually, this group of "free colored men with their white wives" came to the attention of the South Carolina Assembly.[5] In 1731 Gideon Gibson and his clan were ordered to appear before Governor Robert Johnson to explain their intent to settle on the Santee River. The governor was impressed, and decided to let them stay:

---

[1]Hening, ed., *The Statutes at Large* 4:131.

[2]Heinegg, *Free African Americans of North Carolina, Virginia, and South Carolina.*

[3]Mario de Valdes y Cocom, "The Blurred Racial lines of Famous Families: Gibson," PBS Frontline (25 April 1996), edited text online at <http://www.pbs.org/wgbh/pages/frontline/shows/secret/famous/gibsonfamily.html> (updated January 2004; as accessed 3 November 2005); William Anderson LaBach, "Ancestry of Tobias Gibson (1800–1872)," <http://members.tripod.com/~labach/gibsonan.htm> (as accessed 3 November 2005).

[4]Heinegg, *Free African Americans of North Carolina, Virginia, and South Carolina.*

[5]Ibid.

I have had them before me in Council and upon Examination find that they are not Negroes nor Slaves but Free people, That the Father of them here is named Gideon Gibson and his Father was also free, I have been informed by a person who has lived in Virginia that this Gibson has lived there Several Years in good Repute and by his papers that he has produced before me that his transactions there have been very regular. . . . I have in Consideration of his Wife being a white woman and several White women Capable of working and being Serviceable in the County permitted him to Settle in this County.[6]

Infamous Characters, and Notorious Villains

A pattern emerged. First, the *malungu* families arrived on the frontier. They married the Indians of the area and the whites who came with them. Then, as decades rolled by, other whites they had not known arrived. As settlement progressed European civilization crept around them, bringing race- and class-consciousness. This resulted in conflict.

In the wake of Gideon Gibson, descendants of other free *malungu* clans moved farther west into the backwoods of North Carolina where, as later Europeans arrived, they began agitating the British over high taxes and property seizures. By the 1750s reports were filtering into large cities of trouble with free mulattos over taxes and land patents. Local British officials began complaining to the home office that this "mixt crew" was armed and violently opposed to paying the king's taxes. In 1754, alarmed Loyalists in Bladen County, North Carolina described to the governor "50 families a mixt Crew, a lawless People possess[ing] the Lands without patent or paying quit rents; shot a Surveyor for coming to view vacant lands being inclosed in great swamps."[7]

The "mixt Crew" of "lawless People" were still shooting at surveyors nineteen years later and, in December 1773, Loyalists appealed to the Assembly for action, complaining "of the number of free negroes and mulattoes who infest that county and annoy its Inhabitants."[8]

Six years later, Bladen County sought militia assistance a third time. Petitioner Capt. Jacob Alford complained of a company of whom the "most

---

[6]Ibid.

[7]William Laurence Saunders, *The Colonial Records of North Carolina*, 10 vols. (Raleigh: P. M. Hale [etc.] State Printer, 1886–1890) 5:161.

[8]Ibid. 9:768.

part of The Robbers Are Molattoes" described as "infamous characters, & notorious villains." Capt. Alford informed the North Carolina Assembly:

> Your petitioners are in constant dread & fear of being robbed and murdered by a set of Robbers And Horse Thiefs, which have been among us this week to the number of About Forty, who have Commited A Great deal of Mischief Already. We Understand by Some of them They Soon Intend to Ruin us Altogether In the Borders of our District and Anson County. The Robbers Are Molattoes. Whether you may Allow us to Get Arms to Defend Ourselves, Or Youl Order Some Oyrs [others] to protect us the Orders Must be Speedy otherwise we are Outerly undone.[9]

By "Horse Thiefs," Alford meant the mulattos were recovering their own livestock that Loyalists had seized over unpaid taxes.

The Revolution-era Melungeons descended from free ancestors who were not timid despite vulnerability as an anomalous minority. Philip Mongon, when fined for allegedly stealing an Englishman's hogs a century earlier, disdainfully threw a pair of pigs' ears on the bar where sat the judges.[10] In Sussex County, Delaware, in December 1680, John Johnson was fined for singing "a scurlous disgracfull song" about a white man and his wife.[11] Johnson Driggers of Northampton County, Virginia, appeared in court in 1702 for stealing a hog and then threatening whites "in an insolent manner."[12]

Their *malungu* descendants were just as aggressive. After the Revolution in places such as Hancock County, Tennessee Melungeons would stand trial for illegal voting.[13] In another place they shot a white lawman

---

[9]"Jacob Alford et al., Bladen County, to North Carolina Assembly, 1779. Bladden County, January 23d Day 1779. . . . The Petition of Jacob Alford Captin [*sic*] & The Inhabitants of the Upper part of Bladen County. . . . to the North Carolina General Assembly, 30 January 1779, Records of the General Assembly, Session Records, NCDAH PAR #11277901," cited in *The Southern Debate over Slavery*, vol. 1: *Petitions to the Southern Legislatures, 1778–1864*, ed. Loren Schweninger (Urbana: University of Illinois Press, 2001).

[10]Deal, *Race and Class in Colonial Virginia*.

[11]Sussex County, Virginia Court Records 1680-99, 2, 23, cited by Deal, *Race and Class in Colonial Virginia*. See also Heinegg, *Free African Americans of North Carolina, Virginia, and South Carolina*.

[12]Deal, *Race and Class in Colonial Virginia*. See also Heinegg, *Free African Americans of North Carolina, Virginia, and South Carolina*.

[13]Goins, "History of the Melungeons."

attempting to bar them from election polls.[14] In North Carolina they would form a company to attack Confederates abducting their sons for forced labor.[15] In Louisiana they picked up guns to expel encroaching whites.[16] In the twentieth century they surrounded and attacked the Ku Klux Klan at a memorable battle.[17]

Direct descendants of Gowen, Cumbo, Driggers, and other *malungu* clans of the first generation of British Virginia didn't view themselves as aliens. Even before the Boston Tea Party and the Battle of Bunker Hill, Americans of *malungu* descent such as Capt. Winslow Driggers and Capt. Gideon Gibson II actually led companies of armed white men raiding Loyalist strongholds in the South.[18]

But the Revolution did not solve conflicts with the "mixt crew" in Robeson County, formed from Bladen County, who in 1805 said they were being unfairly treated because of their color. Free mulattos seized the county court and fined their enemies.[19] Maj. William Odom protested that

> at the last October Term of the Superior Court of Fayette Ville District, your Petitioners was try'd for a Riot [and] prosecuted by a Mullattoe by the name of Elisha Cumboe. In the Neighborhood where your petitioners lives, there also lives a family of these Mullattoes, who are well known to be of Infamous Characters. Your petitioners proceeded to apprehend said Cumboe, perhaps without the Legal process of Law; for which he pre-ferred a Bill of Indictment and succeeded so far as to get the above named Maj. William Odom fined in the Sum of Fifteen Pounds, & each of your other petitioners Ten pounds. These Cumboes are of Infamous characters, & Notorious Villains. Your Petitioners pray your Honorable Body will

---

[14]Ivey, "Oral, Printed, and Popular Culture Traditions Related to the Melungeons of Hancock County."

[15]Sider, *Lumbee Indian Histories: Race, Ethnicity, and Indian Identity in the Southern United States.*

[16]J. A. Crawford, *Redbones in the Neutral Strip, or No Man's Land, between the Calcasieu and Sabine Rivers in Louisiana and Texas Respectively, and the Westport Fight between Whites and Red Bones for Possession of this Strip on Christmas Eve, 1882* (Lake Charles LA: pub. by the author, 1955).

[17]"Ku Klux Klan Routing," *Fayetteville Observer*, 18 January 1958.

[18]R. M. Brown, *The South Carolina Regulators* (Cambridge MA: Belknap Press of Harvard University, 1963) 29-31.

[19]Heinegg, *Free African Americans of North Carolina, Virginia, and South Carolina.*

grant us relief by remitting the fine. William Odom, 15th November 1805.[20]

Surprisingly, the legislature rejected Maj. Odom's petition and found for the mulattos. The lead "infamous character," Elisha Cumbo, was the son of the free mulatto Cannon Cumbo who married a white woman.[21] Cannon descended from the seventeenth-century Angolan American *malungu* Manuel Cumbo. Although Elisha was legally barred from testifying, his mixed frontier community was strong enough to challenge its enemies.

Carried Away in the Night

On April 10, 1778, an ad was placed in the *North Carolina Gazette* by Johnson Driggers, a desperate Melungeon father:

> Saturday night, April the 4th, broke into the house of the subscriber at the head of Green's Creek, where I had some small property under the care of Ann Driggers, a free negro woman, two men in disguise, with marks on their faces and clubs in their hands, beat and wounded her terribly and carried away four of her children, three girls and a boy, the biggest of said girls got off in the dark and made her escape, one of the girls name is Becca, and other is Charita, the boy is named Shadrack.

After an abduction on March 12, 1754, John Scott of Berkeley County, South Carolina alerted authorities in Orange County, North Carolina that "Joseph Deevit, Wm. Deevit, and Zachariah Martin, entered by force the house of his daughter, Amy Hawley, and carried her off by force with her six children, and he thinks they are taking them north to sell as slaves." Records show only his son, "a mulatto boy Busby, alias John Scott" was rescued and returned home from the ordeal.

By 1750, these and other free Melungeons lived in constant fear of abduction and loss of liberty during the long night of American slavery when the slightest trace of African blood might lead to abduction. After the

---

[20]"William Odom et al., Robeson County, to North Carolina Assembly, . . . 30 November 1805, Records of the General Assembly," as cited in *The Southern Debate over Slavery*, vol. 1: "1. Despite testimony from a number of witnesses that members of the Cumboe family were of 'Infamous Character' and carried on 'illicit trade,' the Committee of Propositions and Grievances in the House of Commons ruled that the evidence was not sufficient to grant the request" (n. 1).

[21]Heinegg, *Free African Americans of North Carolina, Virginia, and South Carolina.* See "Cumbo."

United States banned the importation of African slaves in 1807, the lucrative domestic slave market tempted man-stealers to prey on mixed people regardless of their free status. Drury Tann of North Carolina recounted how

> he was stolen from his parents when a small boy by persons unknown to him, who were carrying him to sell him into Slavery, and had gotten with him and other stolen property as far as the Mountains on their way, that his parents made complaint to a Mr. Tanner Alford who was Then a magistrate in the county of Wake State of North Carolina, to get me back from those who had stolen me and he did pursue the Rogues & overtook Them at the mountains and took me from Them.[22]

For this and other reasons the *malungu* claimed non-African descent. They were compelled to get certificates in court stating they were Portuguese and not African.

The American Revolution

Despite the 1729 law forbidding arms to free people of color, many Melungeon ancestors did in fact enlist and fight in the American Revolution. Brutus Johnson, son of freeborn parents of Hyde County, North Carolina was described by Charles Wood as "a man of colour who died at Valley Forge while serving as a soldier in the North Carolina Line of the Continental Army."[23] Brutus descended from Anthony and Mary Johnson— free blacks of Northampton County, Virginia who had been among sixty Ndongo prisoners stolen from the Portuguese slave ship *St. John the Baptist* by pirates on July 15, 1619 and brought to Virginia in the 1620s. Paul Heinegg, in *Free African Americans of North Carolina, Virginia, and South Carolina*, says their free mulatto grandson named his plantation, "Angola" in 1660.

Another *malungu* ancestor was John Kecatan, freed from the Charles City County, Virginia plantation of Rice Hoe about 1650. His son, Anthony Tann produced many patriots, including Benjamin Tann who supplied the North Carolina Army in 1783. Benjamin's son Joseph served in the North

---

[22]Heinegg, in the introduction to his *Free African Americans of North Carolina, Virginia, and South Carolina from the Colonial Period to about 1820*, as posted online at <http://www.genealogy.com/genealogy/12_heing.html>.

[23]Heinegg, *Free African Americans in North Carolina, Virginia, and South Carolina*. See under "Johnson." <http://www.freeafricanamericans.com/Jeffrey_Johnson.htm>.

Carolina Continental Line and his heirs received 640 acres. Another son, Ephraim, enlisted in Baker's Company in 1778. His heirs also received 640 acres. Another son, James Tann, was killed in the war. James's niece Hannah Tann received 640 acres from the U.S. Government for his sacrifice. His cousin Drury Tann fought the British with North Carolina's 10th Regiment.

Moses Carter fought in the American Revolution and established a *malungu* settlement. He descended from Paul and Hannah Carter, freed servants from the Littleton Plantation, circa 1640, Northampton County, Virginia. Moses was a "man of color" in Capt. Joseph Rhode's 1st Regiment from July 1782 to July 1783. Five years later he obtained 100 acres near Six Runs and Rowan Swamp and received an army pension in Sampson County in October 1820. His cousin John Carter enlisted in the war and, in Capt. Quinn's 10th Regiment, saw action at West Point and at Kings Ferry. Another cousin, Isaac Carter, described as a "mulatto," was taken prisoner by the British and later released in 1780. He married into another historic *malungu* clan, the Perkinses.[24]

John Gowen and Margaret Cornish, early Angolans of seventeenth-century Virginia produced many patriots in the eighteenth century. Edward Gowen Jr. enlisted in Bute County, Virginia and, in 1791, sold his claim for Revolutionary War pay to John Hall.[25] Edward was a great grandfather of Daniel Goins, who in 1882 Randolph County, North Carolina reported that his ancestry was, "slitly mixt about an eight."[26]

Edward's brother Reeps Gowen served in Capt. Thomas Hall's Second South Carolina Regiment beginning in 1779. A third brother, Jenkins was listed as a seventeen-year-old "mullato" in the Granville County Militia Company of Capt. John Rust. David Gowen, son of Shadrack Gowen, joined in the same county. His cousin Anne married another Melungeon named Dudley Miner in 1795 in Henrico County.[27]

Another cousin, Frederick Gowen married a Chavis girl in Mecklenburg County, Virginia in 1789. He had fought the British at the age of

---

[24]Heinegg, *Free African Americans of North Carolina, Virginia, and South Carolina*.

[25]Heinegg, *Free African Americans of North Carolina, Virginia, and South Carolina*. See also Gowen Research Foundation archives online at <http://bz.llano.net/gowen/>.

[26]Virginia DeMarce, "Very Slightly Mixt: Triracial Isolate Families of the Upper South—A Genealogical Study," *National Genealogical Society Quarterly* (March 1992).

[27]Heinegg, *Free African Americans of North Carolina, Virginia, and South Carolina*. See also Gowen Research Foundation archives online.

sixteen. A large free community of color existed on the banks of the Meherrin River where he was born.[28]

Patrick Mason married Patsey Gowen in 1790. In Person County he filed on May 12, 1828 for his Revolution pension. Patrick was the grandson of a white woman named Sarah Mason who was living in St. Ann's Parish, Essex County, Virginia on 21 June 1743 when the court sold her for five years as punishment for having a 'Mulatto' child."[29] The "Person County Indians" are kinsmen of the Melungeons.

John "Buck" Gowen rose to the rank of major in the Revolution. His kinsmen fought in his company. His cousin Zephaniah Goins saw Cornwallis surrender at Yorktown and moved to Hancock County, Tennessee after the War and was known as a Melungeon.[30]

According to Mary Elizabeth Motley Beadles, a descendant and a member of the Daughters of the American Revolution, Drury Going was born in Brunswick County, Virginia in 1749 and moved to the Camden District of South Carolina with a number of other mixed clans. In 1767 Drury married seventeen-year-old Sarah "Sallie" Baxter of Granville County, North Carolina. The young couple settled down to build a farm and a family.

However, duty called and Drury Going was soon fighting the British in the brigade of the famous "Swamp Fox," Gen. Francis Marion. Marion took rough frontiersmen who could ride and shoot and forged them into a deadly guerilla army slashing into British strongholds in the South. The brigade's lightning-fast attacks at Georgetown, Ft. Watson, Ft. Motte, and Eutaw Springs divided British forces and were responsible for boosting the morale of the Continental Army then losing battles everywhere. Marion's Brigade won a stunning victory at the Battle of Parker's Ferry and the U.S. Congress awarded a Congressional Medal to all of Marion's men.[31]

Drury Going and his cousin James Goyne (from "Gowen") fought in Col. Winn's South Carolina Regiment under Gen. Marion's command.[32]

---

[28]Heinegg, *Free African Americans of North Carolina, Virginia, and South Carolina*.

[29]Heinegg, *Free African Americans of North Carolina, Virginia, and South Carolina*.

[30]"Major John 'Buck' Gowen," *Gowen Research Foundation Newsletter* 2/1, ed. Arlee Gowen (September 1990). See also "Zephaniah Goins Fought in Yorktown Campaign," *GRF Newsletter* 5/3, ed. Arlee Gowen (November 1993).

[31]"Brunswick County, Virginia," *Gowen Research Foundation Manuscript*, ed. Arlee Gowen. <http://freepages.genealogy.rootsweb.com/~gowenrf/Gowenms133.htm>.

[32]"Brunswick County, Virginia," *Gowen Research Foundation Manuscript*, ed. Arlee

Tactics learned from the 'Swamp Fox' would aid Melungeons known as Red Bones in defeating whites who encroached upon their territory in Louisiana and Texas a century later. Today, "Francis Marion" remains a common Christian name for Red Bone descendants in Louisiana and Texas.[33]

In 1787, Drury Going used his Army grant to obtain more than 300 acres from Merry McGuire on the south side of Broad River. The following year he bought an additional 100 acres on Turkey Creek in Chester County. On July 8, 1788 he confessed to having an illegitimate child by a white woman named Sarah Golden. Required to pay a fine of five pounds in addition to Sarah's fine, he also agreed to provide for the welfare of the child. Chester County owed him money and his fines were deducted from that amount.[34]

These were the freeborn patriots of color who descended from *malungu* African pioneers brought to Virginia in the seventeenth century by pirates. They used their war pensions to migrate and acquire land east of the Appalachian Mountains after the young states forgot about their sacrifice. In the twentieth century, Virginia would call them "mongrels."

Exile

Slave-holding states, particularly those from the original colonies, believed free people of color like the Melungeons stirred up the slaves. The Nat Turner Rebellion turned that fear into fanaticism. In 1831 a petition to the state legislature was introduced by a delegation from Northampton County, Virginia calling for immediate plans to send all free Americans of color to Liberia, Africa. The mixed families they wanted to deport had lived in America for two centuries at the time and many had fought for independence.

Relying on information obtained by the federal census, the petition declared:

Gowen. <http://freepages.genealogy.rootsweb.com/~gowenrf/Gowenms133.htm>.

[33]Don C. Marler, "The Louisiana Red Bones," a paper presented at the First Union, a meeting of Melungeons, at Clinch Valley College, Wise, Virginia, July 1997, posted online at <http://dogwoodpress.myriad.net/dcm/redbone.html> and on the <multiracial.com> website. For updated information on Red Bones, see Marler, *Red Bones of Louisiana* (Hemphill TX: Dogwood Press, 2003).

[34]"Brunswick County, Virginia" (see n. 32).

By the last census of the United States it appears that there are in this county 3,573 whites, 3,734 slaves, and 1,334 free persons of colour. By a comparison with the census of preceding years it also appears that the proportion of free persons of colour to our white inhabitants is annually increasing. A fact of this sort under any circumstances would be a source of well founded uneasiness. The free persons of colour in Virginia form an anomalous population, standing in a relation to our society, which naturally exposes them to distrust & suspicion. Inferior to the whites in intelligence & information; degraded by the stain which attaches to their colour; excluded from many civil privileges which the humblest white man enjoys, and denied all participation in the government, it would be absurd to expect from them attachment to our laws & institutions nor sympathy with our people.

Fearing that free people of color would lead slaves in rebellion, Northampton County petitioned to send them back to Africa:

It is absolutely necessary, not only to the correct government of our slaves, but also to the peace & security of our society, that all free persons of colour should be promptly removed from this county. That the free negroes of our county ought, if practicable, to be sent to Liberia in Africa.

After obtaining a loan for the removal, the committee was to "make known the same to the free negroes, & to make arrangements for their removal to Liberia of such of them as are willing to go there." Whites intended to coerce those reluctant to leave:

After the arrangements for their removal have been made, we pledge ourselves not to employ, or have any dealings with any free negros in the county . . . we pledge ourselves not to rent to any free negro any house or land, and that we will forthwith give notice to those with whom we have contracted to quit on the 1st day of June next.[35]

Most free people of color after 200 years considered themselves Americans. Instead of getting on the boat, many got in their wagons and moved west.

---

[35]*The Southern Debate over Slavery*, vol 1: *Petitions to the Southern Legislatures, 1778–1864*, ed. Schweninger.

Westward Yo

In 1741, an ad in the *South Carolina Gazette* read: "Help Wanted, a Man use to a Cow Pen and of good Character." The ancestor of the Ashworths of Texas was James Ashworth, described as a "tall, lusty man, of swarthy complexion, and short black hair."[36] James Ashworth was a skilled cattleman in the Carolina backcountry in the 1760s. He enlisted with Capt. James Leslie of the South Carolina Militia in the campaign against the Cherokees in 1759, and in 1810 Ashworth and his wife Keziah Dial Ashworth, of the *malungu* Doll family of seventeenth-century Virginia, moved to St. Landry Parish, Louisiana with their four sons William, Aaron, Abner, and Moses.[37]

One son married into the Perkins family, descended from Esther Perkins, a white indentured servant who in 1730 bore a mulatto child in Accomack County, Virginia. Another Ashworth son married into the Bunch clan. This family came from John Bunch, a mulatto born in Virginia in 1684 who in 1705 had petitioned the Virginia Council to be allowed to marry a white woman, Sarah Slayden, after the minister of Blisland Parish refused to perform the ceremony. Bunch families are also found among the Tennessee Melungeons and the Red Bones of Louisiana.

In the early nineteenth century, the Ashworths drove their cattle across the Sabine River into Texas. In *North American Cattle-Ranching Frontiers*, Terry G. Jordan-Bychkov[38] wrote that these Ashworths were Melungeon-Red Bones and were the first non-Mexican ranching families in Texas. By the early 1830s they had settled near present-day Orange, Texas. The Ashworth brothers integrated the cattle-tending system they had developed on South Carolina's Peedee River with the Spanish cattle culture to

---

[36]Terry G. Jordan-Bychkov, *Trails to Texas: Southern Roots of Western Cattle Ranching* (Lincoln: University of Nebraska Press, 1981); W. T. Block, "The Meanest Town on the Coast," *Old West* (Winter 1979); Heinegg, *Free African Americans of North Carolina, Virginia, and South Carolina*; Nolan Thompson, "Ashworth Act," *The Handbook of Texas Online* <http://www.tsha.utexas.edu/handbook/online/articles/AA/mla3.html> (accessed 9 November 2005); Marler, "The Louisiana Red Bones"; Scott Withrow, "Red Bones: The Appalachian Connection," a paper read at Fourth Union, 22 June 2002.

[37]Heinegg, *Free African Americans of North Carolina, Virginia, and South Carolina*.

[38]Terry G. Jordan-Bychkov, *North American Cattle-Ranching Frontiers: Origins, Diffusion, and Differentiation*, Histories of the American Frontier (Albuquerque: University of New Mexico Press, 1993; repr. 2000).

produce the epic Anglo-Texas cattle drives into Missouri and Kansas years later. Innovations such as cattle drives on horseback, open ranges, corrals, summer and winter pastures, bulldogging, and steer wrestling originated in seventeenth-century Virginia with Angolan *malungu* cattle herders. The bullwhip is a colonial American invention of rawhide plaited in strips up to twenty-five feet in length. Jordan says the free-black Carolina cowboys also used leopard dogs: "fierce cur-dogs, one of which accompanies each cattle-hunter, and is taught to pursue cattle, and to even take them down by the nose." Lacking the Spanish lariat, the South Carolina cowboy developed steer wrestling to force cattle into the pens. The colonial cowherd also used the salt lick in the absence of fences to control wandering cattle. The Ashworths first introduced these practices into Texas and they became successful early cattle barons.

Jordan-Bychkov also cites the word "buckaroo" as coming from the South Carolina *bockorau*, which originated with the Angolan-African word *buckra* and not the Spanish word *vaquero* as commonly claimed. The word *buckra* referred to whites and to mixed people roughly the same as the word "cracker" was used to describe those who herded cattle with whips. Livestock pens in South Carolina were called "craul" or "crawl." The word was derived from the African word *kraal* and was brought in with the *malungu*. Angolans in North America originated the South Carolina "crawl" for "cowpen" just as Angolans in Central America gave the Spanish the word *corral*.[39]

William and Aaron Ashworth moved to the Zavala Colony in southeast Texas in 1831 during the Comanche-Kiowa wars. When the War for Texas Independence began, William, as many whites did, paid a kinsman named Gibson Perkins to fight in his stead. As his name suggests, Gibson Perkins was related to both the Melungeon Gibsons and the Perkinses of Tennessee and Louisiana. Perkins served in the Beaumont Volunteers company in 1836 until the end of the Texas war with Mexico. Even though the Beaumont District had previously barred free persons of color from immigrating, the Ashworths were allowed to settle and William Ashworth won an important contract from Jefferson County in 1838 to operate a ferry between Lake Sabine and Beaumont.

William eventually accumulated vast tracts of land and herds of cattle, but in 1840 the Republic of Texas, alarmed by the growing number of non-

---

[39]Jordan-Bychkov, *North American Cattle-Ranching Frontiers.*

white immigrants and fearing a Nat Turner-inspired slave rebellion, enacted legislation ordering all free blacks and mulattos to leave the country or face slavery. White friends persuaded the Texas Congress to exempt the Ashworths. The legislature passed the *Ashworth Act*, which allowed free people of color living in Texas before 1836 to remain. On December 12, 1840, Texas president Mirabeau B. Lamar signed the first petition. But two years later in 1842 color discrimination returned front and center. The Texas Land Board refused to acknowledge ownership of lands claimed by the Ashworths, saying the regulations of the board did not include ownership by free blacks. Friends again petitioned the Texas Congress to go over the land board's head and pass an act certifying the Ashworths' claims. Then Texas President Sam Houston signed the bill into law.

Sixteen years later, the Ashworths faced their greatest race challenge. Texas had become a state in the Union and by 1850 Aaron Ashworth was the wealthiest man in Jefferson County, Texas. Many Ashworths married white women and the older whites from the days of the Texas Republic accepted the mixed marriages. But a new breed of Anglo settlers from east of the Appalachians was arriving. They had nothing but open contempt for the early pioneers of color. The Ashworths were compelled to organize a Regulator company for self-protection when their white enemies formed as Moderators in the Orange County War of 1856. Newspapers were pro-Moderator and official versions of the war were usually slanted in favor of whites.

Madison, Texas, now named Orange,[40] was a prosperous, pretty town in 1856 with

> white fairy-tale cottages pleasantly situated along a cypress-studded mile-long crescent of the Sabine River. . . . Population 600, the town owed its existence to the lumber industry and led the state in manufacturing and exporting wood products. A half-dozen sawmills and shingle mills, two shipyards, stores, and cotton warehouses stretched along the river where

---

[40]The following account of Madison/Orange, Texas and the Orange County War of 1856 is based on Block's "The Meanest Town on the Coast," *Old West* (Winter 1979): 10ff.; as posted online at <http://www.wtblock.com/wtblockjr/mulattoe.htm>. Sources: the *Galveston Weekly News* and the *Tri-Weekly News*, 1 June to 15 July 1979. Also see A. F. Muir, "The Free Negroes of Jefferson and Orange Counties, Texas," *Journal of Negro History* 35 (April 1950); Johnnie Blair Deen, "Trinity County Kinsearching," four-part series, *Groveton* (Texas) *News*, 1–22 October 1998; and William Ashworth, "The Handbook of Texas Online" <http://www.tsha.utexas.edu/handbook/online/articles/AA/fas6.html>.

steamboats and sailing vessels docked to export timber throughout the nation.

But according to historian W. T. Block, beneath the town's idyllic setting lay a quiet storm of prejudice, envy, and ugliness that would blow up into race violence that year.

Numbering about 100, in 1856 there were more free people of color in Orange County than anywhere else in Texas and they were led by the Ashworth brothers and their in-laws Hiram Bunch, Gibson Perkins, and Elijah Thomas. The old Melungeon settlers held land grants given to them by the Republic of Texas for service in the 1836 war with Mexico. They also held even older Mexican land grants. Late-arriving whites starting from scratch envied those prosperous black men who came to town with white wives on their arms. Accusations of stealing and counterfeiting began circulating.

Trouble started on May 15, 1856 when Deputy Sheriff Samuel Deputy (his real name) arrested Clark Ashworth for allegedly stealing a white man's hog.

Judge A. N. Reading released the defendant into the custody of his kinsman Sam Ashworth. But seething over the arrest of his cousin, Sam Ashworth got a gun. Confronting Sam Deputy in Madison he challenged him to a gunfight. Deputy declined and promptly arrested Sam under a "statute providing against abusive language from Negroes."

Presiding Justice Reading subpoenaed witnesses who testified that Sam was "of mixed blood, or a Mulatto." The judge ordered Ashworth be given "30 lashes on the bare back" and turned him over to the sheriff, a friend of the Ashworths. When Sam Ashworth escaped jail some suspected Sheriff Edward C. Glover had intentionally released him.

Free again, Ashworth and his eighteen-year-old cousin Jack Bunch rowed a skiff to Cow Bayou to await Officer Deputy who habitually took that route home. After a few hours Sam Deputy and a friend named A. C. Merriman rowed up. Ashworth shot him dead. Merriman furiously paddled back to town. Pressed to act, Sheriff Glover gathered a posse to go after Ashworth and Bunch. When Glover returned empty-handed, Deputy's friends demanded another posse be raised. The new posse led by Joshua Harmon heard the two fugitives were hiding at the Empire Sawmill Company. On May 31 the frustrated posse lit a match to the mill, said to be the best in the state. According to Block, 100,000 feet of fine-cut lumber went up in smoke. Ashworth and Bunch were miles away.

Vigilantes calling themselves Moderators began ransacking and burning Melungeon houses and barns at will. Bunch was eventually captured in Montgomery County, Texas and returned to Madison where he was lynched by the Moderators. Sheriff Glover, sensing the murderous mood of the Moderators, fled town while Melungeons began moving their families across the Sabine River into Louisiana. Hearing that Glover had raised a band of Melungeons at Ballew's Ferry, dozens of Moderators with "double-barrel muskets, knives, and a general assortment of Colt jewelry" gathered in town. Among them was a stranger recently arrived, a cold-blooded killer named Jack Cross who was running from murder warrants in West Texas. The Moderators issued

> an ultimatum warning all Mulattoes and their white associates (including the Sheriff and his posse) to remove themselves fifty miles beyond the county borders within twenty-four hours on penalty of death.
> Many mulattoes crossed the river to safety, but Glover and his men remained hidden in the vicinity of Brandon's and Moore's log cabins near Ballew's Ferry, about ten miles north of Madison.

On June 15, at one in the afternoon, a friend of the Ashworths named Bennett Thomas got into a gunfight with a Moderator named Willis Bonner and left him dead in the streets of Madison. That sparked a second duel an hour later when killer Jack Cross ran into Ashworth ally Burwell Alexander on Front Street and shot him in the neck. As Dr. Andrew Mairs knelt to help his mortally wounded friend, Cross killed him in cold blood.

On June 22, dozens of Moderators rode north searching for Sheriff Glover and his Regulator posse. Two strangers passing through the country were mistaken for Regulators and were murdered on the spot. Locating the hideout near the Ferry, the Moderators surrounded the cabins where the Regulators were holed up. After exchanging gunfire the outgunned Regulators surrendered on terms they be escorted to the county line with the promise of never returning. However, the whites were intent on taking Sheriff Glover and his uncle, John C. Moore back to stand trial.

Knowing he would be lynched, Moore resisted. Several Moderators fired and Moore "died on the floor of his cabin with the cocked revolver still clenched in his fist." Outlaw Jack Cross then pulled his pistol and casually murdered the unarmed sheriff. This act signaled the end of the shooting.

Cross had worn out his welcome and he crossed the Sabine into Louisiana. He killed Jake Morrison in 1857, but this time the odds were with the Melungeons. A quick verdict in Red Bone country "left him swinging from the broad branch of a live-oak tree."

In the 1850 census, Aaron Ashworth was listed as the richest man in the county, but by 1860 his estate had been cut in half and an entire herd of 3,000 cattle completely vanished. Elderly William Ashworth had to take a job as a day laborer to support his white wife, Layde. Decades later, the nation's first oilfield, Spindletop, sprouted derricks where Ashworth cattle once grazed.

One year after the Orange County War, a wagon train of Melungeons left Georgia for Texas. Alfred Franklin Mayo led the party until it halted near Valentine, Louisiana. Before going their separate ways, all men and boys older than twelve gathered apart from the circled wagons and swore an oath to conceal their past.[41]

Then, the war over slavery began.

---

[41]Johnnie Blair Deen, "Trinity County Kinsearching."

Chapter 4

Civil War Struggles

In the Civil War, Melungeons produced a Medal of Honor recipient. Harrison Collins, born in Hawkins County, Tennessee, enlisted in the 1st Tennessee Cavalry Regiment, USA. Collins earned the nation's highest award for capturing Chalmer's divisional flag at the battle of Richland Creek. He was described in his enlistment papers as "dark complexion, blue eyes, light hair, farmer."

Melungeons not only fought in the Civil War, they participated in the event that ignited it. John Anthony Copeland, Jr. and Lewis Sheridan Leary descended from free, mixed families with *malungu* roots.[1] On October 16, 1859, John Brown and twenty-one men seized the U.S. Armory at Harper's Ferry, West Virginia. With him were Copeland and Leary.[2]

Harper's Ferry

John Copeland was from Raleigh, North Carolina. His family had moved to Oberlin, Ohio in 1842 and while attending Oberlin College his uncle introduced him to John Brown. In September 1859 Copeland joined Brown's cause but he was no recent convert to abolition. He and thirty-six other men had rescued a fugitive slave named John Price, a deed for which Copeland served time in a Cleveland prison.

Copeland's uncle, twenty-five-year-old harness maker Lewis Leary, was another free Melungeon of North Carolina. He too had moved to Oberlin, Ohio where he married and had a child. In 1857, Leary met John Brown in Cleveland and became one of his first lieutenants. Leary's ancestor was an Irishman named Jeremiah O'Leary who married a woman of Melungeon ancestry said to have descended from Raleigh's "lost

---

[1]Heinegg, *Free African Americans of North Carolina, Virginia, and South Carolina.*

[2]William Elsey Connelley, *John Brown* (Topeka KS: Crane & Co., 1900); see also Oswald Garrison Villard, *John Brown 1800–1859: A Biography Fifty Years After* (1910; repr.: Gloucester MA: P. Smith, 1966).

colonists" of Roanoke Island. This Melungeon White Doe tale is very early and elusive. Virginia Dare, first English child born in North America (in 1587), was torn between one young Indian of the Chesapeake and another of the Hatteras tribes. She was transformed into a white doe said to still haunt the area of Roanoke.

In October 1859, Brown's twenty-one abolitionists began moving towards Harper's Ferry to take the arsenal and summon slaves from nearby plantations to join them. Whites had feared such a scheme for decades. With surprise on their side, the raiders seized several objectives. But before the slaves could rally, the militia responded and cut off the roads. The siege lasted three days. Leary was severely wounded and lingered eight hours before dying. His final words in a message to his wife were, "I am ready to die." On the morning of the 18th, the Marines broke through the barricaded door and captured the surviving raiders, including John Copeland.

Brown and his men were quickly tried in Charlestown. Convicted, they were sentenced to hang in December of the same year. During the trial John Copeland won the admiration of his enemies, including the judge and the prosecuting attorney. James Monroe, who was sent to Virginia by Copeland's parents to retrieve his body, wrote:

> Mr. Andrew Hunter, who was the State prosecutor at the trial, in communications given to the press a few years since, says: "Copeland was the cleverest of all the prisoners. He had been educated at Oberlin. He was the son of a free negro, and behaved better than any man among them. If I had had the power and could have concluded to pardon any, he was the man I would have picked out. He behaved with as much firmness as any of them, and with far more dignity."

Judge Parker in the St. Louis *Globe Democrat* in 1888, said: "Copeland was the prisoner who impressed me best. He was a free negro. He had been educated, and there was a dignity about him that I could not help liking. He was always manly."[3] Lewis Leary's widow, Mary, later married a man named Langston. Their grandson was the great poet, Langston Hughes.

---

[3]James Monroe, "A Journey to Virginia In December, 1859," in his *Oberlin Thursday Lectures, Addresses, and Essays* (Oberlin OH: E. J. Goodrich, 1897) 158-59; this address is also published online at <http://www.oberlin.edu/external/EOG/History268/monroe.html>.

Bridge Burners

On June 8, 1861, the state of Tennessee voted to secede from the Union. However, voters in the eastern third of the state near its borders with Virginia and Kentucky opposed leaving the Union by a margin of 2 to 1. This was the heartland of "Melungia," and from it came a Melungeon who personally presented President Lincoln a daring plan to divide East Tennessee from the rest of the state and place it back in Union hands.

William Blount Carter was a free descendant of Paul and Hannah Carter, two early seventeenth-century Angolan *malungu* of Northampton County, Virginia. By the 1860s many of the Carters had assimilated into white society, rising to great prominence and influence. But two of W. B. Carter's friends were simple potters who shared a 200-year-old link with the famous clergyman. Jacob Harmon and his son Henry descended from the old Angolan William Harman. In the mid-seventeenth century William Harman married a free black woman named Jane Gussall, the twenty-two-year-old daughter of Emanuel Driggus. They settled in the *malungu* community on King's Creek in Northampton and joined other early mulatto families, including the Carters.

Tennessee Governor William Brownlow hated Presbyterian minister William Blount Carter who called him "King" Brownlow because of the power he had amassed. Gov. Brownlow was the same "Parson" Brownlow who two decades earlier, in the *Knoxville Whig*, taunted an "impudent Malungeon" as a "kinky-headed villain." With equal venom the *Whig* launched a crusade against William Blount Carter, attacking his ancestry:

> Reverend! W. B. Carter, one of the orators of the late Johnson meeting in this city, is a very dark-skinned man. He has always been called "Black Bill Carter." But for the straightness of his hair he would pass anywhere for a negro. No mulatto or half-breed in the South is darker than "Black Bill Carter." In his speech here he complained that "though an original Union man, he was disfranchised under the laws of Tennessee, while Judge George Brown, who was a rebel, could vote." He added that his only consolation and hope of being permitted to vote, was that "his skin was black." He thought this would pass him with the Radicals. We can tell the Reverend!! gentleman he is mistaken. His black skin will not be a

passport with Tennessee Radicals, because they know his heart is blacker than his skin, or that of any negro in the State.[4]

East Tennessee was a vital railway link for the Confederacy, but previous Union plans to capture the region were unfeasible. W. B. Carter believed there was a way however, and in September 1861 approached Gen. George Thomas of the 2nd Tennessee Infantry Regiment with his plan. Gen. Thomas was impressed and wired Gen. George B. McClellan in Washington:

> I have just had a conversation with Mr. W. B. Carter, of Tennessee, on the subject of destruction of the Grand Trunk Railroad through that State. It would be one of the most important services that could be done for the country, and I most earnestly hope you will use your influence with the authorities in furtherance of his plans, which he will submit to you, together with the reasons for doing the work.[5]

W. B. Carter was summoned to Washington where, before President Lincoln, he laid out the scheme to split East Tennessee from the Confederacy. Lincoln approved and authorized Union forces to assist. Back in Kentucky, Carter began collecting volunteers in Tennessee and Virginia. The plotters from those states faced treason charges if caught.

The bold plan was large scale: the main railroad bridges in a 150-mile area between Virginia and Georgia were targeted for destruction and several small teams of civilian saboteurs would be required. Scheduled for the night of November 8, 1861, the burning bridges would signal Union sympathizers in the South to take up arms against the Rebels. Without bridges, the Confederacy could not send in reinforcements, and the 2nd Tennessee Infantry USA would march in to occupy East Tennessee. Jacob Harmon and son Henry were to destroy the vital Lick Creek bridge.

On the appointed night the teams of East Tennessee saboteurs destroyed half of the bridges targeted and damaged the remaining. But with the inefficiency that would plague it throughout the war, the Union Army hesitated, marched, hesitated again, and then retreated as Gen. Thomas decided at the last moment that he did not have the necessary forces despite Gen. McClellan's urgent order to proceed.

---

[4]*East Tennessee Union Flag*, 5 October 1866, reprinted from the *Knoxville Whig*.

[5]Richard Current, *Lincoln's Loyalists: Union Soldiers from the Confederacy* (Boston: Northeastern University Press, 1992; New York: Oxford University Press, 1994).

The U.S. Army abandoned the civilian bridge saboteurs to their fate. The Confederacy responded quickly, pouring troops into East Tennessee and repairing bridges. Precious seconds passed. Carter's brother wrote,

> Recruits are arriving almost every day from East Tennessee. The Union men coming to us represent the people in East Tennessee as waiting with the utmost anxiety for the arrival of the Federal forces. If the loyal people who love and cling to the Government are not soon relieved they will be lost.

The Confederates arrested several of the bridge burners, including Jacob Harmon and his son. Col. W. B. Wood wired Confederate Secretary of War Judah P. Benjamin on November 20, 1861 for permission to hang the conspirators for treason:

> The rebellion in East Tennessee has been put down in some of the counties, and will be effectually suppressed in less than two weeks in all the counties. . . . We have now in custody some of their leaders, Judge Patterson, the son-in-law of Andrew Johnson, Col. Pickens, the senator from Sevier, and others of influence and some distinction in their counties. . . . They really deserve the gallows, and, if consistent with the laws, ought speedily to receive their deserts.

The order came back: "All such as can be identified in having been engaged in bridge-burning are to be tried summarily by drum-head court martial, and, if found guilty, executed on the spot by hanging in the vicinity of the burned bridges."

Hundreds who had exposed themselves as Union sympathizers were arrested in East Tennessee, and most of those who had actually carried out the bridge burnings were tried. Confederate guards at the Lick Creek Bridge identified the Harmons and on December 12, 1861 Jacob Harmon, his son, and three others were executed by hanging.

The U.S. Congress had the five men posthumously enrolled in the Union Army and their sacrifice became a rallying cry for the 2nd Tennessee Infantry USA to regain its honor.

Lumbees and Rebels

"There is not, probably, a negro in Scuffletown who would betray him, and his prowess is a household word in every black family in seaboard

Carolina." George Alfred Townsend in 1872 was describing Henry Berry Lowery of North Carolina.[6]

Claiming descent from Raleigh's Roanoke colony, they were once known as "Croatoan Indians," and in the twentieth century, as Lumbee Indians. Forbidden to testify against whites, the Lumbees suffered much abuse in the nineteenth century. For example, a white man would tie up his mule on the land of a Lumbee and then complain to the sheriff that the landowner had stolen his mule. Lumbees were then coerced into turning over land to settle the dispute. According to Gerald Sider,

> Land loss, particularly for Scuffletown's larger landholders, began after the Revolutionary War and increased dramatically following the 1835 statewide disfranchisement of free persons of color, and the inclusion of the ancestors of the present-day Lumbee and Tuscarora in that category. Free persons of color lost the right to keep and bear arms, to vote, to testify against whites in court, to sit on a jury, to attend state-supported schools and to select ministers for their churches.[7]

The Civil War placed Robeson County, North Carolina directly in the line of fire. Confederate patrols seized Lumbee men to work in labor camps because they held Lumbee lives to be less valuable than the lives of African slaves. Sider continues:

> The most important merchant port in the Upper South was at Wilmington, North Carolina about seventy miles east of the center of

---

[6]Heinegg, *Free African Americans of North Carolina, Virginia, and South Carolina*. The Lumbee and Melungeons, according to Heinegg, are related through many of the same families—Bennett, Berry, Chavis, Cole, Cumba/Cumbo/ Cumbow, Goins, Graham, Lucas, Martin, White, and Wright. Today Lumbees are recognized as "Indians" by the state of North Carolina. In Heinegg, see "Chavis," "Dolls," and "Locklear." See also George Alfred Townsend, *The Swamp Outlaws: Being a Complete History of the Modern Rob Roys and Robin Hoods* (New York: M. DeWitt, 1872); Karen I. Blu, *The Lumbee Problem: The Making of an American Indian People*, Cambridge Studies in Cultural Systems 5 (Cambridge and New York: Cambridge University Preess, 1980; repr. with an afterword by the author: Lincoln: University of Nebraska Press, 2001); Loren Schweninger, "Maroonage and Flight: An Overview," paper presented at the Fourth Annual International Conference at the Gilder Lerhman Center for the Study of Slavery, Resistance, and Abolition . . . at Yale University, 6 December 2002, online at <http://www.yale.edu/gle/maroon/schweninger.pdf>; and Sider, *Lumbee Indian Histories: Race, Ethnicity, and Indian Identity in the Southern United States*.

[7]Gerald M. Sider, *Lumbee Indian Histories: Race, Ethnicity, and Indian Identity in the Southern United States* (New York: Cambridge University Press, 1993).

Robeson County's Indian settlement, then called Scuffletown, and they were directly connected to each other by the Wilmington, Charlotte, and Rutherford Railroad which passed right through, and had several small stations within the center of the Indian settlement. To protect this port during the war the Confederacy built an enormous sand and dirt fortification—Fort Fisher, one of the largest engineering projects ever undertaken at the time—at the pestilence-soaked mouth of the estuary, requisitioning slaves from surrounding plantations for the work. After the yellow fever epidemic of 1862–1863 substantially increased the already high mortality of the fort's laborers, slaveowners complained even more strongly about the use of their slaves for this work.

Free persons of color were thus in serious trouble, being people who could be forced to work much like slaves and simultaneously people whose deaths were far less costly to the White elite. Robeson County, with one of the largest "free colored" populations in the state, suffered the brunt of the labor impressment . . . people who resisted or who fled could be and were summarily shot for such crimes as "desertion."

In 1864 a white neighbor named James Barnes accused a wealthy Lumbee named Allan Lowery of stealing his hogs. Barnes was also directing Confederate labor recruiters to the Lowery family, then numbering ten sons. On Christmas Eve 1864 one of those sons, Henry Berry Lowery, shot and killed Barnes.

Three weeks later Henry Berry Lowery shot down Confederate recruitment officer J. Brantley Harris. Harris wanted a Scuffletown woman that Henry's cousin was seeing and he had murdered one of the Lowery boys out of spite. Harris then arrested two other Lowery brothers, fearing they would take vengeance against him, and then he shot them both in cold blood with their hands tied behind their backs. An all-white Robeson County grand jury refused to indict Harris so, after warning him, Henry Berry Lowery shot Harris in broad daylight. Both sides unanimously agreed that Lowery, however violent, always warned his enemies in advance that he was coming.

Three weeks later the local Home Guard militia was dispatched to the prosperous farm of Henry's father, Allan Lowery, on a tip that he was concealing a cache of weapons. Free people of color were forbidden to own guns. No weapons were found but the militia shot down Allan Lowery in cold blood and then murdered another one of his sons. As father and son lay dying, the militia members tied Henry's mother Maria Cumba Lowery and her daughters to posts, shamefully assaulted the blindfolded women and then, pretending to execute them, fired a volley over their heads to frighten them into revealing the location of the phantom hoard of guns.

Henry Berry Lowery, away from home at the time, vowed revenge and that day the Lumbee clans deep in the heart of the South began to breathe fire. First, they needed guns: "Henry Berry and a group of followers almost immediately raided the courthouse in Lumberton, seizing for themselves and their community a large supply of modern, breech-loading rifles destined for the local militia and the war was on."[8]

The band of kinsmen, friends, free mulattos, and slaves included the Oxendines and the old free *malungu* Chavis, Cumbo, and Dial families. Hiding out in the swamps near Moss Neck, the band would launch sudden attacks against plantations and whites who pointed out Lumbee men for the deadly Confederate work brigades. They successfully robbed the Confederate arms depot twice. The Confederates stepped up raids on Lumbee farms in March 1865 but stopped as Gen. Sherman approached.

Henry Berry Lowery was never caught and no one has yet documented his end. Lumbees say that his spirit still lives. It would flame again when the Lumbees confronted the Ku Klux Klan in the twentieth century.

Battle of Newman's Ridge

The Clinch, heart of Melungia, was a vital crossroads between Virginia, Kentucky, and Tennessee as the Indians knew back when Daniel Boone discovered it. As such, the area witnessed many Civil War battles. Melungia was unique, Southern by culture yet populated by "Lincoln Loyalists"—an island surrounded by enemies.

It was inevitable that the war would come to Newman's Ridge when the Confederates learned that Melungeons were supplying regular soldiers and guerrillas to the Union cause. John Mullins lived with his wife, Appalachian legend Mahala Collins Goins Mullins, on Newman's Ridge overlooking the valley community of Vardy. The couple had twenty children and many of their sons fought for the Union cause.

In 1863, Confederate guerillas from Virginia climbed Newman's Ridge to kill the sons of Haley Mullins. The raiders

> came looking for two of her sons, probably Larkin and Jim, and one son-in-law, Howard Collins, Union soldiers that were home on leave. Howard

---

[8]The previous account is based on Sider, *Lumbee Indian Histories*.

Collins's wife, Jane Mullins, saw the bushwackers coming up the Ridge, and screamed to her husband, who picked up his gun and took a shot at them. They fell back a little to size up the situation. Meanwhile, Haley's boys escaped over a low bluff. The raiders came to the bluff, but didn't get to get a shot off. Howard Collins sprained or broke a finger while escaping, but they got a shot off at the raiders, and got safely away. The sons escaped, but the house was burned, along with most of their possessions. They [the Rebel guerillas] let the family take their burning bedclothes, but fire broke out in them again. A light blanket of snow was on the ground, and the children were barefooted. Old John was so mad, he loaded up a muzzle with about all it could hold. Then, as the raiders were leaving through the Blackwater Valley below them, he fired at them from the bluff. But, in his anger, he left the ramrod in the gun, and loaded it so heavily it burst at the end of the muzzle. The ramrod, however, flew all the way across the valley, and stuck in a rail fence, near where the Becky Hurley house was, a short distance west of Vardy Church.[9]

---

[9]William P. Grohse, William P., Grohse Papers, Tennessee State Library and Archives, Microfilm #501.

Chapter 5

Jim Crow Struggles

The North's stand against slavery did not mean Northerners accepted people of color as equals. They certainly did not. Even after the Civil War, the South *and* North enforced rigid segregation laws that came to be known as "Jim Crow" laws. But Melungeons proved even Jim Crow was not bulletproof.

School Halls

Shortly after Tennessee restricted the rights of free people of color, Thomas Hall got a "proof of race" affidavit on September 19, 1835, from Judge James L. Crawford of Maury County, Tennessee which declared that he was "Portuguese."[1] Thomas Hall was in fact not Portuguese. His ancestors were a white woman of seventeenth-century Virginia and a black man she was forbidden by law to marry.[2]

Thomas Hall was a farsighted Melungeon who made sure to file and refile his "proof of Portuguese" documents when he moved to Yelleville, Arkansas in 1843, then to Oregon County, Missouri in 1850, and finally to Howell County, Missouri in 1890.[3] The affidivit read:

> State of Tennessee, Maury County, The said Thomas Hall is entitled to all of the privileges of a free citizen. Thomas Hall's great grand father on his father side was portagee [Portuguese] and his great grand father on his mother's side was an Englishman and Thomas Hall's grand father on his

---

[1]In addition to the Crawford affidavit, William Allen Holmes found another document supporting the first. "The second document seems to be a certification by William E. Erwin, clerk of the Court of Pleas and quarter session for Maury County, that James L. Crawford had full authority to issue the Proof of Race document. This document was dated October 13, 1835." William Allen Holmes, contributor, "Maury County TN — Court — Thomas Hall, Proof of Race Affidavits," online at <http://ftp.rootsweb.com/pub/usgenweb/tn/maury/court/hall02.txt>.

[2]Heinegg, *Free African Americans of North Carolina, Virginia, and South Carolina.*

[3]Holmes, "Thomas Hall, Proof of Race Affidavits."

father's side was of the portagee descent and his grand father on mother's side was an Irishman and his own father was of the portugee decent and his mother was a white American woman. Sworn to and subscribed before me this the 19 day of September 1835. James L. Crawford J.P.[4]

A thorough examination of Hall's genealogy fails to reveal a single Portuguese ancestor but the Tennessee judge had ruled that he and his family were entitled to "all the privileges of a free citizen" and Hall passed the affidavit to his children.[5] When the obviously mixed Hall descendants were refused entry to white schools in Missouri, Oklahoma, and elsewhere, they promptly produced the affidavit and sued Northern school districts. Jim Crow or not, they won again and again. The Halls became famous in the West for their much-publicized battles with different white school districts. More than 100 related Halls would appear at a trial to testify. Not only did they force the white schools to accept their children, they won large cash awards.

On August 23, 1906 the *Howell County Gazette* of Missouri reported one such trial:

Questions about Henderson Hall Descendants — In the Indian Territory Wesley Hall Children Were Excluded from the White School. Wesley Hall, a former resident of Howell county, and one of the descendants of the late Henderson Hall, has come into prominence at Okmulgee, Indian Territory near which place he resides. Mr. Hall has brought suit for damages against the board of school directors in the district in which he resides for ejecting his children from the white schools.

The reason Hall children were ejected from the school is that the directors claim the children are negroes and not entitled to attend the white schools. In 1889 a suit similar to this one was filed in circuit court here by Jeff Hall, a relative of Wesley Hall, because his children were refused admission to the Spring Creek school. The board of directors said the children looked so much like negroes that they must stay out. Hall brought suit to mandamus the directors to permit his children to attend the school. All the Hall tribe in this county, and they number quite a few, were present and crowded the courtroom.

The jury after hearing all the evidence decided that the Halls are not negroes and were entitled to attend the white schools. Henderson Hall, the ancestor of these people, came to Howell county from Tennessee before

---

[4]Holmes, "Thomas Hall, Proof of Race Affidavits."
[5]Heinegg, *Free African Americans of North Carolina, Virginia, and South Carolina.*

the war. He knew little of his folks, only that they had resided in the United States for many years and that they came from Portugal. They were seafaring people and traveled a great deal. Henderson Hall married a daughter of Fred Colyer, a Howell county pioneer, who refused to speak to Hall after he married his daughter, for he believed that Hall was of negro descent. Many children were born of the marriage and from this family came the Hall tribe of Howell county.

In addition it was shown that Jeff Hall has photographs and locks of hair of a number of his ancestors and he even introduced land titles which were given members of his family in Tennessee before the war showing conclusively that they were not negroes, for blacks could not own land in those days. Wherever they have gone the Halls have had difficulty with the school boards for refusing to permit their children to attend the white schools. In every instance they have won their case for they are able to prove that they are of Portuguese origin instead of having negro blood course through their veins, as many might believe from their appearances.[6]

The descendants of Thomas Hall even filed a lawsuit when they were barred from a literary society in 1910. The Halls, according to the Missouri newspaper, were Portuguese adventurers who, incredibly, "came to America soon after the discovery of the country by Columbus." This was the old 1848 Hancock County, Tennessee "Portuguese pirate" tale handed down from the *malungu* of seventeenth-century Jamestown, resurrected in the Show Me State in the twentieth century. The June 16, 1910 edition of the *Howell County Gazette* reported:

> Halls Ostracized — Down in Muscogee county, Oklahoma, damage suit for $10,000 for which the "Jim Crow" law of that state is responsible. They are suing a school board because the directors have refused to permit the Halls to take part in a literary society that meets each week at the schoolhouse. One of the family was met at the door by a director who told him that he could not be admitted because he was "part nigger." Then the ostracism was declared against the whole colony and they were barred from the white school.[7]

Once again, the Halls were successful in court.

---

[6]"Halls," *Howell County Gazette* (West Plains MO), 23 August 1906, cited by Holmes, "Thomas Hall, Proof of Race Affidavits."

[7]"Halls," *Howell County Gazette*, 16 June 1910.

Red Bones in the Neutral Strip

Shortly after the American Revolution, several free Melungeon clans known as "Red Bones" left the Carolinas and moved to Louisiana where they came to rule over wide stretches of unsettled territory. Though the name they were called changed from place to place, Red Bones, Melungeons, and Lumbees all descended from the same families—from the free *malungu* of old Jamestown.[8]

Between the Calcasieu River of southwestern Louisiana and the Sabine River that now marks the southern border of Texas-Louisiana lies a long stretch of wild pine, cypress, and swamp country once called the Neutral Strip. At one time the Neutral Strip served as the buffer zone along the disputed border between Spanish-controlled Texas and French Louisiana. Later, both Spain and the U.S. purposefully avoided the region to avoid an international confrontation and it soon became a base for outlaw bands and a haven for fugitives. Many *malungu* villages in several states are located in impassable or hard-to-reach places such as the Cumberland Gap, the Great Dismal Swamp, and the Neutral Strip, or near state and county borders where jurisdiction was in question, and enforcement of white law was, therefore, "iffy."

South Carolina Melungeons settled together in the Louisiana parishes of Opelousas, Natchitoches, and Rapides in 1810 and in St. Landry in 1820. In the 1830s some of these Louisiana families moved again to East Texas and established a settlement west of the Sabine River in the swamps of eastern Newton County, Texas.[9] Another community settled along Bear Head Creek east of the Sabine in Calcasieu Parish about 1830. But the largest Melungeon settlement was scattered through the Cherry Winche country, a densely wooded region of about 150 square miles in southwestern Rapides Parish.[10]

---

[8]For another "history" of the Red Bones and their trek from Virginia and Carolina to Louisiana and on to Texas, see Patricia Ann Waak, *My Bones Are Red: A Spiritual Journey with a Triracial People in the Americas* (Macon GA: Mercer University Press, 2005).

[9]Deen, "Trinity County Kinsearching." See also N. Brent Kennedy and Robyn Vaughn Kennedy, *The Melungeons: The Resurrection of a Proud People: An Untold Story of Ethnic Cleansing in America*, 2nd rev. and corr. ed. (Macon GA: Mercer University Press, 1997).

[10]Frederick Law Olmsted, *A Journey through Texas; or, A Saddle-Trip on the Southwestern Frontier, with a Statistical Appendix*, (series) Our Slave States 2 (New York: Dix, Edwards Co.; London: S. Low, 1857). Marler, "The Louisiana Red Bones." Deen, "Trinity

From the 1830s through the 1890s several race wars erupted in the Neutral Strip between early Red Bones and late-arriving whites. Many were killed on both sides, but unlike the Orange County War in pre-Civil War Texas, the Louisiana Red Bones remained and the Anglo settlers fled.

The Red Bone wars, forgotten now, were recorded by Frederick Law Olmsted who toured the violent Strip in the 1850s about the time of the Ashworth War in East Texas. In *A Journey through Texas; or, A Saddle Trip on the Southwestern Frontier*, Olmsted stated:

> The country is but thinly settled. The people are still herdsmen, cultivating a little cotton upon the riverbanks, but ordinarily only corn, with a patch of cane to furnish household sugar. We were told that there were a number of free negroes in the country, all mulattoes.[11]

Olmsted shared the prejudice of the whites of his time in his opinions about Melungeons.

> There were some white people, good-for-nothing people that married in with them but they couldn't live in Texas after it; all went over into Louisiana. This country has been lately the scene of events which prove that it must have contained a much larger number of free negroes and persons of mixed blood than we were informed on the spot, in spite of the very severe statute forbidding their introduction, which has been backed by additional legislative penalties in 1856. Banded together, they have been able to resist the power, not only of legal authorities, but of a local Vigilance Committee, which gave them a certain number of hours to leave the state, and a guerilla of skirmishes and murders has been carried on for many months upon the banks of the Sabine.[12]

J. T. Crawford who lived among Red Bones in the early twentieth century described them as prone to feud with each other but united against outside invasion: "clannish guerilla warriors" living in "lonely scattered habitations," always quick to avenge insult.[13]

County Kinsearching."
[11]Olmsted, *A Journey through Texas*.
[12]Olmsted, *A Journey through Texas*.
[13]Marler, "The Louisiana Red Bones."

The Westport War

Westport, Louisiana was the largest Red Bone settlement in the Neutral Strip. At the height of the Jim Crow era, a bloody war erupted there on Christmas Eve 1881 when words broke into action between Red Bones and white settlers who had gradually encroached into the Cherry Winche. A young white man named Frank Taylor met a pretty Red Bone woman while working on a government surveying party and his attempt to woo her put him in the line of fire when the war erupted. Taylor told his story to Webster Talma Crawford sometime around 1930.[14]

The Red Bone Dyal clans in Taylor's account were the Dials who descended from the seventeenth-century Angolan, Benjamin Dolls of Virginia. The Red Bone Perkins family was related to the Lowrey clan of the Lumbees in North Carolina as well as to the Goins and Chavises of the Brass Ankles in South Carolina. The Perkinses were also related to the Melungeon Bunch family of Tennessee, the Melungeon Carters, and the Sweat family that originated in seventeenth-century Tidewater Virginia with the black slave Margaret Cornish and the white gentleman, Robert Sweat.[15] Many of these Melungeon—Red Bone families had fought in the American Revolution under the wily Swamp Fox, Gen. Francis Marion.

The Louisiana Red Bones waged a fierce battle against Anglo invaders in the 1830s. It was called a "rawhide fight"—a final pitched battle after which wives and daughters toted away the bodies of dead warriors in cowhides. A rawhide fight was to the death.

The Red Bones won in the 1830s, and for almost fifty years kept the Cherry Winche cleared of Anglos.[16] Eventually two white men named Moore and Hamilton set up a general store in Westport near Hineston, Louisiana. Red Bones had banned whites from settling west of the "Quelqueshoe" (Calcasieu River) but Moore and Hamilton had delicately refrained from questioning Red Bone ancestry. These white men had also built a gristmill and were doing a good business. The land was then a thick

---

[14] As told by Frank Taylor to Webster Talma Crawford, and recounted by J. A. Crawford in *Redbones in the Neutral Strip, or No Man's Land, between the Calcasieu and Sabine Rivers in Louisiana and Texas Respectively, and the Westport Fight between Whites and Redbones for Possession of This Strip on Christmas Eve, 1882* (Lake Charles LA: pub. by the author, 1955). Houston Public Library, Clayton Genealogy Library, Houston, Texas.

[15] Heinegg, *Free African Americans of North Carolina, Virginia, and South Carolina.*

[16] Crawford, *Redbones in the Neutral Strip.*

vast tract with pine and cypress and the Red Bones shared it with "only the panthers and wolves."[17]

The Louisiana Neutral Strip was a haven for illegal traffic, much like Jamestown in 1619. Tough men such as Jim Bowie made fortunes in the Neutral Ground, transporting the stolen loot of pirate Jean Lafitte to New Orleans, running slaves or making moonshine. White law was not welcome.

The Cherry Winche was a land of plenty coveted by white settlers beyond the Sabine and Calcasieau Rivers:

> The valley of the Cherry Winche was a fine grazing country; sheep and cattle thrived; land cleared of its thick growth was productive of bountiful crops; hogs fattened to solid grease in the creek bottoms; and deer, turkey, and all manner of other wild game provided an easy living.[18]

The incident that reignited conflict between Red Bones and whites in 1881 began with a loudmouth white man named Gordon Musgrove. Musgrove had moved to Louisiana about five years earlier and had settled just across the northwestern border of the so-called Red Bone Dead Line:

> But it was not in Gordon Musgrove's mind to stop at either an imaginary or a real line of demarcation. Nor was he inclined to call a spade a handshovel or a Red Bone an "Israelite." The beginning of the actual trouble which led up to the Westport fight occurred at a camp meeting when Musgrove stoked the fire by suddenly leaving the building which was packed with Red Bones, after making the statement that the "Smell of Nigger" always made him ill.[19]

A few weeks later, ten days before Christmas, a Red Bone named Henry Perkins and a white farmer named Buck Davis staged a horse race. The Red Bone horse was declared the winner and new white settlers who had bet on Davis's steed started a bitter argument with the Red Bones that almost disintegrated into a gunfight right then. Taylor reported that both

---

[17]Withrow, "Red Bones: The Appalachian Connection."

[18]As told by Frank Taylor to Webster Talma Crawford and recounted by J. A. Crawford in *Redbones in the Neutral Strip, or No Man's Land, between the Calcasieu and Sabine Rivers in Louisiana and Texas Respectively, and the Westport Fight between Whites and Redbones for Possession of this Strip on Christmas Eve, 1882* (Lake Charles LA: pub. by the author, 1955). Houston Public Library, Clayton Genealogy Library, Houston, Texas.

[19]As told by Frank Taylor to Webster Talma Crawford and recounted by J. A. Crawford in *Redbones in the Neutral Strip*.

factions "went away to their homes with much snarling and rancor of heart."

The girl that Frank Taylor was chasing against her father's wishes was named Ruth Dial. Taylor heard about a dance at the home of a Red Bone farmer named Bob Wray on the December 23rd just before Christmas. It was to be a "Red Bone only" dance but the smitten young white man jumped on his horse and went to see Ruth. He was unwelcome.

> Upon reaching the Wray place I found it a focus of excitement somewhat stronger than I had ever before observed. It was a cold crisp night. In a corner of the yard a big pine knot fire was going and a crowd of men were standing around it, drinking and "Whooping it Up" in general revelry.
>
> I tied my horse to a sapling and joined the crowd by the fire. I found a cool greeting and an almost hostile attitude. Thinking that all the "White" men probably were in the house, I made my way through the pack of men on the porch and into the front room of the building, where the dance was in progress. On the hearth of the immense dirt chimney at the end of the room, a great fire of pine knots was roaring, while couples were shuffling over the rough boards to the spirited strains of a veteran darkey's fiddle. He alone comprised the orchestra. And what man of mature years who was reared in Western Louisiana has not danced to the music supplied by that lovable old slave negro, "Uncle Rube." Later, "Pete" joined Rube with the guitar and it was "Pete and Rube" playing for the country dances for years on years.
>
> Red likker was the universal drink throughout the backwoods of that day and a dance near Christmas was the supreme occasion for its use. Wine was tolerated, for the women folks. So, on an inverted dry-goods box in one corner of the big room, two kegs were set enthroned, one of whiskey and the other of wine, and beside this box, next to the broad fire place, old Rube sat with his fiddle; the kegs and the old darkey being joint rulers over the conviviality of the merrymaking crowd.
>
> At first glance I saw no one whom I recognized and I was about to pass out into the yard when I caught sight of my sweetheart dancing with a strapping young Red Bone. The girl saw me about the same time, immediately disengaged herself from her partner and returned to the seat near the door, where I joined her and asked for a dance.
>
> "No, no, we mustn't dance together here," Ruth replied. "I am afraid all my people dislike you Frank, and you had better leave."
>
> But I insisted, so when the next dance we waltzed out on the floor. After finishing the set, my girl's father, old Eph Dyal, told me he wanted to talk with me a little, so I followed the old man outside.

"I'm a thinkin' you had better git on ter hoss and ride stranger," old Eph declared as soon as we had cleared the room.

"Why?" I asked him.

"Because I ainter goin' to have you a dance with my gal and because we unses don't want you here no how."

"All right, I'll be going then," I told him.

Being unarmed, I knew it would be unwise to remain and so assented to his demand. But I decided to ask Ruth first, if she thought I was really in danger.

Ruth told me that I must not remain another minute, else her father send someone out to waylay me on the way home. So, with hurried words of parting, I left my sweetheart with her Red Bone lover and rode swiftly out of the Cherry Winche Country.[20]

As the fiddle played and the young people danced to calls of "Skip fire in a fen, swing your partner and swing him again," Red Bone elders began talking among themselves in low tones. Simon Morrows had a plan to ambush the whites at sunrise on the country road near Chinquapin Gulch. Some white settlers passed that way to Hatch's general store. Being Christmas Eve they would head for the store for their holiday shopping.

After the dance broke up everyone went home. But the plan had been overheard by "old Uncle Rube who was sawing valiantly away on his fiddle, beating time with his feet and ostensibly oblivious to everything but his own paramount part in the success of the evening. But old Rube's hearing was more acute than his years belied."

When the dance ended about midnight, "no one saw Rube and his mule slip silently through the gap and into the woods behind the barn lot, nor did anyone see them steal silently back again, after a ten-mile circuit, which ended just as the sun broke over the Cherry Winche swamp, Christmas Eve morning."

Alerted whites took another road to the Hatch store the next morning. A few hours later in the clearing in front of the store white men drank and enjoyed the festive gathering, unaware of the Red Bones regrouping among the pine trees at the fringe of the clearing. At ten o'clock Gordon Musgrove drove up in his wagon and saw Buck Davis who had lost the horse race:

---

[20] As told by Frank Taylor to Webster Talma Crawford and recounted by J. A. Crawford in *Redbones in the Neutral Strip*.

The talk between the two men soon turned to the horse race, and whether by design or by chance, it was just as Marion Perkins stepped out of the store that Musgrove spoke the words which precipitated the inevitable battle. Marion Perkins was an older brother of the jockey whose horse had won the race, and he was a somewhat larger man. He held a new bullwhip in his hands which he had just bought.

Musgrove said, "You won that race clean, Buck. And if I'd bin a ridin' instid o' you, I'd er had that money or a whipped Henry Perkins." It was a straight challenge to Marion Perkins's hot Red Bone blood, and he didn't hesitate a moment. Tossing his new bullwhip to the floor, he faced Musgrove arrogantly. "Mabby you wanta whap his brother now," he roared. Without further word the men charged each other.[21]

Musgrove swung at the Red Bone but

Perkins ducked under it and grappling the timber man around the waist, lifted Musgrove off his feet and hurled him to the floor, the Red Bone driving his own head into the pit of the under man's belly as he fell.

With the breath knocked out of him by the fall, Musgrove was unable to retain the hold he had secured on Perkins who lost no time in taking full advantage of what he had gained by gripping his prostrate opponent between his knees, and driving his heavy fists into the unyielding face pillowed on the rough board floor.[22]

Just as the Red Bone was about to win the fight a white man named John Watson attacked Perkins from behind with a savage kick. Musgrove was unconscious and Perkins dazed. The whites at the store were still gathered after enjoying the entertaining fight, oblivious to the ominous mutterings of the Red Bones who encircled them. Dr. Hamilton just happened to be riding by and got down to see to Musgrove. He, Moore, and Watson became aware of the piercing looks from the group of Red Bones and quickly forced the still-dazed Red Bone into the store where they disarmed and "arrested" him.

Frank Taylor was at the store hoping to rendezvous with Ruth Dial when he saw the fight and realized the "long-festering wound was emi-

---

[21]As told by Frank Taylor to Webster Talma Crawford and recounted by J. A. Crawford in *Redbones in the Neutral Strip*.

[22]As told by Frank Taylor to Webster Talma Crawford and recounted by J. A. Crawford in *Redbones in the Neutral Strip*.

nent." The Red Bones were now deadly intent on running all whites out of the Cherry Winche.

As Moore, Watson, and Hamilton detained Perkins in a room in the second story of Hatch store, the drunken whites outside, many of whom had lost money on Davis' horse, were beginning to work up some wrath of their own and wanted to get their hands on the defenseless Red Bone:

> Half an hour passed. Tom Perkins the elder, father to Marion and Henry, rode up to the Hatch store, dismounted, and went in. Old man Tom had heard of the fight between Musgrove and Marion; had heard that his son was being held a prisoner in the store. The old Red Bone's face was set and tense as he approached the proprietor, Joe Moore. Dr. Hamilton caught his attention and suavely nodded to old Tom to come over into the vacant corner of the store. Apart from the boisterous crowd which stood about the counters drinking, Dr. Hamilton hoped to allay Perkin's anger. Hamilton poured a glass of his best wine and extended it to Perkins.
>
> "Mr. Tom," the doctor said soothingly, "We have assured Marion that we will see that he is not harmed and now that you have come and can go with him, we will send the boy for his horse and keep the crowd occupied up front while Marion slips out the back door and gets away. Where shall we say that you will meet him?"[23]

According to Taylor,

> Pushing back the proffered glass of wine, old Tom straightened his heavy shoulders with the cold arrogance of his proud Moorish lineage: "Dr. Hamilton," he said, "this ain't no time for drinkin.' My boys have done run away for the last time and nothing but a rawhide fight is goin' ter do now." And turning about, the old Red Bone strode silently the length of the store and out to his horse. Mounting the cayuse, Perkins drove his spurs viciously into the animal's flanks as the pony wheeled from the hitch rack and dashed away through the trees.[24]

Tom Perkins sent a call out to gather all the men of the Red Bone clans at the store to "Fight it out," the declaration of a rawhide war. The drunken boisterous white men around the store suddenly realized the danger as Red

---

[23] As told by Frank Taylor to Webster Talma Crawford and recounted by J. A. Crawford in *Redbones in the Neutral Strip*.

[24] As told by Frank Taylor to Webster Talma Crawford and recounted by J. A. Crawford in *Redbones in the Neutral Strip*.

Bones poured down the roads towards Westport carrying "guns of every description, some with barrels as long as hoe handles." Red Bone women came too, armed and raising the war cry. Taylor figured about fifty Red Bones had answered.

A dozen or more Red Bones boldly rode up to the store and dismounted. They were led by Tom Perkins, Simon Morrows, and Hamp Dial. The Creole man Louis Lacaze joined Moore, Watson, Hamilton, Sam Nolen, Hugh Sanders, and Moore's three sons as they dashed into the store and barred the doors. The Hatch and Moore store at Westport supplied the whole territory and it was fully stocked with firearms, ammunition, and liquor to fortify the spirits of the men inside. The whites trapped outside in the clearing were not so fortunate and ran in all directions seeking cover as Red Bones opened fire.

Meanwhile, Marion Perkins, still imprisoned upstairs, suddenly made a break for it as the shooting started. One of the white men in the store fired and wounded him, but Perkins, armed with a "Double derringer," scattered his attackers with two shots and burst through a window, "his coat having been shot to threads."

Almost immediately someone inside the store unloaded buckshot into old Tom Perkins, killing him instantly. Once outside, his son Marion Perkins fired and killed a white man named Hance Dykes. Racing around the corner of the store, Marion Perkins happened upon his foe Gordon Musgrove frantically scrambling for a place to hide. Marion cut him down with several shots and continued on. Another Red Bone named Matt Johnson next came upon the prostrate Musgrove, saw him move, and shot him again. Then Johnson picked up a knotted pine limb and began pummeling him until he believed the white troublemaker to be surely deceased. This was a false assumption.

After the initial bloodletting the gun battle settled down into a steady exchange of fire between the white defenders inside the store and the Red Bone attackers in the surrounding woods. Simon Morrows and his men dashed from tree to tree sniping off shots into the windows of the store. Morrows, who had planned the ambush at Chinquapin Gulch that morning, was enraged that the Frenchman Louis Lacaze had eluded him. While dashing for a better shot, Simon left himself exposed and Lacaze fired from the store and killed the Red Bone leader. As Hiram Morrows stepped up to lead the Red Bones, he judiciously kept to the old ways of the Swamp Fox of firing from cover.

For hours the Red Bone clans peppered the store, firing at every window where a shadow could be glimpsed. Then as the sun began to set, the gunfire outside slowly tapered off. The besieged whites inside the store heard the clatter of Red Bone ponies on the roads as they broke off the battle. After waiting hours, cautiously assuring themselves that no Red Bone had lingered, the white men emerged from the store to view their losses.

> Dykes was dead, but wonder of a Frenchman, Musgrove still lived. Gordon Musgrove was removed to his home, and in spite of the desperate condition in which his assailants had left him, he eventually recovered. Musgrove became a Baptist minister of the gospel and lived to the venerable age of eighty-nine. The old fiddler Uncle Rube was ordered to saddle his mule and ride for the White settlement of Sugartown to bring a relief party to Westport in case the Red Bones resumed the battle the next day. A half-dozen men would answer the call and the vigil continued at Hatch's bullet-riddled store. But it was Christmas Sunday and the Red Bones were burying their dead.[25]

During the coming days, the white settlers, their farms widely dispersed, realized their vulnerable position. The trees were thick about them, providing perfect concealment for ambush. Soulonge Lacaze was chosen to ride to the home of Hiram Morrows to propose a truce. But, the Red Bones angrily rejected it. The whites had to leave, and any white man who stayed was fair game. Taylor observed,

> Soulonge Lacaze had demanded peace while he lived in the Red Bone country, but after making his mandate he did not long continue to reside there. Had he done so, the brave cajun doubtless would have been blessed with that eternal peace which came to the other settlers who continued to live in the Cherry Winche Valley, for bushwhacking went on apace. A convenient time came and Lacaze moved away from the Red Bone settlements. Wives often have their way; they don't like to have their husbands left in the woods, and so forth. Musgrove went away. The Davises moved; old Rube moved.
>
> Not long after the Westport Fight, the Moore & Hatch Store burned to the ground. A little later Hatch's historic old mill disappeared in another conflagration. The site became known as the "Old Burn Down." Hamilton, Moore, and Hatch all escaped and never came back. They used good

---

[25]As told by Frank Taylor to Webster Talma Crawford and recounted by J. A. Crawford in *Redbones in the Neutral Strip*.

judgement. Watson continued to be fast on the draw, but he camped one night alone on the borders of the Cherry Winche country. In the glow of his campfire he was a plain target. I have had pointed out to me the hollow where he was killed. It is in the pine hills near the site of the old "New Hope" church.

What the combined attack failed to do, Red Bones working singly and in squads of twos accomplished. By deed and by warning, the "White" settlers were slowly but effectively ousted from the region by the Red-bones, described by Taylor as "lone scouts, sharpshooters, snipers, and true unknown soldiers" par excellence. Gathered into battalions, Simon's men are poor soldiers, but one Red Bone can carry on a war. And how![26]

The Pattern

A pattern of migration and eventual conflict began in seventeenth-century Jamestown and followed Melungeons in every generation. Their children moved to the next frontier with the earliest white pioneers, cleared the land, and planted their crops. In time white strangers arrived and soon persecution followed, as in South Carolina in 1790 when Melungeons were hit with harsh "free Negro" taxes to make them leave the state.

Anna Going Friedman found that Georgia was first open to the *malungu* fleeing Virginia and the Carolinas.[27] In 1810 there were more blacks in Georgia than whites. Alarmed, the state in 1818 limited the rights of free blacks just as colonial Virginia did in 1670 and South Carolina in 1790. They had to register their names twice a year and have them published in newspapers. Many left Georgia for (at the time) more-liberal Alabama, Mississippi, Kentucky, Louisiana, and Texas. But, during 1830–1840 after Nat Turner, these states also enacted race laws.

The Civil War ended Melungeon migration. If not for the War, no doubt Melungeons would have continued west to California. However, some never moved, but stubbornly fought to keep their old colonial lands.

---

[26]As told by Frank Taylor to Webster Talma Crawford and recounted by J. A. Crawford in *Redbones in the Neutral Strip.*

[27]Friedman et al., "Going Family Futily Criss-Crossed America to Escape Racial Discrimination."

The Battle of Hayes Pond

The Lumbees endured insults and double taxes to hold their ancestral lands. Nearly a century after the Civil War career of Henry Berry Lowery, the Lumbees of North Carolina showed that his spirit was indeed still burning.

It would become known as the Battle of Hayes Pond, a gunfight in a cow pasture on a cold winter night in Robeson County, North Carolina, 1958. Once again the old Lowery bunch was at the center of the storm. The *Fayetteville Observer* newspaper reporter Pat Reese and photographer Bill Shaw were sent to Hayes Pond following rumors of a pending confrontation between Lumbees and the KKK. Klansmen had burned crosses in Lumberton and St. Pauls a few days earlier with the warning that they were going "to teach the Indians of Robeson County a lesson."[28]

One of the crosses was burned in front of a house where a Lumbee woman and a white man lived. The Klan burned the second cross in the yard of a Lumbee family that had recently moved into an all-white neighborhood. The Lumbees then got hold of KKK fliers promoting a rally and cross burning at Hayes Pond on January 18, 1958.

Reese reported that Lumbee leaders, including Neill Lowery and Sanfor Locklear, had decided to run the Klan out of the county. Willie Lowery's barbershop in Pembroke became the Lumbee planning room for the upcoming battle. From there the call went out for volunteers and according to Reese, more than 1,000 Lumbees answered the alarm.

The Klansmen were outsiders. Their leader, James "Catfish" Cole of Marion, South Carolina brought a flatbed truck with a portable generator for powering a light bulb and a public address system that night. 'Onward Christian Soldiers' poured from a scratchy phonograph, and the cow pasture echoed with amplified rants. They wore hooded white robes and carried rifles. The Lumbees, the Klan assumed, were cowering in their homes.

But the Lumbees were assembling less than a mile away at an abandoned shack. Reese described an eerie moment of silence as the song ended and then on cue the Lumbee Christian soldiers began to march forward. Small groups armed with rifles and shotguns converged on the white-robed gathering. Neill Lowery leveled his shotgun at his hip and blasted out the Klan's power-generated single light bulb. The field went dark.

---

[28]"Ku Klux Klan Routing," *Fayetteville Observer*, 18 January 1958.

Lumbees began firing and shotgun pellets and bullets flew wildly at any flash of light. The reporter was slightly wounded. Klansmen scattered, their figures weirdly illuminated by the headlights of their circled cars. Some had brought their wives and children who began to wail in fear as dark-faced Lumbees curiously milled around their cars and pointed their flashlights at them.

Robeson County Sheriff Malcom McLeod, a white Southerner who had warned the KKK to stay away, led his men forth to escort terrified Klansmen from the field. The sheriff blithely ignored Lumbees overturning Klan cars as he led the way out. One Klansman cursed a Lumbee blocking the road. The Lumbee punched him through the open car window and blood flew. Lumbees seized KKK banners and paraded through town. Word flashed across the nation, and *Life* magazine published a photograph of the battle on the cover. Klan leader Catfish Cole got eighteen months in prison for inciting a riot.[29]

The End of American Apartheid

In 1958 the Lumbees clashed with the Klan over integration and mixed marriage. In 1967, in the case of *Loving v. Virginia*, the U.S. Supreme Court ended Jim Crow's ban on mixed marriage, halting centuries of apartheid in the commonwealth where it had begun.

---

[29]This account is based on "Ku Klux Klan Routing," *Fayetteville Observer*, 18 January 1958.

Part two

Children of Perdition

Chapter 6

Mythic Origins

Melungeons once claimed descent from Sir Walter Raleigh's mysterious "Lost Colony of Roanoke." White Americans believed these survivor yarns for reasons of their own.

After the American Revolution, John Sevier, early Tennessee governor and ruthless land-grabber, promoted tales of pre-Columbian "Welsh" lost colonists as an excuse for his war on the Cherokees. When President Thomas Jefferson, a Welshman, sent two Welshmen named Lewis and Clark to explore the Northwest, he first had them consult with Gov. Sevier about the Welsh myths. Sevier, who once spent the night with a Melungeon family, pointed out strange stone forts in Tennessee and Kentucky as "proof" that the Welsh "discovered" America. Sevier's popular Welsh tales got him elected governor with a mandate to remove or kill Cherokees to get the land.

Thomas Jefferson did not invent the Welsh theory. Two centuries earlier, Queen Elizabeth I sought a legend of one of her early Welsh kinsmen, a relative of King Arthur named Prince Madoc who supposedly sailed to America around 1000 AD. Elizabeth's historians presented the saga to strengthen her claim on North America against France and Spain. President Jefferson revived the claim when the U.S. contested France and Spain for western North America. Rumors of King Arthur's remains and the Holy Grail buried in a Kentucky cave were strengthened by the coincidental presence of a nearby village of "mysterious" Melungeons said to be "Keepers of the Grail."

Supported by monarchs, presidents, and governors, the lost colony legends had great credibility. Ironically, dark-skinned Melungeons were cited as "evidence" of European claims. Melungeons perpetuated the myths for different reasons.

Refuge in a Lost Colony

An old poem describes the contempt that black slaves and their descendants felt for mixed freeborn Melungeons, Lumbees, and Brass Ankles.

Calls dey self white—
Brass ankles dey is—
White wid a little tech er yellow,
Niggers dat's passed on up.[1]

Life was no less difficult for Melungeons seeking to assimilate into black society as for Melungeons seeking to become white: "the line of demarcation was rigidly drawn—not by the fairer children, but by the darker ones." In her essay "Brass Ankles Speaks," Alice Dunbar-Nelson (1875–1935), a Melungeon essayist and poet, revealed bitter experiences of mulattos who were identified as African American, only to be rejected by darker blacks.

In her prefatory note to Dunbar-Nelson's "Brass Ankles Speaks," editor Gloria T. Hull described Dunbar-Nelson's story as an

> outspoken denunciation of darker-skinned black people's prejudice against light-skinned blacks told by a "brass ankles," a black person "white enough to pass for white, but with a darker family background, a real love for the mother race, and no desire to be numbered among the white race." This brass ankles recalls her "miserable" childhood in "a far Southern city" where other schoolchildren taunted and plagued her because she was a "light nigger, with straight hair!"
>
> This kind of rebuff and persecution continued into a Northern college and her first teaching job: "Small wonder, then, [Dunbar-Nelson remarks,] that the few lighter persons in the community drew together; we were literally thrown upon each other, whether we liked or not. But when we began going about together and spending time in each other's society, a howl went up. We were organizing a "blue vein" society. We were mistresses of white men. We were Lesbians. We hated black folk and plotted against them. As a matter of fact, we had no other recourse but to cling together." And she states further that "To complain would be only to bring upon themselves another storm of abuse and fury."[2]

---

[1]Edward Clarkson Adams, "Brass Ankles," *Nigger to Nigger* (New York and London: Charles Scribner, 1928) 163.

[2]Gloria T. Hull, ed., introduction to "Brass Ankles Speaks," in vol. 2 of *The Works of*

In her essay, Alice Dunbar-Nelson remarks that:

My earliest recollections are miserable ones. I was born in a far Southern city, where complexion did, in a manner of speaking, determine one's social status. . . . I was sent to the public school. It was a heterogeneous mass of children which greeted my frightened eyes on that fateful morning in September, when I timidly took my place in the first grade. There were not enough seats for all the squirming mass of little ones, so the harassed young teacher . . . put me on the platform at her feet. I was so little and scared and homesick that it made no impression on me at the time. But at the luncheon hour I was assailed with shouts of derision— "Yah! Teacher's pet! Yah! Just cause she's yaller!" Thus at once was I initiated into the class of the disgraced, which has haunted and tormented my whole life—"Light nigger, with straight hair!"

This was the beginning of what was for nearly six years a life of terror, horror and torment. . . .

. . . I essayed friendship with Esther. Esther was velvet dark, with great liquid eyes. She could sing, knew lots of forbidden lore, and brought lovely cakes for luncheon. Therefore I loved Esther, and would have been an intimate friend of hers. But she repulsed me with ribald Laughter— "Half white nigger! Go on wid ya kind!" and drew up a solid phalanx of little dark girls, who thumbed noses at me and chased me away from their ring game on the school playground.

Bitter recollections of hair ribbons jerked off and trampled in the mud. Painful memories of curls yanked back into the ink bottle of the desk behind me, and dripping ink down my carefully washed print frocks. That alone was a tragedy, for clothes came hard, and a dress ruined by ink-dripping curls meant privation for the mother at home. How I hated those curls! Charlie, the neighbor-boy and I were of an age, a complexion, and the same taffy-colored curls. So bitter were his experiences that his mother had his curls cut off. But I was a girl and must wear curls. I wept in envy of Charles, the shorn one. However, long before it was the natural time for curls to be discarded, my mother, for sheer pity, braided my hair in a long heavy plait down my back. Alas! It, too, was ink-soaked, pulled, yanked, and twisted.[3]

Alice Dunbar-Nelson, 3 vols., The Schomburg Library of Nineteenth-Century Black Women Writers (New York: Oxford University Press, 1988). Now available online at <http://www. english.uiuc.edu/maps/poets/a_f/dunbar-nelson/essays.htm> (as accessed 5 December 2005).
[3]Dunbar-Nelson, "Brass Ankles Speaks."

Late nineteenth-century scholars and journalists studying lost colonies from court documents did not take into account the bitter ostracism Melungeons hoped their legends would help them overcome. Some understood. Lawyer Lewis Jarvis of Hancock County, a neighbor of Melungeons attempted to ease their plight by offering an Indian origin to hide their African roots. Abraham Lincoln claimed a Melungeon client was Portuguese, as attorney John Netherland once said of the Hancock County Eight. Attorney Lewis Shepherd of Chattanooga argued Melungeons were Portuguese-Phoenicians. Senator Hamilton McMillan of North Carolina persuaded the legislature that Melungeons were mixed English and Indian descendants of Roanoke.[4]

Scientists such as Dr. Swan Burnett and Stephen Weeks accepted the stories and gave them academic stamps of approval that popular writers like Will Allen Dromgoole were able to cite as authoritative academic sources.

These scientists and writers were as much the children of their generation as scientists and writers today are of ours. In 1889, Dr. Burnett, an anthropologist, joined a researcher from the Smithsonian Institution to study a community of Melungeons. Presenting his report to the American Anthropologist Society of Washington D.C., Burnett raised several origin theories including Portuguese, Roanoke, and even Romani Gypsy. A native of Tennessee, the anthropologist recalled his childhood terror of the name Melungeon:

> I first heard it at my father's knee as a child in the mountains of Eastern Tennessee, and the name had such a ponderous and inhuman sound as to associate them [Melungeons] in my mind with the giants and ogres of the wonder tales I listened to in the winter evenings before the crackling logs in the wide-mouth fireplace.

Burnett matured to regard Melungeons not as demons but as a lost race:

> In the course of time, however, I came to learn that these creatures with the awe-inspiring name were people somewhat like ourselves, but with a

---

[4]The preceding is a summary of material previously documented in chap. 1, above. But see esp. L. M. Jarvis interview in the *Hancock County Times* (Sneedville TN), April 1903; Swan Burnett, "Notes on the Melungeons"; and Lewis Shepherd, "Romantic Account of the Celebrated 'Melungeon' Case," *Watson's Magazine*. See also Shepherd, *Personal Memoirs of Lewis Shepherd*; Virginia Easley DeMarce, *Gowen Research Foundation Newsletter* (April 1994); and Hamilton McMillan, *Sir Walter Raleigh's Lost Colony*.

difference. I learned, too, that they were not only different from us, the white, but also from the Negroes—slave or free—and from the Indian. They were something set apart from anything I had seen or heard of. Neither was the exact nature of this difference manifest even in more mature years, when a childish curiosity had given way to an interest more scientific in its character.[5]

The anthropologist had in fact, rejected a superstition in favor of a myth.

People fell into two camps on the question of Melungeon origin. One said they were onto the game, that Melungeons were simply mulattos, hardly a mystery. Parson Brownlow's 1840 political editorials are the earliest in the first category. Later, twentieth-century scholars developed this into the "tri-racial isolate theory."[6]

The second category, beginning with the 1848 *Knoxville Register* version, stemmed from testimony at race trials, and eventually entertained a mob of opinions that Melungeons began with a mysterious, forgotten non-African origin that had occurred in obscurity off the scope of recorded history, "long before the white man came"—that is, Portuguese pirates, the lost Roanoke colony, Phoenicians, Turkish galley slaves, survivors of the expeditions of Ponce de DeLeon, Juan Pardo or De Soto, and so forth. This category survived into the twentieth century to include theories that Melungeons descended from pre-Columbian settlers such as the Vikings, the Welsh Prince Madoc, exiled Templar Knights, and Chinese merchants. Some tales were also motivated by Masonic symbolism, such as the Phoenician theory; or by pseudotheologians seeking to prove that Northern Europeans were the "lost tribe of Israel"; or by Islamists promoting Moslems as discoverers of America.[7] Melungeons either gave a

---

[5]Swan M. Burnett, "Notes on the Melungeons," *American Anthropology* 2/21 (October 1889): 347-49.

[6]The term "triracial isolate" was coined by Calvin Beale in 1957. Calvin L. Beale, "American Triracial Isolates, Their Status and Pertinence to Genetic Research," *Eugenics Quarterly* 4/4 (December 1957): 187-96. See Wayne Winkler, "A Brief Overview of the Melungeons," online at <http://www.melungeons.com/articles/jan2003.htm>.

[7]Will Allen Dromgoole, "The Malungeons," *The Arena* 3/3 (March 1891): 470-79; Louise Davis, "The Mystery of the Melungeons," *Nashville Tennessean Sunday Magazine*, 22 September 1963; Manuel Mira, *The Forgotten Portuguese* (Franklin NC: Portuguese-American Historical Research Foundation, Inc., 1998); William L. Worden, "Sons of the Legend," *Saturday Evening Post* (18 October 1947); Shepherd, "Romantic Account of the Celebrated 'Melungeon' Case"; Everett, "Melungeon History and Myth"; "Melungeon," *Dictionary of Genealogy and Archaic Terms* (online at <http://freepages.genealogy.

rootsweb.com>), cites, among others, local historian Mary Sue Going, of the Watauga Association; John Fetterman, "The Mystery of Newman's Ridge," *Life Magazine*, 26 June 1970; Cyrus Thomas, *Report on the Mound Explorations of the Bureau of Ethnology*, Twelfth Annual Report of the Bureau of American Ethnology to the Secretary of the Smithsonian Institution, 1890–1891 (Washington DC: Government Printing Office, 1894; repr., Washington DC: Smithsonian Institution Press, 1985); J. Huston McCulloch, "The Bat Creek Inscription: Cherokee or Hebrew?," *Tennessee Anthropologist* 13/2 (1988): 79-123; see also Robert C. Mainfort, Jr. and Mary L. Kwas, "The Bat Creek Stone: Judeans in Tennessee?" *Tennessee Anthropologist* 16/1 (Spring 1991): 1-19; see reply by McCulloch in *Tennessee Anthropologist* (Spring 1993): 1-16, and rejoinder by Mainfort and Kwaw in *Tennessee Anthropologist* (Fall 1993): 87-93; see also J. Huston McCulloch, "The Bat Creek Inscription: Did Judean Refugees Escape to Tennessee?" *Biblical Archaeological Review* (*BAR*) 19/4 (July/August 1993): 46-53 (and see comment by P. Kyle McCarter, *BAR* [Jul/Aug 1993]; 54-55; reply by McCulloch, *BAR* [Nov/Dec 1993] 14-16; and numerous letters in *BAR* [Nov/Dec 1993 and Jan/Feb 1994]); Cyrus Herzl Gordon, *Before Columbus: Links between the Old World and Ancient America* (New York: Crown, 1971); Jan Harold Brunvand, "Modern Legends of Mormonism, or Supernaturalism Is Alive and Well in Salt Lake City," in *American Folk Legend: A Symposium*, ed. Wayland Debs Hand (Los Angles and Berkeley: University of California Press, 1971); Lowell Kirk, "The Bat Creek Stone," <http://www.telliquah.com/Batcreek.htm> (accessed 10 November 2005); Robert C. Mainfort, Jr. and Mary L. Kwas, "The Bat Creek Fraud: A Final Statement," *Tennessee Anthropologist* 18/2 (Fall 1993); Ivey, "Oral, Printed, and Popular Culture Traditions Related to the Melungeons of Hancock County," cites the Shapira Scrolls, the Paraiba Stone, and the Bat Creek Stone, in addition to other controversial discoveries of supposed early European, African, and Mediterranean artifacts in America claimed by others; George Chapman, Ben Jonson, and John Marston, *Eastward Ho*, a play performed in London, 1604 (London: William Aspley, 1605; repr., ed. R. W. van Fossen, Manchester UK: Manchester University Press; Baltimore: Johns Hopkins Press, 1979); Kennedy, *The Melungeons*; Samuel Cole Williams, *Early Travels in the Tennessee Country, 1540–1800: with Introductions, Annotations, and Index* (Johnson City TN: Watauga Press, 1928); Michael S. Steely, *Swift's Silver Mines and Related Appalachian Treasures* (Johnson City TN: Overmountain Press, 1995); Amos Stoddard, *Sketches, Historical and Descriptive, of Louisiana* (Philadelphia: Mathew Carey, 1812); Noel Bertram Gerson, *Franklin: America's "Lost State"*, America in the Making (New York: Crowell-Collier Press, 1968); see also Samuel Cole Williams, *History of the Lost State of Franklin* (Johnson City TN: Watauga Press, 1924; rev. ed., New York: Press of the Pioneers, 1933; repr., Bowie MD: Heritage Books, 2002); see also Carl Samuel Driver, *John Sevier: Pioneer of the Old Southwest* (Chapel Hill: University of North Carolina Press, 1932; repr., Nashville: Charles and Randy Elder Booksellers, 1973); Donald Dean Jackson, ed., *Letters of the Lewis and Clark Expedition, with Related Documents, 1783–1854*, 2nd ed. (Urbana: University of Illinois Press, 1978); see also Meriwether Lewis and William Clark, *The Journals of the Lewis and Clark Expedition*, 13 vols., ed. Gary E. Moulton and Thomas W. Dunlay (Lincoln: University of Nebraska Press, 1983–2001); Geoffry A. Wolff, "The Story of Madoc," *Washington Post*, 5 February 1967; "The Legend of Prince Madoc" <http://data-wales.co.uk/madoc.htm>; Robert Johnson, *Nova Britannia:*

noncommittal "could be" response, or told what they had been told.

In fact, both camps were partly correct. Melungeons were "mulattos" as Brownlow said, but their origin was also obscure and fantastic, beginning at Jamestown in 1619 with "pirates." The myths erred by missing the African element in mixed Melungeons.

As Dr. Burnett readied his research for the American Anthropologist Society in 1889, journalist Will Allen Dromgoole set out for the Southern Appalachian Mountains to find Melungeons. For weeks she struggled along rutted timber roads, forded rapid mountain streams, climbed steep ridges and descended sheer ravines until at last the unearthly beauty of the misty lonely Clinch stretched before her. Scaling one last rockslide, the breathless reporter came face to face with the legend.

To say she didn't find what she expected is putting it mildly. For a century before her coming, the name Melungeon had appeared and disappeared, marveled at and then forgotten by the outside world. But Dromgoole's epic journey assured, for good and bad, that the Melungeons would never be lost again. Her series would ignite a controversy and an explosion of books and articles on the so-called mystery that reverberates even today. Melungeons are not pleased with what she wrote.

Offering Most Excellent Fruites by Planting in Virginia: Exciting All Such as Be Well Affected to Further the Same, 1609 letter/pamphlet addressed "To the Right Worshipfull Sir Thomas Smith of London, Knight of one of his Majesties Councell for Virginia" [then treasurer of the Virginia Co. of London and Alderman Johnson's father-in-law] (London: printed for Samuel Macham, 1609); Adrian Gilbert, Alan Wilson, Baram Blackett, *The Holy Kingdom: The Quest for the Real King Arthur* (London: Transworld Publishers; UK: Bantam Press, 1998; repr., Montpelier VT: Invisible Cities Press, 2002); see also Tim Matthews (<www.kingarthur-online.co.uk>), "Evidence Britons Were in the US in the 6th Century," posted 25 August 2002 <http://www.rense.com/general 28/britd.htm> (accessed 10 November 2005); see also Mark K. Stengel, "The Diffusionists Have Landed," *Atlantic Monthly* (January 2000); S. D. Allen, "More on the Free Black Population of the Southern Appalachian Mountains: Speculations on the North African Connection," *Journal of Black Studies* 25/6 (July 1995): 651-71, abstract online <http://linux.library.appstate.edu/lumbee/16/ALLE001.htm>; Glenn Ellen Starr Stilling, "The Lumbee Indians: An Annotated Bibliography Supplement" <http://linux.library.appstate.edu/lumbee/credits.html>; George E. Butler, *The Croatan Indians of Sampson County, North Carolina: Their Origin and Racial Status: A Plea for Separate Schools* (Durham NC: Seeman Printery, 1916; electronic ed. online <http://docsouth.unc.edu/nc/butler/menu.html>).

Preconceptions

For 200 years, Appalachian stereotypes in literature and popular media described "hillbillies" in a very negative light, and that continues to be the norm. CBS President Les Moonves announced what one newswire headline described as a "hick hunt," a national search for a poor rural family.[8] Producers of "The Real Beverly Hillbillies" reality show proposed to have a family live in a Beverly Hills mansion, showing their awkwardness amid opulent surroundings and sophisticated neighbors. But before the program could air, the network was drawing boos and catcalls for promoting blatant stereotypes.[9] The Kentucky-based Center for Rural Strategies advocacy group organized protests with legislators from states such as Tennessee, Kentucky, and West Virginia, and introduced motions condemning CBS. "Airing such a TV show," one said, "involves humiliating, stereotyping, and discriminating against persons of extreme poverty."[10]

Melungeon literary characterizations are even more extreme than "hillbilly" stereotypes. A recent book on lost Melungeon treasure claimed: "Some believe that small groups of them [Melungeons] still live a primitive, semiferal existence in the mountains of Kentucky, Tennessee, and Virginia, directly descended from the original Melungeons."[11] Semiferal existence? Melungeons today own businesses, teach school, and pastor churches. Melanie Sovine describes outside preconceptions about Melungeons in print:

> The problem derives from a discrepancy that exists between the imagery one obtains from reading the literature: "There were tales of blood-drinking, devil worship, and 'carryings on that would freeze a good Christian's spine,' and whispered conversations of Big Betsy, the she-devil moonshine queen"; and the impression one forms by casual observation within the designated Melungeon communities: "I have lived here all my

---

[8]"CBS Heads for Hills in Hick Hunt," Logan WV (AP), 18 November 2002, posted at <www.cbsnews.com/stories/2002/08/29/entertainment/main520227.shtml>.

[9]Meg James, " 'Beverly Hillbillies'? CBS Has Struck Crude," *Los Angeles Times*, 11 February 2003.

[10]Joal Ryan, "Cajuns Ragin' at 'Hillbillies,' " Eonline News, 10 April 2003 <http://www.eonline.com/News/Items/o,1,11604.html> (as accessed 5 December 2005).

[11]W. C. Jameson, *Buried Treasures of the Appalachians: Legends of Homestead Caches, Indian Mines, and Loot from Civil War Raids* (Little Rock AR: August House Publishers, June 1991).

life and I never heard of such things as this monstrosity tells of. I have
some almighty good friends who bear the names given here, and I do not
think Hancock County is a place like this 'booger' describes." The dis-
crepancy between the imagery and the impression raises a question as to
whether the expansive body of Melungeon-related literature is representative of the people it purports to describe. It is my contention that the literature offers a mythical image that is rarely congruent with the empirical
reality corresponding to the people who are labeled "Melungeons."[12]

Example: Will Allen Dromgoole wrote of Melungeons after her short
visit in 1890:

> They are exceedingly lazy. They live from hand to mouth in hovels
> too filthy for any human being. They do not cultivate the soil at all. A
> tobacco patch and orchard is the end and aim of their aspirations. I never
> saw such orchards, apples and apples and apples, peaches and peaches and
> peaches, and soon it will be brandy and brandy and brandy. They all drink,
> men, women and children, and they are all distillers; that is, the work of
> distilling is not confined to the men. . . . They are very dishonest, so much
> so that only a few, not more than half a dozen, of the best are admitted into
> the house of the well-to-do native. I could run on forever telling you of
> these queer, queer people, who are a part of us, have a voice in our politics
> and a right to our consideration. They are a blot on the state. They are
> ignorant of the very letters of the alphabet, and defiant (or worse, ignorant)
> of the very first principles of morality and cleanliness. It is no sensational
> picture I have drawn; it is hard truth, hard to believe and hard to under-
> stand. In politics they are Republican to a man, but sell their votes for 50
> cents and consider themselves well paid. . . . They are totally unlike the
> native Tennessee mountaineer, unlike him in every way. The mountaineer
> is liberal, trustful, and open. The Malungeon wants pay (not much, but
> something) for the slightest favor. He is curious and suspicious and given
> to lying and stealing, things unknown among the native mountaineers.[13]

A 1947 article in the *Saturday Evening Post* retorted:

> Miss Dromgoole is gone and there is no practical method of checking
> her theories or even her facts now. But her final estimate of the Malun-
> geons did not please them, and they had a sort of revenge. Milum Bowen

---

    [12]Melanie Lou Sovine, "The Mysterious Melungeons: A Critique of Mythical Image"
(Ph.D. diss., University of Kentucky, 1982).
    [13]Will Allen Dromgoole, "Land of the Malungeons," *Nashville Sunday American*, 31
August 1890, 10.

remembers that the ridge people created a jingle about the poetess and repeated it endlessly to each other. "I can't remember the rest of the words," he says, "but the last of it was 'Will Allen Damfool.' "[14]

Had Dromgoole accurately described Melungeons? Walter E. Precourt, a behavioral scientist, identified an ideological bias in Appalachian literature. Writers of Appalachian articles and books gave

> excessive and distorted generalizations about the character, mental capabilities, psychology, or emotional patterns of the people described [implying] that there is a biological basis of observed behavior, not characteristic of the human species as a whole, but characteristic only of a particular population or populations. [They made] negative judgments or condemnations of native customs, manners, values, beliefs, and general lifestyles, assumptions regarding poverty and cultural deprivation, statements in support of, or against, a particular political group or ideology.[15]

Dromgoole's articles featured many such "excessive" and "distorted" ethnocentric generalities. In her view, shared by her generation, character traits resulted from biology and ethnicity, as in one example: "He was of a roving, daring disposition, and rather fond of the free abandon which characterized the Indian." She spoke of "his love for freedom and sport, and that careless existence known only to the Indians."[16] She also claimed, "The Mullins and Collins tribes will fight for their Indian blood . . . only in this matter of blood will they 'show fight' . . . their customs have lost but little of the old primitive exclusive and seclusive abandon characteristic of the sons of the forest." Dromgoole added strangeness to ethnicity: "The Malungeons are a most peculiar people. . . . Many of the Malungeons claim to be Cherokee and Portuguese. Where they could have gotten their Portuguese blood is a mystery. . . . The most that can be said of them is, 'He is a Malungeon,' a synonym for all that is doubtful and mysterious."[17]

---

[14]William L. Worden, "Sons of the Legend," *Saturday Evening Post*, 18 October 1947. This article is now posted online at <http://journals.aol.com/nmorri3924/Melungeon Research/entries/646> and at <http://www.geocities.com/ourmelungeons/post.html> (as accessed 5 December 2005).

[15]Walter E. Precourt, "Ideological Bias: A Data Quality Control Factor for Cross-Cultural Research," *Behavioral Science Research* 14 (1979), cited by Sovine, "The mysterious Melungeons."

[16]Will Allen Dromgoole, "The Malungeon Tree and Its Four Branches," *The Arena* 3/6 (June 1891): 745-51.

[17]Dromgoole, "Land of the Malungeons"; and "The Malungeons," *The Arena* 3/3

Today, the literary image of the Melungeon still conforms to this description, similar to the "Gypsy" stereotype in literature, but with a subtle, shaded difference—the Melungeon's mysteriousness is not in his roaming, but in his predating the arrival of whites. He's the riddle waiting in mountains and swamps until "civilization" finally arrives, to gawk in wonder, the lost man in the forgotten colony, preserved, timeless.

More recent publications also link strangeness with mixed ethnicity. Phyllis Reynolds Naylor wrote a best seller entitled *Sang Spell*.[18] An outline of this children's novel states:

> Grieving over the sudden death of his mother, Josh Vardy is reluctantly hitchhiking to Dallas (to begin a new life with his aunt), when he is mugged and left beside a remote mountain road. A woman driving a horse and cart takes him to a strange, fog-bound, primitive village, where there are no cars or telephones or electricity. The homespun villagers turn out to be a long-lost people of mixed ethnicity, called Melungeons. They accept Josh into their community, but will only answer his questions with evasiveness and enigmas. Mavis, a broad-shouldered young woman his own age, befriends Josh when he is put to work with the others gathering ginseng, a valuable root they refer to as 'sang and trade once a year to Chinese merchants. Over and over again Josh tries to escape—by road and by river—but finds that somehow all routes lead back to this village that time has forgotten. When Josh finally joins in the villagers' rituals and celebrations, his feelings of despair about his own future begin to transform and heal. And after his loyalty to the Melungeons is tested, Josh finds that he is free at last to make the decision to leave.[19]

Here, the reviewer uses the phrase "mixed ethnicity" to highlight the eerie strangeness of mysterious Melungeons and their magical "Brigadoon-like" village cut off from the real world. These "long-lost" Melungeons of "mixed ethnicity" live in a "strange, fog-bound, primitive village." A Melungeon female is "broad shouldered." They respond to the outsider's questions with "evasiveness and enigmas." When the boy attempts to escape "somehow all routes lead back to this village that time has forgotten." The climax arrives when the protagonist participates in "the villagers' rituals and celebrations."

(March 1891): 470-79.

[18]Phyllis Reynolds Naylor, *Sang Spell* (New York: Atheneum Books for Young Readers, 1998; New York: Aladdin Paperbacks, April 2000).

[19]Patty Campbell, literary critic for *Horn Book Magazine*.

Rituals? Since the American Revolution, Melungeons have been mostly Protestant.

But while Naylor weaves eerie descriptions of the fantastic "Canara" (mythical home of the Melungeons) the Melungeon community in her book is ultimately presented not as sinister, but as compassionate and healing, which is as superficial a treatment of a historical Melungeon community as Dromgoole's. Both Dromgoole and Naylor, though worlds apart, give portraits that are misleading. Dromgoole introduced a myth based on distorted ethnocentricities and mixed "strangeness." Naylor creates a fantasy to teach life-affirming values. But both link weirdness and remoteness with mixed ethnicity, reflecting the urban dweller's fear of the wilderness. Rather than go with either the ghost stories of Melungeon monsters or the myths of Melungeon lost colonies, Naylor and Dromgoole channel the fantasy elements to reach the same conclusion still present in the American perception—race mixing, whether acceptable or not, is "uncivilized."

Folk Tales and Superstition

European conquest over less technologically advanced continents in the seventeenth and eighteenth centuries ironically agitated European xenophobia—the fear that the "civilized" European ethnoculture would be contaminated by contact with dread "sauvages."

According to the earliest legend after the American Revolution, Melungeons were born of a devilish mixed marriage on a high bald knob in Appalachia. Lively and wild and full of deceit, the mixed offspring were called "children of perdition." The phrase "children of perdition" means they came from unblessed, and therefore uncivilized, unions, common-law marriages—the only way mixed couples could marry. Even before Melungeons became a lost colony, black and white storytellers just a hop, skip, and jump from the nation's capital were scaring children with Melungeon bogeyman stories—"Be good or a Melungeon will grab you!"—as Burnett and Dromgoole recalled from their youth.

In the eighteenth and nineteenth centuries, Europe produced Gothic horror novels and chilling shockers presenting the half-breed as the Unnatural, the Monster, the Abnormal deviant of nature evoking horror, the allegorical union of the sacred with the profane; a loathsome creature capable of moving between worlds.[20]

---

[20]Howard L., Malchow, *Gothic Images of Race in Nineteenth-Century Britain* (Stanford

The Middle English "monstre" originated from Middle French which came from the Latin word for "omen," or "warning."[21] Howard L. Malchow says early Gothic horror stories reflected Northern European fears of cultural upheaval resulting in race mixing, written in "a language that could be appropriated by racists in a powerful and obsessively reiterated evocation of terror, disgust, and alienation."[22] As Europeans conquered North America, traded in the Far East, and enslaved Africa they were drawn closer to strange customs that shocked them. The Gothic xenophobia of the eighteenth century was born in "the context of an expanding experience of cultural conflict, of the brutal progress of European nationalism and imperialism, and was in part a construct of that phenomenon."[23]

Nurtured in a twilight world mingling fantasy and science, Gothic racism bridged

> the imagined world of literature and the "real" world of historical experience, between fiction and romance on the one hand, and the "parallel fictions" of the human sciences, of anthropology and biology, between popular representations of the "unnatural" at home and abroad, between domestic environment and that of empire.

The Gothic imagination of half-humans like Dracula and Jekyll and Hyde was rooted in the perceived horrors of mongrelization during colonialism, and later during the industrial revolution. In the twentieth century, wielding the power of Virginia's Racial Integrity Act, influential white segregationists warned of Melungeon "mongrels" more cunning than Indians and Africans because of their infusion of white blood. Science legitimized the myth. Virginia State Registrar Dr. W. A. Plecker, who loathed Melungeons like the fictional Prof. Van Helsing abhorred vampires, warned during the 1924 annual conference of the American Public Health Association that, "Mongrels are superior in mental power to the lower race. They are more cunning and more capable."[24] Marcus Garvey, the black

---

CA: Stanford University Press, 1996).

[21]"Monster," *Merriam-Webster Dictionary* online <http://www.m-w.com/dictionary/monster>.

[22]Malchow, *Gothic Images of Race in Nineteenth Century Britain.*

[23]Malchow, *Gothic Images of Race in Nineteenth Century Britain.*

[24]Walter Ashby Plecker, "Virginia's Attempt to Adjust the Color Problem," read before the 53rd annual meeting of the Public Health Administration and Vital Statistics Section of the American Public Health Association, Detroit, Michigan, 23 October 1924, as published in *Eugenics in Relation to the New Family and the Law on Racial Integrity, Including a*

separatist with whom the white racist Dr. Plecker plotted, warned in New York in 1927 that integration created, "disease, mongrels—social disgrace."[25]

A consistent thread in the earliest Melungeon folk superstition was the claim by blacks and whites that the strange Melungeon was a "born rogue . . . mean as the devil . . . dark and treacherous as their mammy," and anyone who was pulling a fast one was said to be "tricky as a Malungeon."[26] James Aswell, who visited Hancock County, Tennessee in the early 1900s, collected folk tales from blacks and from whites. His story "God Bless the Devil" retells an early Appalachian tale about the origin of the Melungeons. Their birth was declared illegitimate, unblessed, evil:

> The old grannies say one time Old Horny [the Devil] got mad at his shrew-wife and left Hell and wandered all over the earth till he reached Tennessee. He set on a high bald and looked around him. "I declare to Creation!" he says, "This place is so much like home I just believe I'll stay awhile." "So Old Horny found him an Indian gal and started in housekeeping. Time came time went. Everybody knows the Devil's always busy, and soon the house was full of children. And mean! Law! They was every one as mean as the Devil—which is natural, seeing as he was their pappy—and as dark and treacherous as their mammy. They beat and hammered at Old Horny day and night. They tricked and mortified him till it was pitiful. Finally he just couldn't stand it no longer at all. "I might as well be in Hell with my old crabby wedlock wife," says he. So he packed his traps and sneaked out of the house and went a skillyhooting back to Hell as fast as ever he could. And they do say it was them offspring of Old Horny that growed up and started the Melungeon kind. . . .

Paper Read before the American Public Health Association, 12-28 (Richmond: D. Bottom, supt. public printing, 1924) and in *The American Journal of Public Health* (1925). Now online at <http://www.webcom.com/~intvoice/powell5.html>.

[25]Marcus Garvey, *The Tragedy of White Injustice* (New York: Amy J. Garvey, 1927).

[26]James R. Aswell (of the Tennessee Writers' Project), *God Bless the Devil!: Liars' Bench Tales*, Tennesseana Editions, facsimile edition (Knoxville: University of Tennessee Press, 1985; orig., Chapel Hill: University of North Carolina Press, 1940). See also, Dromgoole, "Land of the Malungeons." James Mooney cited Swan Burnett's "Notes on Melungeons" in *American Anthropology* (1889), and added that the Croatans (Lumbees), Red Bones, and Moors of Delaware, "seem to be the same mixture" as the Melungeons. James Mooney, *Myths of the Cherokee; and Sacred Formulas of the Cherokees*, reprint of the 1900 and 1891 editions respectively, which were published in the 19th and 7th Annual Reports, Bureau of American Ethnology (Nashville: Charles and Randy Elder—Booksellers, 1982).

[So] whites left them alone because they were so wild and devil-fired and queer and witchy. If a man was fool enough to go into Melungeon country and if he come back without being shot, he was just sure to wizzen and perish away with some ailment nobody could name."[27]

Aswell added, " 'sons of perdition' the East Tennessee mountaineers call the Melungeons, a dark, strange folk living principally in the high ridges and back coves of Hancock and Rhea Counties."

In 1889, Dr. Swan Burnett reported that as a child before the Civil War he had heard frightening Melungeon tales at his father's knee.[28] In 1890, the thirty-year-old Will Dromgoole wrote that the previous generation of parents had heard supernatural Melungeon tales when they were children.[29] This suggests Melungeon "bogeyman" stories were told at least as early as the 1840s when the slavery issue was dividing the nation. During the same decade, Melungeons in Hawkins County, Tennessee produced the counter-myth that they were "Portuguese."

The Melungeon tale Dr. Burnett heard had mixed elements of African and Indian lore:

And when I chanced to waken in the night and the fire had died down on the hearth, and the wind swept with a demoniac shriek and terrifying roar around and through the house, rattling the windows and the loose clapboards on the roof, I shrank under the bedclothes trembling with a fear that was almost an expectation that one of these huge creatures [Melungeons] would come down the chimney with a rush, seize me with his dragon-like arms, and carry me off to his cave in the mountains, there to devour me piecemeal.[30]

Like many affluent white Southerners, Walter Plecker, born ten days before the Civil War started, was raised on stories told by a black slave in

---

[27]James Aswell, *God Bless the Devil!, Liars' Bench Tales*; Aswell, "Lost Tribes of Tennessee's Mountains," *Nashville Banner Magazine*, 22 August 1937. In "Mystery of the Melungeons," a story for the *San Francisco Examiner and Chronicle*, 15 November 1970, William Endicott wrote something similar: "Mountain legend says that if a man is fool enough to wander into Melungeon country and if he comes back without being shot, he is sure to wizen and perish with some ailment nobody could name."

[28]Burnett, "Notes on the Melungeons."

[29]"Were you ever when a child half playfully told 'The Malungeons will get you'? If not, you were never a Tennessee child, as some of our fathers were. . . . " Dromgoole, "The Malungeons."

[30]Burnett, "Notes on the Melungeons."

Augusta County, Virginia. After the War, "Delila" remained with the family as a beloved faithful servant. Plecker, one of the most rigid segregationists the U.S. ever produced would later say, "the birth of mulatto children is a standing disgrace."

Tales told to white and black children over hissing embers of the fireplace described monstrous harpy-like Melungeons said to be genetically misshapen. According to another writer, "When I was a child, babysitters used to threaten us with abduction by six-fingered Melungeons who reputedly lived in trees on the ridges ringing town."[31] Melungeons were seen as "untrustworthy, undependable, and inhuman. In fact, tales of six-fingered Melungeons still circulate."[32]

John Shelton Reed also heard of "six-fingered" Melungeons from his father:

> When I was growing up in east Tennessee, I heard about the Melungeons, these strange folk who lived back in the hills and had olive complexions. My father, a doctor, also told me that they often have six fingers. (Now, the literature I've been reading lately doesn't mention that. Some triracial groups like the Wesort of Delaware do have a tendency to polydactylism, but if the Melungeons do, it hasn't made the papers. Nevertheless, as a child I believed what my father told me.)[33]

Another kind of Melungeon folk tale also described mischief and deceit. However, the second genre differs in that it adds the names of real Melungeons. These stories are like the Anansi "trickster" tales told long ago in Angola, Africa and retold by Africans in American as the "Br'er Rabbit" stories. Dromgoole's series in the 1890s stirred a reader at the time to write to the newspaper about hearing such stories from his father's black slaves "long before the war." He was "anxious to know if such people really existed or not." The reader was astonished to read of real Melungeons, having thought they were myths from "the very fertile brain of our

---

[31]Lisa Alther, "Border States," in *Blood Root: Reflections on Place by Appalachian Women Writers*, ed. Joyce Dyer (Lexington: University Press of Kentucky, 1998).

[32]Ed Runyon, "The Melungeons" <http://www.english.vt.edu/~appalach/essaysM/melung.htm>.

[33]John Shelton Reed, "Mixing in the Mountains" (with reference to Beale, "American Triracial Isolates"), *Southern Cultures* 3/4 (Winter 1997): 25, and reproduced at <http://www.bioethics.umn.edu/genetics_and_identity/reed.html>; Joan Vannorsdall Schroeder, "First Union: The Melungeons Revisited," *Blue Ridge Country* magazine (July/August 1991) and online at <http://www.blueridgecountry.com/melung/melung.html>.

imaginative Negro nurse, who used to entertain us with stories of the Malungeons, ghosts, hobgoblins, Br'er Rabbit, Br'er Fox, etc."[34]

The early socialization between African Americans and Southeastern American Indians transferred Angolan trickster stories to Cherokee tales of the *Yunwe Tsunsdie*, or "little people," according to James Mooney.[35] These supernatural creatures lived on bald knobs and, like Melungeons, hunted ginseng, and were said to be cunning and tricky. Lost Indians rescued by Cherokee "little people" could never leave their hidden village, for all the trails were bewitched. Folk tales of the 1800s said Melungeons also put spells on travelers to make it impossible to leave their secret communities and reveal them.

Will Allen Dromgoole related a Melungeon "trickster" story about Vardy Collins and Buck Gibson that she said showed they had inherited the "cunning" of their ancestors:

> Somewhere in the eighteenth century, before the year 1797, there appeared in the eastern portion of Tennessee, at that time the Territory of North Carolina, two strange-looking men calling themselves "Collins" and "Gibson."
>
> Old Buck, as he was called, was disguised by a wash of some dark description, and taken to Virginia by Vardy where he was sold as a slave. He was a magnificent specimen of physical strength, and brought a fine price, a wagon and mules, a lot of goods, and three hundred dollars in money being paid to old Vardy for his "likely nigger." Once out of Richmond, Vardy turned his mule's shoes and stuck out for the wilderness of North

---

[34]Douglas Anderson, "What Do You Know about the Melungeons?" *Nashville Banner*, 3 August 1924; Joel Chandler Harris, *Uncle Remus, His Songs and His Sayings* (1880), ed. Robert E. Hemenway (New York: Penguin Books, 1982); Linda S. Chang, "Brer Rabbit's Angolan Cousin: Politics and the Adaptation of Folk Material," *Folklore-Forum* 19 (1986): 1, 36-50; see also Endicott, "Mystery of the Melungeons"; Stories of "Big Betsy," aka Mahala Mullins, traced to Henry Martin Wiltse of Chattanooga, who—according to Ivey, "Oral, Printed, and Popular Culture Traditions Related to the Melungeons of Hancock County, Tennessee"—described her as such in 1895 in a story entitled *The Moonshiners* (Chattanooga: Times Printing Co., 1895); James Aswell, "Lost Tribes of Tennessee's Mountains," *Nashville Banner Magazine* (22 August 1937); Ivey, "Oral, Printed, and Popular Culture Traditions Related to the Melungeons of Hancock County, Tennessee"; Phyllis Cox Barr, "The Melungeons of Newman's Ridge" (M.A. thesis, East Tennessee State University, 1965); Jim Lynch, "The Melungeons: Who Are These People?" *Tennessee Magazine* (16 August 1973); Pam Vallett, "The Melungeon Mystery: The Making of Myth?" *The Tennessee Alumnus Magazine* (Summer 1977): 12-14.

[35]Mooney, *Myths of the Cherokee; and Sacred Formulas of the Cherokees*.

Carolina, as previously planned. Buck lost little time ridding himself of his negro disguise, swore he was not the man bought of Collins, and followed in the wake of his fellow thief to the Territory. The proceeds of the sale were divided and each chose his habitation; old Vardy choosing New-man's Ridge, where he was soon joined by others of his race, and so the Melungeons became a part of the inhabitants of Tennessee.[36]

The Buck and Vardy story related by Dromgoole had a life long before her visit because both men were of the first generation of Melungeons who came to Southern Appalachia between 1790 and 1810. Vardy Collins was born in 1764 and is believed to have died in the decade between the 1850 and 1860 censuses. Shepard "Buck" Gibson was born in 1765 and died in 1842. The "Buck and Vardy" folk tales originated before the Civil War, and were likely told as least as early as the "Trail of Tears" removal of the Cherokees to Oklahoma. Mahala Mullins, whose story was embellished more than any other, was from the second generation in Tennessee, 1824-1898. Children like the educated Will Allen Dromgoole and W. A. Plecker who heard tales of "sneaky" and "tricky" Melungeon hobgoblins, grew up with preconceptions that turned monsters into tricksters "passing" as white. Decades later, race scientists had a wide-eyed audience on the edge of its seat when they introduced polygenics and eugenics to counter what they perceived were the dangers of "race mixing."

The Storyteller

Suspicion about Melungeon ancestry along with superstition caused trepi-dation: "fathers warned their daughters against "marrying up with that class."[37] Mildred Haun's short story, "Melungeon-Colored,"[38] illustrates the disgrace of Melungeon blood. Haun, an early twentieth century Vanderbilt-educated native of Appalachia told a story of race mixing, attempted abor-tion, and infanticide, decades before such topics were discussed. In her tale, heavy with "signs," the speaker is a white woman whose daughter Effena has rashly married a Melungeon man. The dying Effena, after giving birth to Cordia, a baby girl with white skin, begs her mother to keep her secret. The mother relates what followed:

---

[36]Dromgoole, "The Malungeon Tree and Its Four Branches."

[37]Berry, *Almost White: A Provocative Study of America's Mixed-Blood Minorities.*

[38]"Melungeon-Colored," in Haun, *The Hawk's Done Gone and Other Stories,* ed. Herschel Gower (Nashville: Vanderbilt University Press, 1968).

So when Effena saw she was going to die she asked me not to ever let Cordia know that her pa had been a Melungeon. Said some folks were getting so they held it against a body for being a Melungeon. I reckon it was because of what that ignorant man from down the country said about them having Negro blood in them. Of course I don't know. I never have seed a Negro. But I've heard tell of them. Ad sees them sometimes when he goes to Newport. But other folks claimed that Melungeons were a Lost Colony or a Lost Tribe or something. I don't know. I just know Effena said for me to raise Cordia up to think she didn't ever have any other pa or ma. And she said for me not to ever let Cordia get married. I could see how Effena thought. I knowed if Cordia ever had any boy youngons they would be Melungeon-colored and her man might not understand. I knew, and I promised Effena just as the breath went out of her.

I set out to keep the promise. Many was the time it was hard to keep from bawling when Cordia would beg like a pup to go somewhere and would think hard of me because I wouldn't let her. But I made up my mind not to worry till I had something to worry about. I told myself there might not be any youngons, or if there were, they might all be girls.

Eventually, Cordia grows up to be a beautiful young girl, and despite her grandparents' vigilance, runs off and marries a white man and then returns home to her grandparents to announce she is pregnant. Knowing Cordia is part Melungeon, and fearing that the child will be born "melungeon-colored" the grandmother unsuccessfully tries to abort the pregnancy by giving Cordia cups of pennyroyal tea.

On a frightful stormy night nine months later, with a howling black panther trying to get into the cabin, Cordia gives birth. Her grandparents are the only people present as the baby is born. Cordia, like her mother before her, will not survive giving birth. One look at the baby and the grandparents see that the secret is about to be revealed. The grandparents make a terrible decision:

Mos come running with the scissors. "Its skin!" I said. "A Melungeon! I knowedit." I don't know what made me say it. Mos give the baby one look. "That's why that devil [the panther] wanted to stay here," he yelled.

I seed him pick up a stick of stove wood. I didn't know what had made me blurt it out. I just didn't know anything. I reckon Cordia was too weak to pay any attention to what we were saying. She was shaking. I seed she was having convulsions. That was what it was. She had took too much gunpowder.

"Mos!" I yelled. "Don't!"

But it was too late to yell. I stood there like a post, trying to think. I felt Mos take a hold of me. I thought he was going to kill me too.

"Listen to reason," he said to me. "Are you in your right senses?"

I jumped. I don't think I knowed for sure whether I was or not. I saw I would have to quiet myself down. The baby was alive. With Cordia dead. Mos's eyes—they were as green as a glow worm.

"Me and you can bury her up yander on the hill in the morning," he said.

I stood there. But I recollected the hill. Mos's grandpa and grandma were buried up there. It would be for Cordia's good. It would save her name. All that went through my head. Nobody would blame Mos. Nobody would know about the burying. Nobody would come to the burying anyhow. Both creeks were up too high. I seed it was best. We could tell folks that we had to bury her. I thought of the baby.

I've thought about the things that happened that night. All night me and Mos hammered on the coffin. Old rough planks that he tore out of the house loft. Right there in the room where Cordia was. And her more than my girl. And the little funny-colored baby that I prayed the Lord would let die before we got the coffin made. But it didn't. It kept on whimpering and gasping. I never could have stood it if I had been in my right mind. I was scared out of my right senses. Scared Mos would hit me in the head with that hammer. Somehow, I wasn't willing to die, even if I did think I wanted to.

When we got the coffin done we didn't even stuff it and put a lining in it. We piled some quilts down in it and laid Cordia on them. I did wash Cordia and wrap her up in a new quilt. But we had to break her knees to get her legs to go down into the coffin.

And the baby, it kept on living. Mos, he just picked it up and put it on in. I stood and watched him. Stood stone-still and watched him. We nailed the lid down. It was about chicken crow then. I had to stay there in the room while Mos went to dig a grave. And the baby alive.

It poured down rain while Mos was gone. It was dark as pitch outside. And that cat. That cat kept on clawing at the window. It meowed and screamed and went on. Then I heard that panther scream right out there in the yard. It sounded like a woman's screaming.

A big puff of wind come and blew the door open. And that cat kept on. I was afraid the panther would get in the house if I didn't go shut the door. But I couldn't move toward the door. I couldn't move any which way.

The grave, it was full of water by the time me and Mos got Cordia carried up there. About halfway there we had to set the coffin down in the mud so we could rest a spell. And that cat. When we set the coffin down, it jumped upon it. Mos couldn't knock it off. It fit him right back. It followed us every jump of the way. I could hear the baby smothering and that cat meowing.[39]

Many Scots-Irish of Appalachia were uneducated and illiterate at the turn of the century. Their superstitious tales paled, however, next to the myths that educated scholars were beginning to spread as the 20th century dawned.

---

[39]Haun, "Melungeon-Colored."

Chapter 7

Development of Modern Racism

Will Allen Dromgoole had not planned to stir up a race controversy when she set off in 1889 to discover the "mysterious Melungeons." She sought a "lost colony" tucked away in the misty mountains. But that changed a few months after her stories caused a heated public debate in Tennessee.

Dromgoole was born in Murfreesboro, Tennessee, one year before the Civil War. Readers later assumed she was male, according to biographer Vicki Slagle Johns: "She did not need to invent a male pseudonym: her father, wishing his seventh child to be a boy, had already decided on the name William, and that was the name Dromgoole received, even though she turned out to be a girl."[1] She wrote for the *Nashville Banner* and the *Nashville Daily American* and the influential newspaper, the *Boston Arena*, "whose editor, B. O. Flower, enthusiastically pronounced her a "Southern woman of genius."

Biographer Kathy Lyday-Lee says Dromgoole studied law with her father and in 1885 and 1887 won terms as an engrossing clerk in the state Senate. She was defeated "possibly because her unflattering portraits of the Melungeons, an East Tennessee mountain community, in articles published in the *Nashville Daily American* (1890) and the *Boston Arena* (1891) angered the senators who represented them."[2]

Will Allen earned great acclaim and wrote the poem "The Bridge Builder," one of America's best-loved poems. Before she died in 1934, she had been named poet laureate of both Tennessee and the Poetry Society of the South.[3]

---

[1]Vicki Slagle Johns, "Written with a Flourish," *Tennessee Alumnus* (University of Tennessee; Winter 1996); online at <http://pr.utk.edu/alumnus/winter96/local.html>.

[2]Kathy Lyday-Lee, "Will Allen Dromgoole, 1860–1934" The Tennessee Encyclopedia of History and Culture Online <http://tennesseeencyclopedia.net>.

[3]Johns, "Written with a Flourish."

The Passion of Will Allen Dromgoole

Will Allen Dromgoole was a serious turn-of-the-century progressive, a "do-gooder," and the unflattering scenes of rural life she described in "Melungia" ruffled feathers in the state capital of Tennessee. Progressives like Will Allen demanded the government solve social problems. In Boston, her peer, turn-of-the-century Boston feminist Lillian Harman criticized her by name in an article ridiculing progressive movements as "Societies for Meddling with Everybody's Business."[4]

"Social purity" relating to family health and women's health issues was Will Allen's passion. But what was "social purity" and what was early twentieth-century "progressivism"?

The post-Civil War industrial revolution uprooted rural America, and wars abroad increased immigration to American cities which soon thronged with masses looking for work. Slum neighborhoods grew up from which civic leaders feared would pour disease, crime, class warfare, and social decay. Industrialists worried about labor unrest such as the coal-mining wars in Appalachia.

The year the Coal Creek war began was the year Dromgoole skewered the Melungeons in print. While setting about solving the "mystery" of the Melungeons, Dromgoole initially thought Melungeons couldn't be mixed black-and-white mulattos, as some said, because they were obviously fertile and she had been led to believe mulattos were sterile:

> A great many declare them mulattoes, and base their belief upon the ground that at the close of the Civil War negroes and Malungeons stood upon precisely the same social footing, "free men of color" all, and that the fast-vanishing handful opened their doors to the darker brother, also groaning under the brand of social ostracism. This might, at first glance, seem probable, indeed, reasonable.
>
> Yet if we will consider a moment, we shall see that a race of mulattoes cannot exist as these Malungeons have existed. The race goes from mulattoes to quadroons [persons of one-quarter black ancestry], from qua-

---

[4]Lillian Harman, "An 'Age of Consent' Symposium (1896)," *Liberty* (magazine, ed. Benjamin Tucker, 1881–1908) #306 (1896?): 2-5, #314 (1896?): 6-7; reprinted in *Freedom, Feminism, and the State: An Overview of Individualist Feminism*, ed. Wendy McElroy (Washington DC: Cato Institute, 1982). The Harman article was one of several omitted from the 1991 2nd ed. of *Freedom, Feminism, and the State*. Harman's article is also posted online at <http://praxeology.net/LH-ACS.htm>.

droons to octoroons [persons of one-eighth black ancestry], and there it stops. The octoroon women bear no children, but in every cabin of the Malungeons may be found mothers, and grandmothers, and very often great-grandmothers.[5]

That "octoroon women bear no children" is of course erroneous, but it was believed in Dromgoole's day, even by scientists. A mixed person was called a *mulatto* because the *mule*, a mix of a horse and a donkey, was sometimes sterile, as mixed people supposedly were.

Yet Melungeons were clearly fertile and at first Dromgoole believed their fertility proved they were not mixed. However, after her first articles appeared, some readers wrote letters to the editor protesting that Melungeons were indeed mixed. One reader argued that Dromgoole was

coining a new name for these amalgamationists. Will Allen need not have gone to East Tennessee to find these people, they are here under the very dome of the capitol. We recognize them as mulattoes on account of the fusion of Negro blood in their veins. When the fusion is slight they set up a claim of superiority and call themselves Portegee, but, as Will Allen says, it is a mystery where the Portugese comes in. This will remain a mystery until better ethnologists enter the lists than have yet appeared. The Negro blood can easily be traced, as also sometimes the Cherokee.[6]

Following public reaction, Dromgoole reassessed Melungeon ethnicity. With evidence that Melungeons were indeed fertile *and* multiethnic, she proposed a new theory of *two* different groups of Melungeons—in a single county! The first group, the "pure race" of Melungeons, was in her opinion the original "lost colony" community. They lived, in her analogy, "above," on Newman's Ridge. She then proposed that some from this "pure" race

---

[5]Dromgoole, "The Malungeons," *The Arena* (March 1891). Dromgoole's well-known 1891 series of articles in the *Arena* was largely reproduced by her from her earlier lesser-known series of Melungeon articles and letters to the editor she had written for the *Nashville Daily American* beginning on 31 Aug. 1890. She originally described the octoroon sterility theory in a letter to the editor of the *Daily American*, published 9 Sept. 1890 and entitled "Will Allen Comes Back at Her Critics in Gallant Style," after her first article on 31 Aug., in which she described the origin of Melungeons as "mystery," drew the ire of some readers who believed Melungeons were of African and Cherokee origin and hardly mysterious.

[6]Anonymous writer identified as "Twenty-fourth District," to editor of the *Nashville Daily American*, published 7 Sept. 1890 and taking issue with Dromgoole's 31 Aug. 1890 Melungeon article. See also Douglas Anderson, "What Do You Know about the Melungeons?" *Nashville Banner*, 3 Aug. 1924.

mixed with "Negroes" to produce a second group of Melungeons led by the Goinses, who, staying with her analogy, lived "below" in Black Water. That the high ridge was called "new man" (that is, the pure Melungeon race) and the valley was called "black water" (the mixed Melungeons) gave her a convenient analogy.

Of course Dromgoole's new theory of pure and mixed Melungeons was nonsense. All Melungeon ancestors had been mixing since the seventeenth century, and their numbers were flourishing more than ever. Mahala Mullins was the most famous of the Melungeons on Newman's Ridge, and she was a Goins on her mother's side, descended from the Angolan John Gowen of seventeenth-century Jamestown. Nearly everyone on Newman's Ridge as well as down in Black Water was related to the Goinses.

In June 1891, two months after the Coal Creek mining troubles began and after the criticism of her first articles, Dromgoole revealed to her readers that "pure" Melungeons had positive qualities that she credited to their European ancestry. Mixed Melungeons were a later "shiftless" breed who were, she alleged, regarded with "contempt" by pure Melungeons:

> The African branch was introduced by one Goins who emigrated from North Carolina after the formation of the state of Tenn. Goins was a negro, and did not settle upon the Ridge, but lower down the Big Sycamore Creek in Powell's Valley. He took a melungeon woman for his wife (took up with her), and reared a family or tribe. The Goins family may be easily recognized by their kinky hair, flat nose and foot, thick lips, and a complexion totally unlike the Collins and Mullins tribes. They possess many negro traits, too, which are wanting to the other tribes.
>
> The Malungeons repudiate the idea of Negro blood, yet some of the shiftless stragglers among them have married among the Goins people. They evade slight, snubs, censure, and the law by claiming to have married Portuguese, there really being a Portuguese branch among the tribes. The Goins tribe was always looked upon with touch of contempt, and was held in a kind of subjection, socially and politically, by the others.[7]

As DNA recently revealed, Dromgoole was wrong. There were no Portuguese, and the idea of a caste system among Melungeons is refuted not only by DNA but by records revealing a common ancestry shared by both the ridge dwellers and the valley dwellers.

---

[7]Dromgoole, "The Malungeon Tree and Its Four Branches."

Dromgoole predicted "impure" Melungeons would disappear: "They are going; the little space of hills, 'twixt earth and heaven allotted them, will soon be free of the dusky tribe whose very name is a puzzle, and whose origin is a riddle no man has unraveled."[8] And "It will be a matter of some interest to follow them down to the present day."[9]

But the Melungeons, said the *Saturday Evening Post*, had changed Dromgoole:

> Several peculiarities mar the poetess's account of the dark people. One is that she changed her mind. In the *Arena* article of March 1891, she rejected the theory that the Malungeons might be Negroid, basing her rejection on their appearance and on what she stated as a fact—that continuance of such blood would be impossible because octoroon women never had children, and Malungeons families were traceable for numerous generations. She said then that she did not know where the Malungeons had come from or of what blood they were, although she was inclined to believe they were basically Portuguese.
>
> Three months later, however, Miss Dromgoole signed another article on the same subject in the same magazine. But by this time she had decided, among other things, that octoroon women were not necessarily barren after all. She no longer found the Malungeons interesting, friendly, or pathetic. In June they were dirty, thieving, untrustworthy, decadent, and not mysterious at all. In June she knew their exact history. . . .[10]

Francis Galton's[11] new Darwinian eugenics theory was starting to replace polygenetics based on the discredited mulatto sterility theory. Unlike polygeneticists, Galton did not say mixing led to biological weakness and eventual race suicide. Rather, he said, mixing led to intellectual, social, and cultural weakness, and eventual race suicide. The nineteenth-century race scientists passed the scepter to the twentieth-century race scientists with hardly a ripple. To Galton, who was Charles Darwin's nephew, mixing lowered the sum intelligence of the white race and thus imperiled white culture and white civilization, which he declared, was the one enlightened civilization preventing the human race from destruction.

Associating mixing with disgrace, Will Allen Dromgoole hinted at her conversion to eugenics: "If the Malungeons are mulattos it is a blot upon

---

[8]Dromgoole, "The Malungeons."

[9]Dromgoole, "The Melungeon Tree and Its Four Branches."

[10]Worden, "Sons of the Legend."

[11]On Francis Galton (1822–1911), see <http://galton.org>.

the name of Tennessee; a disgrace so black that morality would hide her face, and, shrieking, leave the world forever."[12]

The Rise of Race Science

The bastard, eugenicists claim, can never rise above the sire—a saying ironically applicable to eugenics' own pedigree.

Influential early Americans such as Thomas Jefferson introduced race theories based on their perceptions of culture and biology that color America's views to this day. Jefferson, who wrote in 1776 that "all men are created equal," years later added doubtfully:

> Nobody wishes more than I do to see . . . proofs that nature has given to our black brethren talents equal to those of the other colors of men, and that the appearance of a want of them is owing merely to the degraded condition of their existence both in Africa and America.[13]

A theory that blacks, and subsequently mulattos, had no souls came from a Frenchman during the heyday of the French colonial empire, who offered a cruel excuse for making slaves of Africans:

> Charles-Louis Montesquieu (1689–1755), whose influence on early Euro- pean-American thought had been quite substantial, had said that Negroes had no souls. Since Negroes had no souls, they could not be regarded as humans, let alone Christians, and therefore there was no need to treat them humanely. Joseph Arthur de Gobineau, in his 1854 book, *The Inequality of Human Races*, added "The Negroid variety is the lowest, and stands at the foot of the ladder. The animal character, that appears in the shape of the pelvis, is stamped on the Negro from birth, and foreshadows his destiny."[14]

---

[12]Dromgoole, in a letter to the editor, *Nashville Daily American*, 9 Sept. 1890, entitled "Will Allen Comes Back at Her Critics in Gallant Style." See also Saundra Keys Ivey, "Oral, Printed, and Popular Culture Traditions Related to the Melungeons of Hancock County, Tennessee" (thesis, Indiana University, 1976). (That this hinted at Dromgoole's conversion to eugenics was the conclusion of Worden in "Sons of the Legend.")

[13]As quoted in Andrew Hacker, *Two Nations: Black and White, Separate, Hostile, Un-equal* (New York: Scribner's, 1992; pbk. 2003). Original: letter to Benjamin Banneker (1791).

[14]Kortright Davis, in "The Episcopal Face of Ebony Grace," Absalom Jones Lecture, Episcopal Divinity School, 2003, citing Eric Eustace Williams, *From Columbus to Castro: The History of the Caribbean, 1492–1969* (London: Deutsch; New York: Harper, 1970).

To the myth of non-human Africans, Gobineau added the myth of the pure white Aryan race. Herbert Wendt, in *It Began at Babel*, wrote:

> In the years between 1853 and 1857 the French author and diplomat Joseph Arthur Count Gobineau published his four-volume work on *The Inequality of Human Races*.[15] Gobineau invented the concept of the "Aryan Race," by which he understood persons of the white race, possessing long skulls and blond hair, a group which, to Gobineau's regret, was hardly anywhere to be found in its pure state. For the count was of the opinion that humanity owed all its greatest achievements to this race, and that all other races were therefore inferior. Now the concept of Aryans originally referred to an Indo-Iranian caste, and was later used as the name for a family of languages. The long-skulled blonde whites about whom Gobineau was so enthusiastic are neither to be identified with these ancient Aryans nor to be regarded as a pure race themselves. But this was not known in Gobineau's day.
>
> Gobineau believed that all great empires and civilizations had fallen into ruin because they had not preserved the purity of their Aryan blood. If the ruling house of France and the French aristocracy had kept themselves racially pure, then there could have been no French Revolution. And this was really the key to Gobineau's philosophy, he was an aristocrat, through and through. He felt it his duty to show the mob of revolutionary "unwashed plebs" that they were racially inferior and unfitted to govern the country. He divided France into the "yellow" race of the Alpine type, and the "black" race of the Mediterranean type. The common people of these two types might very well mix, but the aristocracy never. So Gobineau was merely upholding what is still sacred to most aristocratic classes, the necessity to preserve caste, an avoidance of marriage with a commoner. His theories are the same as those governing the ruling houses of Europe. His *Essai sur l'Inegalite des Races Humaines* released an avalanche. . . . He would have remained an obscure exception on the margins of history if a few people had not taken up his ideas and turned them into a philosophy of life.[16]

---

[15]The French original was four volumes. The English translation of part one is one volume: *The Inequality of Human Races*, trans. Adrian Collins (New York: G. P. Putnam, 1915; repr. New York: H. Fertig, 1999).

[16]Herbert Wendt, *It Began in Babel: The Story of the Birth and Development of Races and People*, trans. James Kirkup (London: Weidenfeld and Nicholson, 1961; repr. 1963).

This French monarchal theory on race and class affected American science and American law. In the twentieth century, the American architects of "one drop"—Laughlin, Plecker, Cox, Powell and Grant—were quoting this French monarchist:

> In America, a follower of Gobineau, Madison Grant, demanded of the government an increase in the number of Nordic immigrants. America already had a race problem in the Negroes, and had her own fanatics, the Ku-Klux-Klan. But Madison Grant's demands, (expressed in his book, *Passing of the Great Race*[17]) created a new racial problem; in the eyes of people who were of the same mind as he was, immigrants from Mediterranean and East Asiatic regions were degraded to second-class members of American society.[18]

The United States, not Nazi Germany, was the first to legislate based on Gobineau's "pure Aryan" philosophy, when, in 1924, due to the influence of Gobineau's followers, three momentous acts were passed to preserve pure Aryans. (In 1924, Hitler was still in prison writing *Mein Kampf.*) Those three laws were Virginia's "one drop" and sterilization acts, and the federal Johnson Immigration Act. Robert N. Proctor described the Johnson Act: "In the period 1900–1924, immigrants were accepted into the United States at a rate of about 435,000 per year. In the period 1925–1939, however, after quotas were imposed, this figure dropped to 24,430 per year, a tiny fraction of the former rate."[19]

Gobineau's race theories echoed those of some well-known American scientists. Samuel Morton's theory of mulatto sterility influenced several scientists, including Josiah Nott who wrote a paper in 1843 brazenly entitled, "The Mulatto a Hybrid—Probable Extermination of the Two Races if the Whites and Blacks Are Allowed to Intermarry."[20] Melungeons

---

[17]Madison Grant, *The Passing of the Great Race; or, The Racial Basis of European History* (New York: Charles Scribner, 1916); 4th rev. ed., with a documentary supplement and prefaces by Henry Fairfield Osborn (New York: Scribner's, 1921; repr.: North Stratford NH: Ayer Company Publishers, 2000).

[18]Wendt, *It Began in Babel* (see n. 16).

[19]Robert N. Proctor, *Racial Hygiene: Medicine under the Nazis* (Cambridge MA: Harvard University Press, 1988).

[20]Josiah Nott, "The Mulatto a Hybrid: Probable Extermination of the Two Races if the Whites and Blacks Are Allowed to Intermarry," *American Journal of the Medical Sciences* 6 (1843); reprinted in *Boston Medical and Surgical Journal* 29 (16 August 1843): 29-32, and in *Race, Hybridity, and Miscegenation*, vol. 1: *Josiah Nott and the Question of*

at that time felt the heat in the isolated mountains of Hancock County, Tennessee, and elsewhere and began calling themselves "Portuguese." And Jacob Perkins feared for his life when his neighbors said he had no soul.[21]

In support of slavery, Dr. Josiah Nott presented his 1854 best seller, *Types of Mankind.*[22] He produced figures, tables, statistics, and projections that appeared to prove that whites and blacks were of two different species incapable of sustained interbreeding. Nott's book was extremely popular in elite circles throughout the nineteenth century and influenced several states to forbid intermarriage as, for example, Missouri did with its antimiscegenation laws. (In 1883 a Missouri judge prevented an intermarriage, ruling that: It is stated as a well-authenticated fact that if the issue of a black man and a white woman, and a white man and a black woman intermarry, they cannot possibly have any progeny, and such a fact sufficiently justifies those laws which forbid the intermarriage of blacks and whites.") When Missouri made mixed marriage a felony in 1906, it repeated Nott's pre-Civil War sterility theory.[23]

Another of Dr. Morton's disciples, the famous Robert Knox of Scotland's Edinburgh Medical School, said morality was virtually exclusive to the Saxons encircling Melungia. The Saxons' attributions of justice and fair play, said Knox,

---

Hybridity, ed. Robert Bernasconi and Kristie Dotson, 6-12 (Bristol UK: Thoemmes, 2005). Josiah Nott later revised his theory when faced with clear evidence of octoroon fertility. He concluded that only Southern Europeans (those closest to Africa, such as the Portuguese) could make babies with Africans after the eighth generation.

[21]"PERKINS v. WHITE," T. A. R. Nelson Papers at the Calvin M. McClung Historical Collection.

[22]Josiah Nott along with George R. Gliddon published *Types of Mankind: or, Ethnological Researches* in 1854 and included contributions from America's two most famous scientists, Samuel George Morton and Louis Agassiz of Harvard. Charles Darwin would refer to it in 1871 in *The Descent of Man*. The mulatto sterility theory was known before 1850, but *Types of Mankind*, with its heavyweight backing, gave the theory legitimacy with a national audience before the Civil War. Josiah Clark Nott et al., *Types of Mankind: or, Ethnological Researches: Based upon the Ancient Monuments, Paintings, Sculptures, and Crania of Races, and upon Their Natural, Geographical, Philological, and Biblical History, Illustrated by Selections from the Inedited Papers of Samuel George Morton and by Additional Contributions from L. Agassiz, W. Usher, and H. S. Patterson* (Philadelphia: J. B. Lippincott, Grambo, 1954).

[23]H. M. Applebaum, "Miscegenation Statutes: A Constitutional Problem," 53 Geo. L. J. (1964) 49.

distinguish them from all other races of men. Now look at the self-confident Saxon. Does he fear to quit the land of his birth? Not in the least; he cares for it not one straw. Landing in America, he becomes a real American—a Kentuckian, a Virginian, a furious democrat. Jealous on the point of honour, his self-respect is extreme; admitting of no practical jokes; an admirer of beauty of colour, and beauty of form, and therefore a liberal patron of the fine arts. Inventive, imaginative, he leads the fashions all over the civilized world. Most new inventions and discoveries in the arts may be traced to him; they are then appropriated by the Saxon race, who apply them to useful purposes.[24]

Africans, according to Knox, would never become civilized like Europeans and he directly parroted Morton and Nott when he warned mixing the two violated the laws of nature:

Nature produces no mules, no hybrids, neither in man nor animals. When they accidentally appear they soon cease to be, for they are either nonproductive, or one or other of the pure breeds speedily predominates, and the weaker disappears.[25]

Will Allen Dromgoole was in prestigious company comparing Melungeons to their idealized Scottish neighbors:

They (Melungeons) are totally unlike the native Tennessee mountaineer, unlike him in every way. The mountaineer is liberal, trustful and open. The Malungeon is curious and suspicious and given to lying and stealing, things unknown among the native mountaineers.[26]

The ethnocentricities blinding Dromgoole could have been corrected by a tour of the penitentiary.

From his "incessant professional intercourse" Dr. Nott concluded mulattos were the shortest-lived of any class of the human race and intermediate in intelligence between the blacks and the whites. Mixing was ruinous because "Mulatto-women are peculiarly delicate, and subject to a variety of chronic diseases . . . they are bad breeders, bad nurses, liable to abortions, and that their children generally die young." Nott claimed that

---

[24]Robert Knox, *The Races of Men: A Philosophical Enquiry into the Influence of Race over the Destinies of Nations* (London: Henry Renshaw, 1850; 2nd ed. with supplementary chapters, 1862).

[25]Applebaum, "Miscegenation Statutes."

[26]Dromgoole, "The Malungeons."

"when mulattoes intermarry, they are less prolific than when crossed on the parent stocks."[27]

Ominously, at the conclusion of his 1855 book, Dr. Nott wrote, "True philanthropy should not tolerate the existence of a race whose nationality is opposed to progress, and who constantly struggle against the general rights and interests of humanity."

Among those contributing to Nott's 1855 international best seller were fellow scholars Dr. Samuel Morton, Harvard's Prof. Louis Agassiz, LL.D., W. Usher, M.D., and Prof. H. S. Patterson, M.D, who directly influenced Hitler decades later:

> The same inevitable racial amalgamation-degeneration principal which Joseph A. Comte de Gobineau described in 1857 deeply further poisoned by the likes of American slavery-apologist doctors Samuel George Morton and Josiah Clark Nott, who suggested blacks were "proximate species" whose "tainting" blood, they assured would degenerate "white blood" inversely to a "black" ancestor's remoteness, leading to hybrid sterility and eventual extinction—had frightened our great grandparents' generation into erecting Jim Crow racial segregation barriers.

Exploiting the fear, Hitler "spouted de Gobineau, Morton, and Nott's 'one-drop' degeneration theories in his book."[28]

---

[27]Nott, "Types of Mankind."

[28]George Winkel, "Are We Seeing an Unfortunate 'Black' Backlash?" (guest editorial) *Interracial Voice* (Sept/Oct 2002) <http://www.webcom.com/~intvoice/gwinkel12.html> cites *Perex v. Sharp* (1948) 32 Cal. 2d 711, p. 739.

Chapter 8

Scapegoating

By the end of the nineteenth century, increased mechanization had made workers a dime a dozen.[1] Lumber, steel, textiles, and coal suffered from fluctuating prices, and, beginning in 1873 and continuing every decade after, a series of depressions further aggravated labor unrest. Panic led to radical and sometimes cruel solutions which brought violent responses.

Striking Melungeon Coal Miners

The dust and din of the machine age reached all the way out to Appalachia and awakened the Melungeons. It's not surprising they were not discovered until just before the twentieth century. Thanks to mechanization, people were traveling farther afield. Industry came to Appalachia, and Melungeons began leaving the farm for jobs in coal towns springing up in Kentucky and West Virginia. But the work and the conditions were brutal. The United Mine Workers of America organized here in the 1890s. The Coal Creek War on Walden's Creek in "Melungia" was one of the first great labor conflicts in the U.S. It involved more than 3,000 miners from Virginia, Tennessee, and Kentucky against 5,000 state militiamen from Knoxville, Tennessee. Melungeon miners were in the thick of it.

The war erupted when Tennessee began emptying penitentiaries of prisoners to work dangerous substandard coal mines for free. Mine owners paid state inspectors to ignore safety regulations and nearby ridges were rapidly filling up with convict graves.

Miners who had been replaced with prisoners gathered with torches and Winchesters and attacked company goons holed up in stockades. Following several gun battles, the miners forced the surrender of the guards and released the convict laborers with maps to leave the state. Tennessee

---

[1]Ralph Chaplin, *Wobbly: The Rough-and-Tumble Story of an American Radical* (Chicago: University of Chicago Press, 1948).

responded by sending in the state militia. Gun battles and lynching flared for several months.

Finally in 1893, Tennessee capitulated and outlawed convict labor.[2] The bitter war produced an Appalachian ballad, "Coal Creek Troubles."[3] Dromgoole's nephew William E. Beard enlisted in the Tennessee Militia and fought in the Coal Creek War against the miners. Melungeons, men and boys from the families of Adkins, Bennett, Clark, Cox, Evans, Goans (Gowens), and Goodman, several of whom died in the terrible Fraterville mine disaster of 1902, were among the miners battling the Tennessee State Militia.

But victorious miners returned to the same brutal conditions that had claimed the lives of many convicts. Coal supervisors and mine owners responded to new strikes with outside labor from eastern and southern Europe. The race purists regarded the new immigrants with the same contempt they had for Americans of color.

The Elkhorn Coalfield

For less than a dollar a day, Appalachian coal miners worked sunup to sundown under miserable conditions with no medical care, no insurance. Children of miners saw their fathers only on Sundays. Accidents in poorly engineered mines killed or injured thousands, leaving their families destitute.

In this bleak atmosphere a local union organized in Wheeling, West Virginia and quickly became popular. The United Mine Workers of America (UMWA) accepted blacks, whites, and immigrants as equals. Melungeons like Gibson, Mullins, Adkins, Sizemore, and Bunch were found among Jewish, Polish, and Italian miners in small coal towns from West Virginia to Kentucky.

One Melungeon, Perry Adkins, joined the UMWA in the Elkhorn Coal Fields in the 1930s and actively campaigned for the union until he was

---

[2]Chris Cawood, *Tennessee's Coal Creek War: Another Fight for Freedom* (Kingsont TN: Magnolia Hill Press, 1995).

[3]"Coal Creek Troubles," recorded by Jilson Setters, 1937; see Archie Green, *Only a Miner: Studies in Recorded Coal-Mining Songs*, Music in American Life (Urbana: University of Illinois Press, 1972). Score, with lyrics, online at <http://sniff.numachi.com/~rickheit/dtrad/pages/tiCOALCRK;ttCOALCRK.html>.

blacklisted and murdered in a company-staged ambush during the Henry Clay War.[4]

Perry Adkins had started at the Wolfpit coal mine on the Marrowbone Creek where the owners refused to compensate his claim after he broke his foot in a bad mine. So, Perry Adkins joined the UMWA and became an aggressive leader pushing for better working conditions. When the Henry Clay Coal War broke out, the sheriff sided with the operators and soon Adkins's name appeared on a blacklist as a union troublemaker. One morning, from concealment, sheriff's deputies riddled Perry with bullets as he walked down a country road.

By the hundreds, union miners from Kentucky and West Virginia came down dusty dirt roads by wagon to attend his funeral. In the heat of the moment UMWA members vowed to find the sheriff and hang him over Adkins's grave, but, Perry's wife a widow and his children orphaned, no justice was forthcoming in coal country. The union helped Adkins's family a little, but fifty dollars at Christmas didn't go far.[5]

Matewan and the Blair Mountain War

The most infamous battle in the coal wars broke out in West Virginia on May 19, 1920, and led to the second largest U.S. civil war. Matewan was a bump-in-the-road mountain coal town. The gunfight was dramatized in the movie, *Matewan*. A few months before Matewan, the union had won a pay increase and the right to organize in parts of Virginia and Kentucky. But to prevent further unionizing, owners hired the Baldwin-Felts detective agency to provide the muscle.

Several armed detectives arrived on the train in Matewan and began evicting union miners from company houses.[6] One evicted Melungeon, a young man named Bob Mullins, had just joined the union that morning. This time however, the local law was on the side of the union workers.

---

[4]Nyoka Hawkins, *Social History and Cultural Change in the Elkhorn Coal Fields Oral History Project*, Appalachian Oral History Project, University of Kentucky Oral History Program, nonmusical recording on cassettes (18 interviews, 35 hours; 1987, c1988), Special Collections and Archives, University of Kentucky Libraries.

[5]Hawkins, *Social History and Cultural Change in the Elkhorn Coal Fields Oral History Project*.

[6]Lon Savage, *Thunder in the Mountains: The West Virginia Mine War 1920–1921* (repr.: Pittsburg PA: University of Pittsburg Press, 1990; orig.: Elliston VA: Northcross House, 1986; South Charleston WV: Jalamap Publications, 1984).

Matewan police chief Sid Hatfield of the infamous Hatfield-McCoy feud confronted the Baldwin-Felts men. Shooting began and Bob Mullins was the first killed. Two townspeople and seven Baldwin-Felts detectives also lay dead when the smoke cleared.[7]

The Matewan gunfight snowballed into more battles known generally as the Blair Mountain War. The U.S. Army took the field and several months after the Matewan massacre, vengeful armies of union miners numbering more than 10,000, with shotguns and rifles, fought the Army which used airplanes, local militias, and detectives.[8]

As strikes wore on, the outside low-wage replacement miners joined the strikers. Desegregation was breaking out in Appalachia: families of Scots-Irish, African Americans, Southern European immigrants, and Melungeons lived together in tent cities. This mixed arrangement troubled the race-obsessed white gentry who feared the consequences of blacks and immigrants pouring in for jobs and settling down with whites. Northern industrialists were galled to see the immigrants and blacks they used to break up union strikes joining the UMWA. The rural Melungeons working the coal mines found themselves in the middle of swirling twentieth-century conspiracies of Red Communists, insurrection, and desegregation.[9]

The violence at Matewan and Blair Mountain directly led to the U.S. Immigration Act of 1924, a major immigration quota bill. Harry H. Laughlin, a Harvard-educated chicken breeder was the eugenicist consulted by Congress in preparing the law. Laughlin guided the Immigration Act and Virginia's 1924 Racial Purity Act and used these laws as models for similar laws in Nazi Germany in the 1930s.

Government Responds

Prominent progressives promoted thinly disguised racist policies pedaled as public health:

> By 1928, courses on the subject [eugenics] were taught at Harvard, Columbia, Cornell, and 370 other colleges.
>
> At fairs nationwide, fairgoers could learn the "science" of eugenics or read poster messages such as "Some people are born to be a burden on the rest." Others could enter a "Fitter Family Contest," the first being at the

---

[7]Savage, *Thunder in the Mountains.*
[8]Savage, *Thunder in the Mountains.*
[9]Savage, *Thunder in the Mountains.*

Kansas Free Fair in Topeka. Entrants submitted to detailed examinations of their lineage, character, employment, and physical health to win a medal reading, "Yea, I Have Goodly Heritage."

This would be the model for Nazi Germany.

> [In the 1920s and 1930s], ministers preached [Galtonion] eugenics from the pulpits. In schools, textbooks would contain "studies"—thinly veiled cautionary tales—about "defective" and "degenerate" families whose poor genetic stock, it was said, led to generations of alcoholics, criminals, or morons.
>
> Among eugenics' prominent supporters were Alexander Graham Bell, Theodore Roosevelt, Calvin Coolidge, and birth control champion Margaret Sanger.[10]

Some of the attempts at social reform were shortsighted, even monstrous. Forced sterilization and segregation of dysgenic groups were endorsed by, among others, economist John Maynard Keynes and Margaret Sanger, who proposed to "give certain dysgenic [biologically defective or deficient] groups in our population their choice of segregation or sterilization."[11]

Supporters of the "age of consent" law campaigned for the federal government to oversee human breeding based on eugenics theories of racial purity. In 1932, Margaret Sanger outlined a so-called "Plan for Peace," admired in progressive circles. Less than a decade before World War II, Sanger demanded the state force sterilization and isolate segments of the population with unwelcome "hereditary" traits. She sought to control population growth and mixing in the lower social classes which she and likeminded people believed contributed to industrial and social upheaval.

---

[10]Eric Adler, "Missourian Played Key Role in Old-Time Eugenics Movement," *The Kansas City Star*, Saturday 27 April 2002; online at <http://www.newsfrombabylon.com/?q=node/1212>.

[11]Margaret Sanger, "A Plan for Peace," *The Birth Control Review* (April 1932): 107-108, cited as a "Summary of address before the New History Society, January 17th [1932], New York City." (Sanger was the founder/editor of *The Birth Control Review* and helped found the National Birth Control League [1917] which became the American Birth Control League [1921] and then the Planned Parenthood Federation of America [1942].) A critical, annotated edition of Sanger's "Plan for Peace" appears in chap. 6 ("Eugenics Captures Feminism") of John Cavanaugh-O'Keefe's *Roots of Racism and Abortion: An Exploration of Eugenics* (Princeton NJ: Xlibris Corp., 2000) the complete text of which is posted online at <http://www.eugenics-watch.com/roots/chap06.html>.

According to her "Plan for Peace," Sanger, the wife of a leading industrialist, wanted Congress to

> set up a special department for the study of population problems and appoint a Parliament of Population, the directors representing the various branches of science . . . to direct and control the population through birth rates and immigration, and to direct its distribution over the country according to national needs consistent with taste, fitness, and interest of the individuals.
>
> The main objects of the Population Congress would be: . . . b. To increase the population slowly by keeping the birth rate at its present level of fifteen per thousand, decreasing the death rate below its present mark of 11 per thousand. . . .
>
> [She also pressed the government] d. To apply a stern and rigid [!] policy of sterilization and segregation to that grade of population whose progeny is already tainted or whose inheritance is such that objectionable traits may be transmitted to offspring.
>
> e. To insure the country against future burdens of maintenance for numerous offspring as may be born of feebleminded parents by pensioning all persons with transmissible disease who voluntarily consent to sterilization.
>
> f. To give certain dysgenic groups in our population their choice of segregation or sterilization.
>
> g. To apportion farmlands and homesteads for these segregated persons where they would be taught to work under competent instructors for the period of their entire lives.

Isolation wouldn't stop with those Sanger called "morons, mental defectives, epileptics":

> The second step would be to take an inventory of the secondary group such as illiterates, paupers, unemployables, criminals, prostitutes, dope-fiends; classify them in special departments under government medical protection, and segregate them on farms and open spaces as long as necessary for the strengthening and development of moral conduct.
>
> Having corralled this enormous part of our population and placed it on a basis of health instead of punishment, it is safe to say that fifteen or twenty millions of our population would then be organized into soldiers of defense—defending the unborn against their own disabilities. . . .
>
> With the future citizen safeguarded from hereditary taints, with five million mental and moral degenerates segregated, with ten million women

and ten million children receiving adequate care, we could then turn our attention to the basic needs for international peace. . . .[12]

Professional people of all stripes met frequently in Northeastern cities (as they still do) to propose radical social solutions for perceived problems. Dromgoole spoke at a Boston symposium to push a federal "age of consent" law barring young women from marrying before age eighteen. Civil libertarian/feminist Lillian Harman opposed the "age of consent" policy promoted by the *Arena* and mainstream feminists, saying such a law was antifeminist:

> For some time now the *Arena* has been trying to arouse a wider public interest in the age-of-consent laws of the various states, and in the January issue there is a symposium participated in by Aaron M. Powell, Helen H. Gardener, Frances E. Willard, A. H. Lewis, D.D., O. Edward Janney, M.D., Will Allen Dromgoole, and Emily Blackwell, M.D. The demand of the reformers who are represented in this symposium, and of those for whom they speak, is that the [age] limit shall be raised to at least 18 years. There are some who make themselves heard through the press who wish to make it 21 years, and a few would put it still higher. . . . With our numerous Societies for Meddling with Everybody's Business, the lover would probably be hanged or at least imprisoned for rape, and this in spite of the fact that the girl, her parents, and all others immediately interested were perfectly satisfied with their own arrangements.[13]

The "age of consent" may appear progressive, but it adversely affected rural semi-isolated communities such as the Melungeons. Age limits reduced the number of available marriage partners in those tiny islands that hung in limbo between black and white America.

The state of Virginia banned her American Indians and their Melungeon kinsmen from marrying whites, not on age, but because of their mixed African ancestry. As Helen Rountree wrote, the state wanted to force her Indians who historically married whites and African Americans to identify openly with blacks, or become extinct:

> "Racial purity" became an issue over which the Indians were attacked in the public media and over which they themselves became more adamant about their Indian-and-white ancestry. Now, as never before, people's

---

[12]Sanger, "A Plan for Peace."

[13]Harman, "An 'Age of Consent' Symposium (1896)," in *Freedom, Feminism, and the State* (1st ed. only).

genetic makeup, and beliefs about it, in the absence of adequate documents, became a prime determinant of "Indianness" in Virginia.[14]

Virginia Registrar W. A. Plecker defended the state's racial purity policy: "When two races live together there is but one possible outcome, and that is the amalgamation of the races. The result of this will be the elimination of the higher type, the one on which progress depends."[15] And Plecker added, "That the mongrel races are liable to perpetuate the undesirable qualities of both their constituent stocks is abundantly demonstrated by a study of the larger and older of the mongrel groups in Virginia, as well as upon a study on a far larger scale in various other parts of the world."

A month later Plecker addressed a national medical association in New Orleans: "Much of South America and Mexico is today inhabited by a mongrel race of white-black-red mixture, one of the most undesirable racial intermixtures known, as I can testify from my own observation of similar groups in Virginia."[16] Plecker again referred to "mongrels" in his 1943 blacklist that carried Melungeon surnames.[17]

Virginia broadened the designation "dysgenic" to include sane, healthy, and law-abiding people whose only "defect" was that they had "one drop" of African blood. Three centuries after their birth, Melungeons were about to face their most determined enemy to date.

One Summer in a Model T Ford

The 1920s—the roaring decade of Prohibition—saw speakeasies opening faster than the police could shut them down. New Yorkers danced the Charleston till dawn and the toasts of the town were talented Jewish-

---

[14]Helen C. Rountree, *Pocahontas's People: The Powhatan Indians of Virginia through Four Centuries*, Civilization of the American Indian series 196 (Norman: University of Oklahoma Press, 1990).

[15]Plecker, "Virginia's Attempt to Adjust the Color Problem," *The American Journal of Public Health* (1925).

[16]*Virginia Health Bulletin* 17 (November 1925) extra no. 12: "Shall America Remain White?" by W. A. Plecker, M.D., from the booklet, *The New Family and Race Improvement*, New Family series 5, issued by the Bureau of Vital Statistics, State Board of Health, Richmond VA (1925; 2nd ed., 1928). Read before the Section on Public Health, Southern Medical Association, Eighteenth Annual Meeting, New Orleans, 24 November 1924.

[17]W. A. Plecker, M.D., State Registrar of Vital Statistics, "Letter to Local Registrars, etc. Regarding Mulatto Classification," January 1943, online at *The Multiracial Activist* <http://multiracial.com/content/view/985/29/>.

American entertainers like Eddie Cantor, Fanny Brice, Al Jolson, and Irving Berlin. The hit on Broadway in 1928 was the musical *Showboat*. Scored by Jewish songwriters Jerome Kern and Oscar Hammerstein and produced by Flo Ziegfeld, *Showboat* sympathetically portrayed the romance of a white man and a woman with "one drop" of African blood.

That same year New York's Harry Laughlin, director of the Commission of the American Genetic Association addressed the International Federation of Eugenics Organizations in Munich Germany where he stunned Germans by unveiling his proposal that the lowest ten percent of the U.S. population be forcibly sterilized in order to "eradicate" people posing a genetic impurity threat to white society.[18]

One year later, the New York stock market crashed.

In the 1920s, a zoologist named Arthur Estabrook, along with two pretty young assistants, left town and took to the open roads in a Model T Ford. Dr. Estabrook, a field researcher employed by the Carnegie Institution and the Eugenics Records Office in Cold Spring Harbor, New York, intended to visit several mysterious mixed communities from Vermont to the Carolinas in the old British colonies between the Atlantic and the Appalachian mountains. His trip was financed by leading New York industrialists.

The Eugenics Record Office would provide Estabrook to offer "expert" testimony in the 1926 landmark U.S. Supreme Court case of a young Virginia woman named Carrie Buck who had given birth to an illegitimate baby. After a hasty examination, Estabrook, a dedicated eugenicist, told the Court that the family "showed backwardness" and urged that Buck be sterilized under the Virginia law enacted in 1924 to protect the white race.[19]

Dr. Estabrook researched Virginia's historic mixed communities and wrote a book about them with the telling title, *Mongrel Virginians: The WIN Tribe*.[20] (WIN = White, Indian, and Negro.) He also published a race study entitled, *The Tribe of Ishmael*, about another local mixed group.[21]

---

[18]Stefan Kuhl, *The Nazi Connection: Eugenics, American Racism, and German National Socialism* (New York: Oxford University Press, 1994; repr. 2002).

[19]*Buck v. Bell*, 274 U.S. 200, Docket number 292. Argued: April 22, 1927. Decided: May 2, 1927.

[20]Arthur Howard Estabrook and Ivan Eugene McCougle, *Mongrel Virginians: The WIN Tribe*, "This study is a contribution from the Department of Genetics of the Carnegie Institution of Washington" (Baltimore: Williams & Wilkins Co., 1926).

[21]Arthur H. Estabrook, "The Jukes in 1915," Arthur H. Estabrook Papers, 1910–1943, Department of Special Collections and Archives University Libraries, University at Albany, State University of New York. Published as *The Jukes in 1915*, Paper no. 25 of the Station

Estabrook's "analysis" relied heavily on local gossip such as, "The oldest, now 42, is a coarse and shrewish harlot."[22] What in his "expert" opinion recommended one family for compulsory sterilization?

> The second living child of Lloyd, a wandering actor, is married and has four children. He is now attempting to get a divorce in order to marry an actress. The third child ran away from home at 14 and joined her brother's traveling circus. She has an ugly temper.[23]

This was not science. This was a rigged game. The poor and the colored were predestined to lose. Such analysis would have exposed the upper crust of Boston as utterly dysfunctional, but they were funding the eugenicists.

Tooling through the Upper South in search of "hereditary defectives" in his Ford Model T, Estabrook photographed Lumbees and other groups he regarded as candidates for isolation and forced sterilization. He collected clippings and photographs on topics such as the Indian Johns Family; the Melungeon Branham family "of early days"; the Indian families of Pembroke, North Carolina; the Lowrie History of the Lumbee Indians; the Croatans and Hamilton McMillan's theory on Sir Walter Raleigh's Lost Colony; the mixed community of Robeson County; the Triple Crosses; the WINs of Amherst County; Isshies (with keys to surnames and places); typical multiracial Christian names; Indians in Virginia; the Gullahs of the Carolinas; and the "Guineamen" of Virginia.[24]

These mixed groups had a rich history. Their ancestors built America from the foundation—independent, resilient, and innovative pioneers. Yet twentieth-century eugenicists regarded them as contemptible specimens of the human race. Estabrook collected bulletins and news articles with headlines such as "Two Indians Shoot Up Store at Pembroke and Run Folks Away"; "Human Dregs"; "Degenerate Family Costs State Heavily"; "The

---

for experimental evolution at Cold Spring Harbor NY, Carnegie Institution of Washington publication no. 240 (Washington DC: Carnegie Institution, 1916).

[22]Estabrook, "The Jukes in 1915": "The Andrew Carnegie Institution of Washington supported the Station for Experimental Evolution at Cold Spring Harbor on Long Island, beginning in 1904. Other members and estate supporters of eugenics or eugenics societies included Edward Henry Harriman, John D. Rockefeller, Henry Ford, John Harvey Kellogg who pioneered breakfast foods, Clarence J. Gamble of Procter & Gamble, Cleveland H. and Cleveland E. Dodge, J. P. Morgan, Jr. of United Steel, Miss E. B. Scripps of United Press, Margaret Sanger whose husband Noah Slee owned 3-in-One Oil, and Mrs. H. B. DuPont."

[23]Estabrook, "The Jukes in 1915."

[24]Estabrook Papers, 1910–1943.

Half-Breed Jones Family"; "The Half-Breed Brown Family"; "Early Genealogy of the Isshies"; and "Riddle of the Lumbee Indians." Clearly the eugenicist was linking whole mixed communities to crime and social decay.[25] Entire mixed communities were considered for sterilization as if they were animals. And, to repeat, in 1920 Hitler had not yet formed the policies and philosophy of *Mein Kampf.*

After the 1929 Wall Street crash, the U.S. began recalling European loans. The German economy, heavily financed by American banks, collapsed, pushing four million Germans into unemployment and propelling Adolf Hitler into power in 1932.

That year, W. A. Plecker gave a speech in New York at the international eugenics convention on Virginia's efforts to identify and curb her "mongrel" groups. Listening was the man Hitler would call upon a few months later to draft Germany's race laws. Ernst Rudin would receive direct assistance in the Nazi project from Plecker's benefactor, Harry Laughlin, who was the director of Carnegie's Cold Spring Harbor eugenics department. And Arthur Estabrook worked for Harry Laughlin.

---

[25]Estabrook Papers, 1910–1943.

Chapter 9

Race Science and Race Politics

"The Germans are beating us at our own game. The fact that there are 12,000,000 defectives in the United States should arouse our best endeavors to push [forced sterilization] to the maximum."[1] So said Dr. Joseph DeJarnette, director of Western State Hospital of Virginia in 1938, not long before America entered World War II.

But what did Dr. DeJarnette mean by "defective"? Suspiciously, the Virginia Eugenical Sterilization Act curbing "socially inadequate defectives" was passed with the 1924 Racial Integrity Act to stop race mixing. Both laws were written by the same people. Evidence suggests these two laws were used to, among other purposes, isolate and curb descendants of America's colonial Virginia *malungu* pioneers. More than thirty states had similar race laws on the books. But Virginia is singled out here because those other states, and several nations, used Virginia as their model.

Racism Disguised as Science

Virginia's 1924 compulsory sterilization and antimixing acts, along with the 1924 Federal Immigration Act, were the three acts that injected various Jim Crow laws with new vigor.

> Virginia's Racial Integrity Act of 1924 stands out among antimiscegenation laws that can be traced to eugenic advocacy. To fashion a successful legislative strategy, three local Virginia eugenicists—John Powell, Earnest Cox, and Walter Plecker—consulted with Madison Grant and Harry Laughlin. Powell, a celebrated pianist and composer, was the founder of the Anglo-Saxon Clubs of America, an elitist version of the Ku Klux Klan dedicated to maintaining "Anglo-Saxon ideals and civilization in America." . . . Cox's book *White America* emphasized white supremacy and the dangers of racial mixing. Plecker was registrar at the Bureau of

---

[1]Kuhl, *The Nazi Connection: Eugenics, American Racism, and German National Socialism.*

Vital Statistics of the Virginia Board of Health. His ideas on racial interbreeding as the source of "public health" problems appeared in state-published pamphlets distributed to all who planned to marry.

When the Racial Integrity Act became law, it included provisions requiring racial registration certificates and strict definitions of who would qualify as members of the white race. It emphasized the "scientific" basis of race assessment, and the "dysgenic" dangers of race mixing. Its major provision declared: "It shall hereafter be unlawful for any white person in this State to marry any save a white person, or a person with no other admixture of blood than white and American Indian. . . . [T]he term 'white person' shall apply only to such person as has *no trace whatever* of any blood other than Caucasian; but persons who have one-sixteenth or less of the blood of the American Indian and have no other non-Caucasic blood shall be deemed to be white persons. . . . "[2]

The "one-sixteenth or less of the blood of the American Indian" was the "Pocahontas clause" put into the law against the wishes of its architects because some influential "white" Virginia families were descended from Pocahontas and John Rolfe. Virginia's eugenicists believed all of Virginia's Indians had been "tainted" with African ancestry in the past.

For Melungeons, the phrase "no trace whatever of any blood other than Caucasian" was ominous. In the twentieth century, sixty years after the Civil War, a standard for segregation was implemented that was far more rigid than the old antebellum one-quarter blood quantum.

Virginia's race standard was harsher than Hitler's. R. J. Lifton in *The Nazi Doctors* noted that before World War II German race scientists were warning

> unless the Germans made progress in this field, America would become the world's racial leader. Nazi physicians on more than one occasion argued that the German racial policies were relatively "liberal" compared with the treatment of blacks in the United States where a person with 1/32nd black ancestry was legally black, whereas if someone was 1/8th Jewish in Germany . . . that person was legally Aryan.

---

[2]Paul Lombardo, "Eugenic Laws against Race Mixing," Image Archive on the American Eugenics Movement. Dolan DNA Learning Center, Cold Spring Harbor Laboratory. <http://www.eugenicsarchive.org/html/eugenics/essay7text.html>.

Mixed people were seen as a greater threat to white purity than blacks because they could "pass" as white. In 1912, after generations of intermarriage, some Melungeons still had

> a swarthy complexion, with prominent cheekbones, jet black hair, generally straight but at times having a slight tendency to curl, heavy black beards, deep-set dark brown eyes. . . . [But,] the typical physical characteristics are gradually disappearing, as outsiders intermarry with them or as they venture out into the outside world to lose their identity. Many whites have already intermingled and intermarried with them and many children with fair complexions, light hair and blue eyes frolic with their swarthy neighbors.[3]

On the eve of World War II, many Melungeons had "light hair, blue eyes, and fair skin."[4]

Melungeon genealogy going back 300 years to Jamestown was on file in Virginia courthouses and libraries, like a ticking time bomb. In 1942, a Virginia state official chasing Melungeons in Tennessee studied the "free negroes of the 1830 census" by counties and detected

> in that list in Hawkins County, Solomon Collins, Vardy Collins, and Shepard Gibson. We find also Zachariah Minor, probably the head of the family in which we are especially interested at this time. We find also the names of James Moore and Jordan and Edmund Goodman. In the list for Grainger County we find at least twelve Collins and Collens heads of families. This shows that they were evidently considered locally as free negroes by the enumerators of the 1830 census.[5]

Virginia had traced Melungeons back 150 years and turned up the names of the Hancock County Eight and the names of Melungeons born before the American Revolution. To what end?

The state at the front door of America's capital was being guided by rabid race fanatics scouring records for a single drop of blood. They were in communication with Nazi Germany, not seeking advice, but giving it.

---

[3]Paul Converse, "Melungeons," *Southern Collegian* (December 1912): 59-69; and *Dictionary of American History* (New York: Scribner's, 1940) 371-72.

[4]Leo Zuber, "The Melungeons," typewritten manuscript #G.08, W.P.A. Federal Writer's Guide (1939), McClung Historical Collection, Lawson-McGhee Library, Knoxville TN.

[5]Walter Plecker's letter to Tennessee state librarian and archivist regarding Melungeon classification, 20 Aug. 1942. Tennessee State Library and Archives, Nashville.

The threat from inside the U.S. from 1924 until 1945 has never been fully realized. Even the notorious events that actually occurred have been avoided today because of partisan politics over such issues as stem cell research and abortion. In fact, leading conservatives sided with liberals on this issue in the early twentieth century. The fundamentalist Bible-believing Presbyterian Walter Plecker admired Margaret Sanger's progressive segregation plan. Court cases show people were sterilized with the approval of liberals and conservatives seeking a "pure" white America.

The devastating impact of the Racial Integrity Act and laws like it on the American generation of 1924–1967 wrecked the lives of some 8,300 Virginians alone. In the first case in 1926 the state of Virginia was challenged as it prepared to sterilize seventeen-year-old Carrie Buck. Physicians employed by the state claimed Buck belonged "to the shiftless, ignorant, and worthless class of antisocial whites of the South."[6] She had done nothing but suffer rape by her foster parents' nephew, for which she was labeled promiscuous.[7] The eugenicist Harry H. Laughlin called for Buck's sterilization, even though he had never met her, and he sent a written deposition affirming Dr. Albert Priddy's opinion that Buck was feebleminded and morally delinquent as a result of "hereditary promiscuity."[8] *Buck v. Bell*, went to the U.S. Supreme Court, which ruled in favor of the state, clearing the way for the forced sterilization of more than 60,000 other Americans.[9]

Dr. Albert Priddy directed the Lynchburg Training School and Hospital, founded in 1911 as the Virginia Colony for the Feeble-Minded. Priddy began supporting forced sterilization legislation after he was threatened with jail for sterilizing people he had unlawfully abducted; people snatched by police from their homes.[10]

---

[6]Deposition of Dr. Albert Priddy of the Virginia Colony for Epileptics and the Feeble-Minded, *Buck v. Bell*, 274 U.S. 200 (1927), docket number 292. Argued 22 April 1927; decided 2 May 1927. See also the opinion of the court delivered by Mr. Justice Holmes at <http://www.law.du.edu/russell/lh/alh/docs/buckvbell.html>.

[7]Dr. Paul Lombardo met Carrie Buck in 1983 just a few weeks before she died at age 77. Lombardo said that Buck told him she became pregnant at age 17 because she had been raped by her foster parents' nephew. See "Involuntary Sterilization the Focus of Academy's Lilianna Sauter Lecture," the New York Academy of Medicine News & Publications, at <http://www.nyam.org/news/1141.html>.

[8]Lombardo, "Eugenic Laws against Race Mixing."

[9]Lombardo, "Eugenic Laws against Race Mixing."

[10]Robert Reinhold, "Virginia Hospital's Chief Traces 50 Years of Sterilizing the

The first sterilization case resulting from this practice was *Mallory v. Virginia Colony for the Feeble-Minded*, a habeas corpus proceeding brought in 1917 to release Nannie Mallory from the Colony. When George Mallory was at work, plain-clothes police officers came to his house, where his wife, Willie, children, and two boarders resided. They arrested Willie and two daughters, Jessie and Nannie, for keeping a disorderly house, and committed them, putting them to work cleaning and caring for children. Willie and Jessie were sterilized and released. Priddy conditioned Willie's release on sterilization. Despite the sterilizations, Priddy continued making efforts to keep Willie and her daughter away from their husband and fiancé. He spoke of Willie as a prostitute, although her husband, boarders, and employer testified to her good moral character. Treating patients as prostitutes made it easier for Priddy and the other workers at the Colony to control them. The petition was granted, and Nannie's commitment was ruled illegal. But Priddy was not held liable for the steriliations."[11]

Dr. Priddy and the state of Virginia then singled out Carrie Buck as a test case for compulsory sterilization in 1926. The Virginia State Supreme Court assented, saying that it "was not meant to punish, but to protect the class of socially inadequate citizens from themselves and to *promote the welfare of society by mitigating race degeneration* and raising the average intelligence of the people of the state."[12]

To "mitigate" the degeneration of the white race, the Act was to curb a class of people, as U.S. Supreme Court Justice William O. Douglas said when he noted that the state sterilized three-time-convicted chicken thieves, but not three-time-convicted embezzlers.[13]

'Retarded,' " *New York Times*, 23 February 1980, p. 6, col. 3: "Special to the *New York Times*, Lynchburg, Va., Feb. 22 [1980]."

[11]Pamela Berger, "Sterilization in Virginia: Fireships into Hewers of Wood and Drawers of Water (1985)," Georgetown Law, Georgetown University Law Center: <http://www.law.georgetown.edu/glh/berger.htm>.

[12]Reinhold, "Virginia Hospital's Chief Traces 50 Years of Sterilizing the 'Retarded' "; italics added.

[13]"Sterilization of people in institutions for the mentally ill and mentally retarded continued through the mid-1970s. At one time or another, 33 states had statutes under which more than 60,000 Americans endured involuntary sterilization. The *Buck v. Bell* precedent allowing sterilization of the so-called 'feebleminded' has never been overruled." Lombardo, "Eugenic Laws against Race Mixing."

Those targeted were disproportionately poor whites or blacks, of whom 500 died during the operation. The American Eugenics Society dreamed of sterilizing millions of Americans, and doctors and state hospital administrators such as Dr. Priddy and Dr. DeJarnette saw themselves in competition with Germany to produce the fittest white race possible.[14] Modeled after Virginia, Hitler's own eugenics program sterilized 225,000 people in less than three years.[15] Virginia never matched the Nazi program, but the failure was not due to a lack of ambition among some officials and doctors.

Today, the eugenics of the 1920s–1970s sounds like alchemy out of the Dark Ages. At the Second International Congress of Eugenics in 1923, eugenicists offered findings based on the crank science of craniometry that claimed to judge intelligence by the size and shape of the skull, and craniologist Dr. Georges Vacher de Lapouge addressed the threat of mixed populations to the white race. The same de Lapouge had predicted forty years earlier (in 1887): "I am convinced that in the next century millions will cut each other's throats because of one or two degrees more or less of cephalic index." Of course it never happened. Also lecturing at the Congress in 1923 was Robert Bennett Bean who declared that the study of the brains of Africans proved that they should be ranked "between man and the ourang-outang." Jon Alfred Mjoen entitled his lecture, "Harmonic and Disharmonic Race-Crossings," and argued from craniometrics that mixed populations produced more prostitutes and lazy people than "pure" groups.[16]

Eugenics persuaded Supreme Court Justice Oliver Wendell Holmes, Jr. and his fellow justices to legalize forced sterilization. In *Buck v. Bell*, Justice Holmes stated that

> the public welfare may call upon the best citizens for their lives. It would
> be strange if it could not call upon those who already sap the strength of

---

[14]Kuhl, *The Nazi Connection: Eugenics, American Racism, and German National Socialism.*

[15]Lombardo, "Eugenic Laws against Race Mixing."

[16]Frank Hamilton Hankins, *The Racial Basis of Civilization: A Critique of the Nordic Doctrine* (New York: Alfred A. Knopf, 1926), quoted in Allan Chase, *The Legacy of Malthus: The Social Costs of the New Scientific Racism* (New York: Alfred A. Knopf, 1976; repr. 1980). See also *Eugenics in Race and State*, vol. 2 of *Scientific Papers of the Second International Congress of Eugenics: Held at the American Museum of Natural History, New York, September 22-28, 1921*, Committee on Publication, Charles B. Davenport, chairman (Baltimore: Williams & Wilkins, 1923; repr.: New York: Garland, 1985).

the state for these lesser sacrifices. It is better for all the world, if instead of waiting to execute degenerate offspring for crime, or to let them starve for their imbecility, society can prevent those who are manifestly unfit from continuing their kind. The principle that susstains compulsory vaccination is broad enough to cover cutting the Fallopian tubes. Three generations of imbeciles are enough.[17]

Compulsory sterilization was be restricted for use on the feebleminded. In some states "feebleminded" described, among others, white women who had colored babies.

Melungeon Profiling

On July 7, 1943, the superintendent of a county welfare board sent a letter to Dr. Walter A. Plecker, director of the Virginia Bureau of Vital Statistics and sponsor of the Racial Integrity Act, seeking his advice on a case. She described a woman who came to her office with two children who appeared to be mixed. This county official asked Plecker how one might determine if a child was mixed, and how this client should be handled in the future. Plecker said there was no test to determine race but he trusted her assessment of the children's ethnicity to be as reliable as the most learned scientist. And then Dr. Plecker told the county superintendent to incarcerate this mother immediately in a state asylum and have her surgically sterilized under Virginia's Racial Integrity law of 1924.[18]

Plecker ordered that a woman he never met be sterilized simply because an unskilled county worker thought her children were of mixed race. How many times did this happen?

For decades Plecker and others blacklisted, intimidated, threatened, jailed, and sterilized people and altered documents in Virginia's war on mixed people. Among Melungeons, fear of the government was pervasive. "I remember once when the census takers came around, and my grandmother told me to go inside," said Connie Clark of Big Stone Gap, who has what many consider the classic Melungeon look of jet-black hair, dark skin and hazel eyes. "She said, 'They don't need to see you.' "[19] In one case,

---

[17]Holmes, *Buck v. Bell*, 274 U.S 200, 207 [1927].

[18]Plecker correspondence cited by J. David Smith, *The Eugenic Assault on America: Scenes in Red, White, and Black* (Fairfax VA: George Mason University Press, 1993).

[19]Connie Clark, interviewed by Chris Kahn, "Appalachian 'Melungeons' End 2-Year Study into Their Ancestry," Roanoke VA (Associated Press), 20 June 2002 <http://www.oakridger.com/stories/062002stt_0620020089.html>.

Rose Nuckols was sixteen when she was raped by a married man at a truck stop. Nine months later, in January 1958, she gave birth to twin boys. She held them exactly once before the nurse explained that they were headed to foster care in Richmond.

Rose objected, but as an unwed, illiterate teenager, she understood that she had few choices. What she did not know was that these were the first and last children she would ever have. The state made sure of that.[20]

Nuchols, whose family surname appeared on Virginia's 1942 Melungeon blacklist, was deemed by the State as unfit to be a mother, and was sterilized and committed to the Virginia state hospital two months after giving birth:

Hers was a fate shared by more than 8,000 men and women between 1927 and 1979 under Virginia's eugenics law, a statute, upheld by the Supreme Court, aimed at preventing those considered genetically unfit from passing on their traits.

The law's scope was wide, targeting a range of people considered social misfits: the insane and feebleminded; the blind and the deaf; the poor, the orphaned, the antisocial; and those, like Rose, who bore children outside marriage.

[Rose recalled that] "The judge said, 'Rose, you ain't fit to have kids, and you need to have this operation done.'. . . They said it was the best thing for my health." . . .

"Their lives were largely ruined by this experience," [Dr. Paul] Lombardo said of eugenics victims, "I don't know anyone who says they're not due some kind of compensation."

But Rose . . . said it is too late for amends. "It won't help the situation I'm in now," she said. "It can't bring things back to you or your body. . . . It's a shame, all them years. I wasted all them years."[21]

Helen Rountree documented some of the negative effects of state policy on Virginia's Indians during the racial purification era.[22] But Melungeons, though related to Virginia's Indians, had long ago left the reservations and

[20]Leef Smith, "Eugenics, Robbed of the Promise of Life: Victim of Va.'s Old Sterilization Law Says Amends Can't End Pain over Loss," *The Washington Post*, 13 May 2002, B1; now online at <http://loper.org/~george/archives/2002/May/66.html>.

[21]Smith, "Eugenics, Robbed of the Promise of Life."

[22]Rountree, *Pocahontas's People: The Powhatan Indians of Virginia through Four Centuries*.

were harder to identify.[23] Virginia will not release surnames of victims of forced sterilization, citing a law "which exempts from disclosure medical and mental records."[24]

But evidence indicates the possibility of a disturbing story yet untold. Pulitzer Prize-winning Virginia reporter Mary Bishop of the *Roanoke Times* found that in a single year 113 Virginians were incarcerated in state asylums under the catchall diagnosis of "mentally deficient." Of the 113 that year, the majority, 111, were labeled as "mixed" (black and white) and "Negro."[25] This meant only two individuals out of the 113 mentally deficient people put in the state asylum that year were white.

Officials like Plecker liberally assigned such clinical terms as "mentally deficient." But according to eugenics, all people of color were mentally inferior to whites: they would have been considered "mentally deficient" before being tested, if tested at all. Clearly the percentage of black and mixed inmates declared mentally deficient was disproportionate to Virginia's diverse ethnic population. How can more than ninety-five percent of inmates incarcerated as mentally deficient in Virginia asylums in one year be either black or mixed? Vague illnesses such as "mental deficiency" and "feeblemindedness" were listed with dementia praecox (schizophrenia), alcoholism, and syphilis, as common ailments of people targeted for eugenic sterilization.[26] No adequate examination was made to determine if mixed people suffered impairment. Diagnosis relied instead on sight or guesswork. For some like Plecker, just the suspicion of being mixed was reason enough for compulsory sterilization under the theory that all mixed people stripped of their "native good qualities" in the mixing, were born substandard.

---

[23]Letter from Plecker to Tennessee Secretary of State, 5 August 1942.

[24]Lisa Wallmeyer, Assistant Director, Virginia Freedom of Information Advisory Council, 910 Capitol Street, Richmond VA 23219, (804) 225-3056 or 1-866-448-4100 (toll free). E-mail correspondence, "FOIA Denial Justification," 10 March 2003, citing sec. 2.2-3705(A)(5) as the state's reason for withholding names of individuals forcibly sterilized, "which exempts from disclosure medical and mental records."

[25]E-mail correspondence with Mary Bishop, *Roanoke Times*, 17 May 2002.

[26]Emil Guillermo, "Sterilization Used to 'Weed Out the Weak,' " the *Stockton Record* (Lodi CA), Saturday 15 March 2003. Records of the Stockton (California) State Hospital: "The sterilization record of No. 3450, a 29-year-old male born in Arkansas, reads 'Father insane. Brother insane. Paternal aunt insane.' The patient's condition is described as 'Dementia Praecox,' a term indicating schizophrenia. He was given a vasectomy, and his condition afterward is described as 'better.' "

The Dynasty Bluff

Plecker influenced laws. He had the support of high-profile industrialists and confidants of U.S. presidents, senators, and judges. He was a guest speaker at the Third International Congress of Eugenics in 1932 at the invitation of Averell Harriman of Standard Oil, whose mother had funded the Eugenics Record Office as a branch of the Francis Galton National Laboratory in London. Plecker was affiliated with eugenics organizations supported in the 1930s by notables such as Dupont, Kellogg, Harriman, Rockefeller, Ford, Carnegie, Gamble, Pulitzer, and Sanger.

Plecker believed the future of America and indeed of the world, rested on eliminating "mongrels," as he made clear in the American Public Health Association (APHA) speech in 1924 in which he claimed the support of African Americans:

> The white race in this land is the foundation upon which rests its civilization, and is responsible for the leading position which we occupy amongst the nations of the world. Is it not therefore just and right that this race decide for itself what its composition shall be, and attempt, as Virginia has, to maintain its purity? We are glad to say that the *true* negro of Virginia is beginning to appreciate this point and is agreeing to the wisdom of this movement. Our chief trouble is with some of the near-whites who desire to change from the colored to the white class.[27]

Clarence Page said of the sham of "one-drop," "No one says a drop of Native American blood makes you 'Indian.' Nor does anyone call the offspring of white-Asian marriages 'Asian.' Yet, as Langston Hughes once wrote, 'our African blood must be mighty powerful, since only one drop of it is all it takes to make you all black.' "[28]

---

[27]Plecker, "Virginia's Attempt to Adjust the Color Problem." For the high-powered supporters of people like Plecker see *A Decade of Progress in Eugenics: Scientific Papers of the Third International Congress of Eugenics, Held at American Museum of Natural History, New York, August 21-23, 1932*, Committee on Publication, Harry F. Perkins, chairman (Baltimore: Williams & Wilkins Co., September 1934).

[28]Clarence Page, "Biracial People Feel 'Boxed In' by Census Form," *Chicago Tribune*, 28 July 1996. Of course, Page condensed and paraphrased Hughes, who actually wrote: "Negro blood is sure powerful—because just *one* drop of black blood makes a colored man. *One* drop—you are a Negro! . . . Black is powerful" (from Hughes's *Simple Takes a Wife* [1953]).

Snubbing eugenics in the 1930s was Seabiscuit, the "undersized crooked-legged racehorse owned by a bicycle repairman turned automobile magnate, trained by a virtually mute mustang breaker and ridden by a half-blind failed prizefighter."[29] Francis Galton's theory of superior genes was a "projection of the concept of the royal Windsor monarchal dynasty of Britain and several others of Europe, Asia, the Indian subcontinent, and Africa."[30] The idea of genetic excellence, of "blue blood," present in all societies says leaders rise to the top because of "good genes." The idea of genetically superior classes of people (aristocrats) eventually produced theories of genetically superior races—racism, and can be traced back to the ancient Greek philosophers. Galton said superior people passed superior genes to produce dynasties. The popular fad of preserving the sperm of celebrated men began under the dynasty theory.

In October 1998, the board of directors of the American Society of Human Genetics stated that

> By 1883 [Francis] Galton, who then had been studying human heredity for almost 20 years, was convinced that the British upper classes were having too few children to maintain what he considered their crucially important contribution to the gene pool of Victorian England. He exhorted the upper classes to have more children. Over the next 30 years this idea garnered much interest. Among its most famous proponents in the United States was President Theodore Roosevelt, who warned that the failure of couples of Anglo-Saxon heritage to have large enough families would lead to "race suicide." . . . Roosevelt's support of eugenic ideals reflects the popular appeal of eugenics during the first half of this century. Adherents included liberals and conservatives, progressives and libertarians. In the early decades of this century the emphasis on encouraging reproduction among those assumed to possess a superior genetic endowment became known as "postivie eugenics."[31]

---

[29]Laura Hillenbrand, *Seabiscuit: An American Legend* (New York: Random House, 2001).

[30]Herbert Wendt, *It Began in Babel: The Story of the Birth and Development of Races and People*, trans. James Kirkup (London: Weidenfeld and Nicholson, 1961; repr. 1963).

[31]"Statement of the Board of Directors of the American Society of Human Genetics: Eugenics and the Misuse of Genetic Information to Restrict Reproductive Freedom. Approved by the ASHG Board of Directors, October 1998." <http://genetics.faseb.org/genetics/ashg/policy/pol-30.htm> (as accessed 12 December 2005).

A Corrupt Partnership

A science based on inadequate research shook hands with a government looking for cheap solutions. The consequences were far reaching:

> In America, a follower of Gobineau, Madison Grant, demanded of the government an increase in the number of Nordic immigrants. America already had a race problem in the Negroes, and had her own fanatics, the Ku-Klux-Klan. But Madison Grant's demands, (expressed in his book, *Passing of the Great Race*), created a new racial problem; in the eyes of people who were of the same mind as he was, immigrants from Mediterranean and East Asiatic regions were degraded to second-class members of American society.[32]

In his book *Racial Hygiene*, Robert N. Proctor described the impact of the Act that accompanied racial purity and forced sterilization:

> In the United States, immigration of Jews (along with other "undesirable" groups) had already been drastically curtailed by the 1924 Immigration Restriction Act. In the period 1900–1924, immigrants were accepted into the United States at a rate of about 435,000 per year. In the period 1925–1939, however, after quotas were imposed, this figure dropped to 24,430 per year, a tiny fraction (5 percent) of the former rate.[33]

On the eve of World War II, the American Immigration Restriction Act sent back to Europe thousands of Jewish "undesirables."[34]

In several states, domestic enforcement against mixed people suspected of having one drop of black blood filtered all the way down to hospitals, jobs, and the military. Sick people in hospital beds were pushed out of the white wing of hospitals and clinics, and bodies were even dug up and moved out of cemeteries.[35] Versions of Virginia's legislation appeared in more than half of the states of the U.S.

Eugenics scholars presented statistics, tests, and observations flawed by presumptive bias.[36] That all so-called "pure" white Europeans had long

---

[32]Wendt, *It Began in Babel*.

[33]Proctor, *Racial Hygiene: Medicine under the Nazis*.

[34]Smith, *The Eugenic Assault on America: Scenes in Red, White, and Black*.

[35]Berry, *Almost White: A Provocative Study of America's Mixed-Blood Minorities*.

[36]Harry H. Laughlin Papers (files collected by the Eugenics Record Office of Cold Spring Harbor, Long Island, New York, from 1910 to 1939) Pickler Memorial Library,

ago descended from Mongolian and other non-Aryan ethnic groups, and were in fact not "pure stock," was unknown. It wouldn't have mattered. The myth of "pure white" functioned during the eugenics era as a propaganda device of racists, not to preserve a mythical ethnic purity but to stop *further* mixing, and they exploited the fiction of "pure white" to that end.

From the beginning, the modern science of public health was influenced by elitism and racism. Francis Galton created eugenics as "the evolutionary doctrine that the condition of mankind can most effectively be improved by a scientifically directed process of controlled breeding."[37] The lower classes, which Galton described as prone to incompetence, sickness, or despondency, were "producing large numbers of impoverished, sick, and miserable children."[38] This group, Galton believed, should be either induced or compelled to limit their children: "The upper classes, he argued, should be encouraged to have more children, whereas the lower classes should be induced, if possible, or compelled if necessary to have fewer."[39] Even underclass whites were to be *compelled if necessary* to stop breeding. Regarding blacks, Galton wrote that "The average intellectual standard of the Negro is some two grades below our own." He added that Jews were "specialized for parasitical existence upon other nations."[40]

American eugenicists determined that among those to be *compelled if necessary* to stop breeding were Abaneki Indians and French Canadians of Vermont, and the Melungeons and the Indians of Virginia. Progressive Vermont engaged in sterilizing mixed groups by force with a dedicated thoroughness unmatched in the South.[41]

Eugenicists said that churches and civic groups who engaged in charity for the poor were counterproductive to good breeding. When asked to give to charity, Charles Dickens's Ebenezer Scrooge responded, "Let those poor go to the prisons and the Union workhouses. . . . And if they would rather

---

Truman State University, Kirksville MO.

[37]Theodore M. Porter, *The Rise of Statistical Thinking, 1820–1900* (Princeton NJ: Princeton University Press, 1986).

[38]Lenny Lapon, *Mass Murderers in White Coats: Psychiatric Genocide in Nazi Germany and the United States* (Springfield MA: Psychiatric Genocide Research Institute, 1986).

[39]Lapon, *Mass Murderers in White Coats.*

[40]Lapon, *Mass Murderers in White Coats.*

[41]Nancy L. Gallagher, *Breeding Better Vermonters: The Eugenics Project in the Green Mountain State*, Revisiting New England series (Hanover NH: University Press of New England, 1999).

die, they had better do it, and decrease the surplus population."[42] American eugenicists agreed with German eugenicist Dr. Alfred Ploetz who wrote in 1895 that "a misdirected humanitarianism was threatening the quality of the race by fostering the protection of its weakest members."[43]

In the same decade the eugenics director of a Kansas facility for underprivileged minors castrated almost sixty children. A year after engineering the Racial Integrity Act, Dr. Walter Plecker, a devout Presbyterian said, "Let us turn a deaf ear to those who would interpret Christian brotherhood as racial equality."[44]

In 1929, G. K. Chesterton blasted eugenics when he wrote that Scrooge

> utters all the sophistries by which the age of machinery has tried to turn the virtue of charity into a vice. . . . Many amiable sociologists will say as he said, "Let them die and decrease the population." The improved proposal is that they should die before they are born.[45]

By blaming ancestors, the state released itself on the cheap from responsibility. Any lingering revulsion against lobotomies, castrations, hysterectomies, and vasectomies was swept aside by scientific-sounding statistics and government economics.

Defining who was "unfit" would be left to each of the thirty-three individual U.S. states that decided to apply the eugenics philosophy on Virginia's model. The victims of sterilization would range from the mentally ill to children who were simply unwanted. Oregon for example, legalized eugenics-based programs from the 1920s until 1983 and sterilized one hundred teenage girls at a state reform school simply for misbehaving. Children placed in state facilities were refused release until they agreed to undergo the operations. Velma Haynes of Oregon, sent to a state facility as a toddler after her parents decided they could only afford to keep her twin, was forcibly sterilized. The father of Ruth Morris placed her in a juvenile work farm after her mother died. State officials demanded that Ruth be sterilized before being admitted and her father agreed.[46] These victims were

---

[42]Charles Dickens, *A Christmas Carol in Prose: Being a Ghost Story of Christmas* (London: Chapman & Hall, 1843; repr.: London: W. Heinemann, 1948).

[43]Lapon, *Mass Murderers in White Coats.*

[44]Plecker, "Shall America Remain White?" (1924/1925) 137.

[45]Lawrence D. Hogan, "Ebenezer Scrooge at Christmas 1998: Decrease the Surplus Population," *New Oxford Review* (December 1998) online at <http://soli.inav.net/~jfischer/dec98/lawrencehogan.html>.

[46]"Governor Apologizes for Forced Sterilizations," Oregon Advocacy Center <http://

denied the children and families who would have cared for them in their old age and ironically became a burden on local government.[47] There was no national standard and no accountability, victims varied depending on community, and states sometimes targeted groups for no other reason than they considered them to be a public nuisance, as Vermont did with the Abaneki Indians.

In Virginia Dr. W. A. Plecker left no doubt as to the motive for his enforcement of racial purity laws he helped shape.

> The white race in this land is the foundation upon which rests its civilization, and is responsible for the leading position which we occupy amongst the nations of the world. Is it not therefore just and right that this race decide for itself what its composition shall be, and attempt, as Virginia has, to maintain its purity?[48]

Teaching the Nazis

The Virginia law targeting Melungeons was soon targeting others, and

> the most dramatic example can be found in Adolf Hitler's "Law for the Prevention of Offspring with Hereditary Diseases." That 1933 German decree contained language that echoed phrases in the Virginia statute. In only ten years, some two million Europeans underwent forced sterilization as part of the Nazi program. In 1936 Henry Laughlin had received an honorary degree from the Nazi—controlled University of Heidelburg for his contributions to the "science of race cleansing." Laughlin was the author of the model law after which both the Virginia and German sterilization laws were fashioned, and he supplied important testimony in favor of sterilization at the [Virginia] trial of Carrie Buck.[49]

American eugenicists applauded *Mein Kampf*, in which Hitler wrote:

> The demand that defective people be prevented from propagating equally defective offspring is a demand of the clearest reason and if systematically executed represents the most human act of mankind. It will spare millions of unfortunates undeserved sufferings, and consequently

---

www.oradvocacy.org/news/OCA2002Fall/>.

[47]"Governor Apologizes for Forced Sterilizations."

[48]Plecker, "Virginia's Attempt to Adjust the Color Problem."

[49]Paul Lombardo, "Involuntary Sterilization in Virginia: From Buck v. Bell to Poe v. Lunchburg," *Developments in Mental Health Law* (July-September 1983).

will lead to a rising improvement of health as a whole. The stronger must dominate and not blend with the weaker, thus sacrificing his own greatness. Only the born weakling can view this as cruel, but he after all is only a weak and limited man. . . . The folkish state must make up for what everyone else today has neglected in this field. It must set race in the center at all life. It must take care to keep it pure.[50]

Hitler praised the 1924 U.S. Immigration Restriction Act, and the work of Harry Laughlin who served as the eugenics authority for the U.S. House of Representatives, Committee on Immigration and Naturalization, "for excluding 'undesirables' on the basis of hereditary illness and race."[51]

On state letterheads, Virginia's Dr. Plecker encouraged Nazi Germany to forcibly sterilize mixed groups en masse.[52] In his *Virginia Pilot* article, Warren Fiske wrote:

In 1935, Plecker wrote to Walter Gross, the director of Germany's Bureau of Human Betterment and Eugenics. He outlined Virginia's racial purity laws and asked to be put on a mailing list for bulletins from Gross's department. Plecker complimented the Third Reich for sterilizing 600 children in Algeria who were born to German women and black men. "I hope this work is complete and not one has been missed," he wrote. "I sometimes regret that we have not the authority to put some measures in practice in Virginia."[53]

One year later, the same Walter Gross, speaking for the Nazis, stated: "As far as the historical appearance of the Jew in Europe is concerned, we believe that the hour of his death has irrevocably arrived."[54] In 1943, during World War II, Dr. Plecker boasted of Virginia's research of its mixed groups that, "Hitler's genealogical study of the Jews is not more complete."[55]

Utilizing the authority of the state, Plecker, like Pharaoh of old, wielded an iron fist by threatening prison for midwives inclined to docu-

---

[50]Adolf Hitler, *Mein Kampf* (1925), trans. Ralph Manheim (New York: Houghton Mifflin, 1971).

[51]Kuhl, *The Nazi Connection: Eugenics, American Racism, and German National Socialism.*

[52]*A Decade of Progress in Eugenics: Scientific Papers of the Third International Congress of Eugenics.*

[53]Fiske, "The Black-and-White World of Ashby Plecker," *Virginia Pilot*, 18 Aug. 2004.

[54]See, e.g., at <http://www.spartacus.schoolnet.co.uk/GERgross.htm>.

[55]Fiske, "The Black-and-White World of Ashby Plecker."

ment mixed children as white.[56] Upon the passage of the 1924 Racial Integrity Act and for more than thirty years after, county clerks and health officials in Virginia would be trained in the Plecker method of spotting a mixed person posing as white.[57] Plecker's efficiency was legend.

Hitler publicly recognized Laughlin for pioneering the science of "race cleansing."[58] But Harry Laughlin's opinion was that, "doubtless the best headquarters in the world [for studying racial integrity] would be Dr. Plecker's office in Richmond, Va."[59]

Plecker energetically promoted his agenda abroad as a lecturer and a eugenics "expert" on the segregation of marriage, schools, churches, hospitals, and workplaces. At the American Public Health Association conference in Detroit, Plecker urged those states that had not acted that, "the most urgent need is the speedy adoption by these states and the District of Columbia of a law forbidding the intermarriage of the white and colored races."[60] Plecker, like other eugenicists, believed that mixed people were parasites on the white race. As Adolf Hitler wrote, "Where no new blood from the superior race enters the racial stream of the mongrels, and where those mongrels continue to cross-breed among themselves, the latter will . . . die out because they have insufficient powers of resistance, which is Nature's wise provision."[61]

Virginia's Plecker and his fellows felt they needed to be aggressive, or else, as Hitler warned, "in the course of many thousands of years they will form a new mongrel race in which the original elements will become so wholly mixed through this millennial crossing that traces of the original elements will be no longer recognizable."[62]

---

[56]Rountree, *Pocahontas's People: The Powhatan Indians of Virginia through Four Centuries.*

[57]Plecker, "The New Virginia Law To Preserve Racial Integrity," *Virginia Health Bulletin* 16, extra no. 2 (March 1924), from the State Registrar of Vital Statistics, Richmond.

[58]Lombardo, "Eugenic Laws against Race Mixing."

[59]Peter Hardin, "Eugenics in Virginia," *Richmond Times-Dispatch*, 26 November 2000. See also P. R. Reilly, "The Virginia Racial Integrity Act Revisited: The Plecker-Laughlin Correspondence: 1928–1930," *American Journal of Medical Genetics* 16 (1983): 483-92.

[60]Plecker, "Virginia's Attempt to Adjust the Color Problem," Read at the joint session of the Public Health Administration and Vital Statistics Section of the American Public Health Association at the Fifty-third Annual Meeting at Detroit Michigan, October 23, 1924. Published in the *American Journal of Public Health* (1925).

[61]Hitler, *Mein Kampf.*

[62]Hitler, *Mein Kampf.*

Nazi scientist Ernst Rudin was invited to the Third International Congress of Eugenics held in August 1932 at the American Museum of Natural History in New York.[63] One of the featured speakers was Dr. Plecker who boasted of Virginia's firm response to the perceived threat against white America to the enthusiastic applause of scientists, legislators, and philanthropists.[64] A few months later Hitler seized control of Germany. The following year Ernst Rudin authored the first draft of German segregation and compulsory sterilization of the "unfit," using the policies of the state of Virginia as the Nazi model. That same year National Socialist Physicians League official Heinz Kurten lauded the U.S. for stemming the immigration tide of "dirtier southern European stocks" to America, who, according to him, slowed the progress of Aryans who "had originally discovered and conquered [America]." The following year another prominent Nazi, Gerhard Wagner, used America's racial restrictions to prod Germany to follow suit.[65]

The American architects of Nazi Germany regarded race mixing as a *moral* crime. Plecker defined immorality in semiclinical terms: "[N]ot a few white women are giving birth to mulatto children. These women are usually feebleminded, but in some cases they are simply depraved." At the passage of his pet law in 1924 he said, "Young men must be brought to realize that it is as great a crime against their state and race to mix their blood with that of another race, out of wedlock, as in it."[66]

---

[63]*A Decade of Progress in Eugenics: Scientific Papers of the Third International Congress of Eugenics.*

[64]*A Decade of Progress in Eugenics: Scientific Papers of the Third International Congress of Eugenics.*

[65]Lombardo, "Eugenic Laws against Race Mixing."

[66]Plecker, *Virginia Health Bulletin* 11 (1927).

Chapter 10

Word War II and the Nazis

January 29, 1943. At the height of World War II, Germany nears completion of a crematorium at Auschwitz. SS Captain Karl Bischoff writes to his senior, Col. Hans Kammler, detailing the progress:

> Except for some minor construction work, crematorium II was finished by working with all our available forces day and night, despite inexpressible difficulties and freezing weather. The ovens were fired in the presence of the senior engineer Prüfer of the executing firm, Topf and Sons, Erfurt, and they are working faultlessly. The reinforced concrete ceiling of the morgue could not yet be eliminated due to the freezing weather. However, this is not significant, as the gassing cellar can be used for this purpose.[1]

Within days of Bischoff's letter, a bulletin was issued warning of non-Aryans attempting to escape detection:

> Some of these mongrels, finding that they have been able to sneak in their birth certificates unchallenged . . . are now making a rush to register as white. Upon investigation we find that a few local registrars have been permitting such certificates to pass through their hands unquestioned and without warning our office of the fraud. Those attempting this fraud should be warned that they are liable to a penalty of one year in the penitentiary. (Section 5099 of the Code.)[2]

Both letters, one describing work on the crematorium and the second alerting workers to be on the watch for "mongrels" are part of an interna-

---

[1] Jean Claude Pressac, *Auschwitz: Technique and Operation of the Gas Chambers*, trans. Peter Moss (New York: Beate Klarsfeld Foundation, 1989) 432. "Vergasungskeller ["gassing cellar"] Auschwitz Document," the Holocaust History Project, online at <http://www/holocaust-history.org/auschwitz/19430129-vergasunkskeller/>.

[2] Plecker, "Letter to Local Registrars, etc. Regarding Mulatto Classification," January 1943—state bulletin addressed to Local Registrars, Physicians, Health Offices, Nurses, School Superintendents, and Clerks of the Courts.

tional race-purity campaign. However, the second letter was not written by
Nazis, but by Walter A. Plecker, chief registrar of Virginia's Vital
Statistics, alerting state workers to Melungeons.[3]

Competitive Cooperation

If rumors coming out of Germany of atrocities against "mongrels" in 1943
gave Plecker any second thought, his lectures and bulletins certainly did not
reflect it. He and his fellow American eugenical segregationists had entertained and corresponded with Nazis who would be killed in the closing
days of World War II, or who would be executed for crimes against humanity in 1946. Because of the close collaboration, the National Holocaust
Museum Online has devoted a chapter to Virginia's seldom-discussed history of eugenics.[4] American eugenicists chafed with envy as Nazi Germany
began to dominate a field that the U.S. had pioneered.[5] When Hitler
sterilized two million, American eugenicists pushed to sterilize twelve
million "unfit" Americans, a nice round number that would restore the U.S.
to global leadership in the racial purity movement and put U.S. eugenicists
back on the dais at international conventions for social progress.[6]

The contest between Germany and the U.S. was based on mutual
admiration and both countries tried to lure the top scientists in the field.
Hitler awarded honorary Heidelberg University degrees to two Americans.
One went to Harry Laughlin who gladly accepted:

> I consider the conferring of this high degree upon me not only as a
> personal honor, but also as evidence of a common understanding of
> German and American scientists of the nature of eugenics as research in
> and the practical application of those fundamental biological and social
> principles which determine the racial endowment and the racial health—
> physical, mental and spiritual—of future generations.[7]

---

[3]Plecker, "Letter to Local Registrars, etc. Regarding Mulatto Classification," January
1943.

[4]United States National Holocaust Museum: <http://www.ushmm.org/>.

[5]Kuhl, *The Nazi Connection: Eugenics, American Racism, and German National
Socialism.*

[6]Kuhl, *The Nazi Connection: Eugenics, American Racism, and German National
Socialism.*

[7]Kuhl, *The Nazi Connection: Eugenics, American Racism, and German National
Socialism.*

Hitler acknowledged the American architect of "one drop" as the "successful pioneer of practical eugenics and the farseeing representative of racial policy in America."[8] A Harvard alumnus who believed blacks and Jews were inferior to Nordic white people, Laughlin's support for Germany's eugenics program continued after the extent of Nazi plans was revealed. Planning to lecture in Germany even after World War II started, Laughlin was only silenced when the embarrassed Carnegie Foundation of New York finally ordered him into retirement. Laughlin then purchased the Nazi race propaganda film *Erbkrank* (*Hereditary Defective*) to show to the American public.

Hitler's other American honorary-degree recipient was Foster Kennedy, a eugenicist who advocated the lethal state extermination of handicapped Americans.[9]

After World War II, some of the Nazi pals of Laughlin and Plecker were tried as Nazi war criminals and executed for their atrocities. Many Nazi officials were shocked that the U.S. would judge them for "race crimes" which many American leaders had applauded as good public health policy. Testimony in the trials exposed the collaboration of eugenics scientists working together to promote racist legislative policies in both America and Nazi Germany:

> Psychiatrist Edwin Katzen-ellenbogen, former member of the faculty at Harvard Medical School was convicted of war crimes he had committed as a doctor at Buchenwald Concentration Camp. During his trial in Dachau, Germany by the U.S. Army, he testified that he had "drafted for the governor the law for sterilization of epileptics, criminals, and incurably insane for the state of New Jersey, following the state of Indiana which first introduced the law in 1910.[10]

New Jersey governor Woodrow Wilson signed the bill and was later elected president of the U.S. President Wilson's second wife, Edith Bolling Wilson, was a descendant of John Rolfe and Pocahontas. Edith Wilson became the *defacto* president when her husband suffered a stroke in 1919 and she controlled matters brought to his attention, as she acknowledged in

---

[8]Kuhl, *The Nazi Connection: Eugenics, American Racism, and German National Socialism.*

[9]Kuhl, *The Nazi Connection: Eugenics, American Racism, and German National Socialism.*

[10]Lapon, *Mass Murderers in White Coats.*

her 1939 autobiography, *My Memoir*. (Virginia changed the Melungeon surname "Bolling" to "Bolin" on its infamous blacklist.)

Hitler's personal physician Karl Brandt also testified at his war crimes trial of the influence on Nazi policy of American eugenicists such as Madison Grant. Brandt had directed the Nazi program responsible for exterminating the mentally handicapped:

> While a defendant in the Doctors Trial for his role as leader of the euthanasia program and for other crimes, Karl Brandt realized that many of the Nazi ideas concerning "life not worthy of living," sterilization and the ilk, had been based on ideas and writings from the United States. He reminded his U.S. prosecutors of this fact by introducing several of those works as evidence in his defense. One was the book, *The Passing of the Great Race*, by Madison Grant.
>
> Brandt excerpted the following from a 1923 German translation of the American's book: "A strict selection by exterminating the insane or incapable—in other words, the scum of society—would solve the whole problem in one century, and would enable us to got rid of the undesirable elements who people our prisons, hospitals, and lunatic asylums. The individual may be supported, brought up, and protected by the community during his lifetime, but the state must see to it by sterilization, that he is the last individual of his line of descent, otherwise future generations too will be burdened with the curse of an ever-increasing number of victims of misguided sentimentality.[11]

The defense was rejected and Brandt was executed. Other German physicians claimed that the U.S. Supreme Court decision in favor of forced eugenical sterilization served as the precedent for Germany's eugenics policies. The Nazi eugenicists lining up to be executed must have felt betrayed by the earlier hearty backslapping from Plecker, Laughlin, Grant, and Cox who had first urged Germany's segregation and sterilization of "misfits."

> H. H. Laughlin, the Expert Eugenics Agent of the United States House of Representatives Committee on Immigration and Naturalization published the Model Eugenical Sterilization Law. This model formed a basis for many state sterilization laws and for Nazi Germany's 1933 law. . . .
>
> Madison Grant published *Conquest of a Continent: A Racial History of the United States* and had copies sent to Mussolini, Nazi Professor Dr.

---

[11]Lapon, *Mass Murderers in White Coats*.

Eugen Fischer at the Kaiser Wilhelm Institute for the Study of Anthropology, Human Heredity and Eugenics in Berlin, Dr. Alfred Rosenberg (Hitler's chief scientific adviser) and to Nazi race hygienist Professor Dr. Fritz Lenz at the University of Munich. Hitler put into law the Nazi Act for Averting Descendants Afflicted with Hereditary Diseases. This sterilization law was directly based on H. H. Laughlin's U.S. Model Eugenical Sterilization Law of 1922.[12]

Through Laughlin and Grant, Virginia's war on Melungeons is linked to Hitler's atrocities: "To fashion a successful legislative strategy, three local Virginia eugenicists—John Powell, Earnest Cox and Walter Plecker—consulted with Madison Grant and Harry Laughlin."[13] These Americans approved the use of force, though they never achieved the level they sought. Violation of the 1924 Virginia Racial Integrity Act was a felony and an appendix named historic groups suspected of mixed blood.[14]

Stopping the "Inevitable Result"

Immediately after the Racial Integrity Bill was enacted, Dr. Plecker rushed out a state bulletin:

1924, Senate Bill 219. It is estimated that there are in the State from 10,000 to 20,000, possibly more, near white people, who are known to possess an intermixture of colored blood, in some cases to a slight extent it is true, but still enough to prevent them from being white. In the past it has been possible for these people to declare themselves as white, or even to have the Court so declare them. Then they have demanded the admittance of their children in the white schools, and in not a few cases have intermarried with white people. In many counties they exist as distinct colonies holding themselves aloof from Negroes, but not being admitted by the white people as of their race. . . . Their children are likely to revert to the distinctly negro type even when all apparent evidence of mixture has disappeared. The Virginia Bureau of Vital Statistics has been called upon within one month for evidence by two lawyers employed to assist people of this type to force their children into the white public schools, and by another employed by the school trustee of a district to prevent this action. In each case evidence was found to show that either the people themselves or their connections were reported to our office to

---

[12]Lapon, *Mass Murderers in White Coats*.
[13]Lombardo, "Eugenic Laws against Race Mixing."
[14]State of Virginia Racial Integrity Act, 1924.

be of mixed blood. Our bureau has kept a watchful eye upon the situation, and has guarded the welfare of the State as far as possible with inadequate law and power. The condition has gone on, however, and is rapidly increasing in importance.

Unless radical measures are used to prevent it, Virginia and other parts of the Nation must surely in time go the way of all other countries in which people of two or more races have lived in close contact. With the exception of the Hebrew race, complete intermixture or amalgamation has been the inevitable result. To succeed, the intermarriage of the white race with mixed stock, must be made impossible. . . . The public must be led to look with scorn and contempt upon the man who will degrade himself and do harm to society by such abhorrent deeds. The Bureau of Vital Statistics, Clerks who issues marriage licenses, and the school authorities are the barriers placed by this law between the danger and the safety of the Commonwealth. The new law further provides for the registration of all persons who desire it, and who will make application for such registration of color and birth. . . . These births will be permanently recorded and preserved for all time, and will be of great value for many purposes, such as to prove American citizenship when applying for passports to go abroad, and for establishing and preserving the family tree for future generations. . . .

The term "Mixed," "Issue," and perhaps one or two others, will be understood to mean a mixture of white and black races, with the white predominating. That is the class that should be reported with the greatest care, as many of these are on the borderline, and constitute the real danger of race intermixture. The term "Indian" will no longer be accepted for that class, but must be applied only to those of known pure Indian blood, for those mixed with white. If there is a mixture of negro they must not be classed as Indians but as "Negro" or "Mixed Indian."

Bureau of Vital Statistics, W. A. Plecker, M.D.,
State Registrar of Vital Statistics, Richmond, Va.[15]

Plecker next zeroed in on the Melungeons. On August 5, 1942, Plecker sent a letter of inquiry to the state of Tennessee seeking assistance. He wrote:

We have in some of the counties of southwestern Virginia a number of so-called Melungeons who came into that section from Newman's

---

[15]Plecker, *Virginia Health Bulletin* 16, extra no. 2 (March 1924). "The New Virginia Law to Preserve Racial Integrity," Cold Spring Harbor Laboratory, American Philosophical Society, and Truman State University.

Ridge, Hancock County, Tennessee, and who are classified by us as of negro origin though they make various claims, such as Portuguese, Indians, etc.

The law of Virginia says that any one with any ascertainable degree of negro is to be classified as colored and we are endeavoring to so classify those who apply for birth, death, and marriage registrations.

We have a list of the free negroes, by counties, of the 1830 U.S. Census in which we find the racial origin of most of these Melungeons classified as mulattoes. In that period, 1830, we do not find the name of Hancock County, but presume that it was made up from portions of other counties, possible Grainger and Hawkins, where we find considerable numbers of these Melungeon families listed.

Will you please advise as to that point and particularly which of these original counties Newmans Ridge was in.

Very truly yours,
W. A. Plecker, M.D.
State Registrar[16]

In her response, Tennessee State Librarian Mrs Trotwood Moore rehashed the old Melungeon legends from sources like Shepard and Jarvis. Then she made a mistake by adding a mildly sympathetic comment about Melungeons:

> But I imagine if the United States Census listed them as mulattoes their listing will remain. But it is a terrible claim to place on people if they do not have negro blood. I often have wondered just how deeply the census takers went into an intelligent study of it at that early period.[17]

Dr. Plecker responded to Mrs. Moore in a bullying, sneering tone he used on midwives and others he sought to intimidate:

> This group appears to be in many respects of the same type as a number of groups in Virginia, some of which are known as "free issues," or descendants of slaves freed by their masters before the War Between the States. . . . All of these groups have the same desire, which Capt. L. M. Jarvis says the melungeons have, to become friends of Indians and to be classed as Indians. He referred to the effort which the melungeon group

---

[16]"August 5, 1942. Walter Plecker Letter to Tennessee Secretary of State Regarding Melungeon Classification" <http://multiracial.com/content/view/986/29/>.

[17]"August 12, 1942. Mrs. John Trottwood Moore Letter to Walter Plecker Regarding Melungeon Classification" <http://multiracial.com/content/view/982/29/>.

made to be accepted by the Cherokees, apparently without great success. It is interesting also to know the opinion expressed by Capt. Jarvis that these freed negroes migrated into that section with the white people. That is perfectly natural as they have always endeavored to tie themselves up as closely as possible either with the whites or Indians and are striving to break away from the true negro type. . . .

One of the most interesting parts of your letter is that relating to the opinion of the Judge mentioned, in his "Personal Memoirs," who seemed to have accepted as satisfactory certain evidence which was presented to him that these people are of Phoenician descent from ancient Carthage, which was totally destroyed by Rome. . . . We are very much afraid that the Judge followed the same course pursued by one of our Virginia judges in hearing a similar case, when he accepted the hearsay evidence of people who testified that they had always understood that the claimants were of Indian origin, regardless of the documentary evidence reaching back in some cases to or near to the Revolutionary War, showing them to be descendants of freed negroes.

We will require other evidence than that of Capt. Jarvis and His Honor before classifying members of the group who are now causing trouble in Virginia by their claims of Indian descent, with the privilege of inter-marrying into the white race, permissible when a person can show his racial composition to be one-sixteenth or less Indian, the remainder white with no negro intermixture. We have found after very laborious and painstaking study of records of various sorts that none of our Virginia people now claiming to be Indian are free from negro admixture, and they are, therefore, according to our law classified as colored. In that class we include the melungeons of Tennessee.

Very sincerely yours,
W. A. Plecker, M. D.
State Registrar[18]

Plecker's letter reveals the cynical disregard for consistency that was rife among the racists who had come to dominate eugenics by the 1940s. While fretting about "one drop" of the black blood in Melungeons, he was mockingly dismissive of "one drop" of Pocahontas's blood in descendants such as Edith Bolling Wilson:

---

[18]"August 20, 1942. Walter Plecker Letter to Tennessee State Librarian and Archivist Regarding Melungeon Classification" <http://multiracial.com/content/view/987/29>.

We have in Virginia white people, descendants of Pocahontas, who married John Rolfe about 1616. About twelve generations have passed since then, and we figured out that there was about 1/4000th of 1% of Pocahontas blood now in their veins, *though they seem to be quite proud of that*. If you go back to the destruction of Carthage in 146 B.C., or to the destruction of Tyre by Pompey in 64 B C., when all characteristic features of national life became extinct and with it racial identity, you will see that the fraction of 1% of Phoenician blood would reach astronomical proportions and be totally lost in the various mixtures of North Africans, with which the Carthaginians afterwards mixed.[19]

Four months later, on the very day that Nazi *Schutzstaffel* (SS) and police units began deporting 6,500 Jewish residents of the Warsaw ghetto to Treblinka, W. A. Plecker of the Virginia Bureau of Vital Statistics, who described mixed people as "rats," issued the following "emergency bulletin," publishing Melungeon and Indian names and counties of residence he regarded as a threat to the purity of the white race.

Dear Co-workers:

Our December 1942 letter to local registrars, also mailed to the clerks, set forth the determined effort to escape from the negro race of groups of "free issues," or descendents of the "free mulattoes" of early days, so listed prior to 1865 in the United States census and various types of State records, as distinguished from slave negroes.

Now that these people are playing up the advantages gained by being permitted to give "Indian" as the race of the child's parents on birth certificates, so we see the great mistake made in not stopping earlier the organized propagation of this racial falsehood. They have been using the advantage thus gained as an aid to intermarriage into the white race and to attend white schools, and now for some time they have been refusing to register with war draft boards as negroes, as required by the boards which are faithfully performing their duties. Three of these negroes from Caroline County were sentenced to prison on January 12 in the United States Court at Richmond for refusing to obey the draft law unless permitted to classify themselves as "Indians."

Some of these mongrels, finding that they have been able to sneak in their birth certificates unchallenged as Indians are now making a rush to register as white. Upon investigation we find that a few local registrars have been permitting such certificates to pass through their hands

---

[19]Ibid. Italics added.

unquestioned and without warning our office of the fraud. Those attempting this fraud should be warned that they are liable to a penalty of one year in the penitentiary (Section 5099a of the Code). Several clerks have likewise been actually granting them licenses to marry whites, or at least to marry amongst themselves as Indian or white. . . .

To aid all of you in determining just which are the mixed families, we have made a list of their surnames by counties and cities, as complete as possible at this time. This list should be preserved by all, even by those in counties and cities not included, as these people are moving around over the State and changing race at the new place. A family has just been investigated which was always recorded as Negro around Glade Springs, Washington County, but which changed to white and married as such in Roanoke County. This is going on constantly and can be prevented only by care on the part of local registrars, clerks, doctors, health workers, and school authorities.

Please report all known or suspicious cases to the Bureau of Vital Statistics, giving names, ages, parents, and as much other information as possible. All certificates of these people showing "Indian" or "white" are now being rejected and returned to the physician or midwife, but local registrars hereafter must not permit them to pass their hands uncorrected or unchallenged and without a note of warning to us. One hundred and fifty thousand other mulattos in Virginia are watching eagerly the attempt of their pseudo-Indian brethren, ready to follow in a rush when the first have made a break in the dike.

Very truly yours,
W. A. Plecker, M.D.
State Registrar of Vital Statistics[20]

The state of Virginia added to the bulletin the names and counties of mixed people "Striving to Pass as 'Indian' or White." The towns and counties were in the heart of Tidewater Virginia and Melungia: Albemarle, Amherst, Bedford, Rockbridge, Charles City, King William, New Kent, Henrico and Richmond City, Caroline, Essex and King and Queen, Elizabeth City and Newport News, Halifax, Norfolk County and Portsmouth, Westmoreland, Greene, Prince William, Fauquier, Lancaster, Washington, Roanoke County, Lee and Smyth, Scott County, Russell County, Tazewell County, Wise.

---

[20]"Walter Plecker Letter to Local Officials" <http://www.vcdh.virginia.edu/lewisand clark/students/projects/monacans/Contemporary_Monacans/letter.html>.

The Indian and Melungeon surnames included Moon, Powell, Kidd, Pumphrey, Adcock, Beverly, Branham, Duff, Floyd, Hamilton, Hartless, Hicks, Johns, Lawless, Nuckles (Knuckles), Painter, Ramsey, Redcross, Roberts, Southwards (Suthards, Southerds, Southers), Sorrells, Terry, Tyree, Willis, Clark, Cash, Wood, McVey, Maxey, Branham, Burley, Coleman, Duff, Floyd, Hartless, Hicks, Mason, Mayse (Mays), Painters, Pults, Ramsey, Sorrell, Johns, Collins, Dennis, Bradby, Howell, Langston, Stewart, Wynn, Custalow, Dungoe, Holmes, Miles, Page, Allmond, Adams, Hawkes, Spurlock, Doggett, Bradby, Wynn, Adkins, Langston, Byrd, Fortune, Cooper, Tate, Hammond, Brooks, Boughton, Prince, Mitchell, Robinson, Epps (Eppes), Stewart (Stuart), Coleman, Johnson, Martin, Talley, Sheppard (Shepard), Young, Sawyer, Bass, Weaver, Locklear (Locklair), King, Bright, Porter, Worlds (or Worrell), Atwells, Butridge, Okiff, Shifflett, Shiflet, Tyson, Segar, Hoffman (Huffman), Riley, Colvin, Phillips. Dorsey (Dawson) Beverly, Barlow, Thomas, Hughes, Lethcoe, Worley, Gibson, (Gipson), Moore, *Goins, Ramsey, Delph, Bunch, Freeman, Mise, Barlow, Bolden (Bolin), Mullins, Hawkins, Dingus, Keith, Castell, Stillwell, Meade, Proffitt, Hammed, Duncan.[21] (Note that "Goins" is the surname of the descendants of John Gowen and Margaret Cornish who came to America on the *White Lion* in August 1619.) Gibson, Collins, Bunch, Bass, and many more of these families descended from free people of color of seventeenth-century Tidewater Virginia.

Early Ethnic Documentation

The state of Virginia trailed only California in the number of compulsory sterilizations. Why should Virginia, the suburban home of Washington senators, congressmen, and superior court justices, have placed so high in such a grisly category? Virginia was the first colony successfully established in English-speaking North America, more than a decade older than Massachusetts. Virginia received the first Africans on board the *White Lion* in the summer of 1619. Virginia was the site of the birth of the seventeenth-century Angolan *malungu* settlements on King's Creek. Virginia had more time than any other to make peace with her people of color.

---

[21]"Walter Plecker Letter to Local Officials," "Page 2. Surnames by Counties and Cities, of Mixed Negroid Virginia Families Striving to Pass as 'Indian' or White" <http://www. vcdh.virginia.edu/lewisandclark/students/projects/monacans/Contemporary_ Monacans/letter.html>.

But, the first commonwealth, within sight of the White House, basked in the nation's envy of its elitism, gentility, and "good breeding," and this may explain its disturbing twentieth-century agenda "to promote the welfare of society by mitigating race degeneration and raising the average intelligence of the people of the state."[22] Here was a twisted pride.

Immediately after the American Revolution, the young United States initiated a national census to be taken every ten years beginning in 1790. In those early records census takers marked American Indians, blacks, mulattos, and any other nonwhite as "free people of color." From these records, black historian Carter G. Woodson in 1925 published *Free Negro Heads of Families* in which he listed the surnames of all families listed as "mulatto" in 1830.[23] Plecker used this book to identify mixed surnames for Virginia's blacklist.

Virginia's Indians

Melungeons descended not only from seventeenth-century African Americans, but also from the American Indians of Virginia, Maryland, North Carolina, South Carolina, and Delaware. Dr. Virginia DeMarce, a historian with the Bureau of Indian Affairs in the U.S. Department of the Interior, and a past president of the National Genealogical Society, found several Upper South Indian tribes contributing to mixed black, white, and Indian, or "triracial," communities such as the Brass Ankles of South Carolina, the Guineas of West Virginia, the Haliwas of North Carolina, the Lumbees of North Carolina, and South Carolina, the Melungeons of Tennessee and Kentucky, the Red Bones of South Carolina and Louisiana, and the Turks of South Carolina. In her article, "Very Slightly Mixt: TriRacial Isolate Families of the Upper South—A Genealogical Study," Demarce identified these Indians as the Chickahominy, Gingaskin, Mattapony, Nansemond, Nanticoke, Nottaway, Pamunkey, Rappahanocks, Saponi, Weanick, and Werowocomo.[24] The markers that distinguish the historic mixed groups from the Upper South Indians can at times be so faint as to be practically irrelevant.

---

[22]Lapon, *Mass Murderers in White Coats.*

[23]Carter Godwin Woodson, *Free Negro Heads of Families in the United States in 1830, together with a Brief Treatment of the Free Negro* (Washington DC: Association for the Study of Negro Life and History, 1925).

[24]Virginia DeMarce, "Very Slightly Mixt: Triracial Isolate Families of the Upper South—A Genealogical Study," *National Genealogical Society Quarterly* (March 1992).

The engineers of the 1924 Racial Integrity Act in Richmond, Virginia used the same methods for dealing with both Melungeons and Powhatan Indians: segregation and attempted destruction of their self-identity. Melungeons and Virginia's Indians were the same mixed people with identical surnames who chose different paths. Dr. Plecker decided that Melungeons must not be allowed to claim they were white, and that Powhatans must not be allowed to claim they were Indian. The goal of Virginia was to force both groups, Melungeon and Indian, to admit on paper that they were black. If they refused to admit it, bureaucrats like Plecker actually scratched out "white" or "Indian" on official documents, or superimposed "colored" or "mixed" in place of Indian.[25] Plecker and his officials did this many times, as existing state records reveal. The process is called "paper genocide,' but it was meant to have a very literal consequence.

The state decided the ethnic identification of mixed Americans. Ethnic profiling in criminal investigation is decried today by certain ethnic and religious groups. Yet many who criticize criminal ethnic profiling insist on other forms of ethnic profiling, as, for example, Tiger Woods and others can attest.

In the twentieth century, Virginia maintained that her Indians were "tainted" by black ancestry and could no longer intermarry with whites.[26] The tribes who had lived in Virginia for more than 400 years suddenly found themselves in a fight for their very survival as a separate people.

When English colonists had first arrived in tidewater Virginia in 1607, the tribes of the Chesapeake Powhatan Indians were believed to number about 15,000 people. Because of disease and war, by 1670 their population was drastically cut to about 1,800.[27] In the following centuries their numbers would fall even lower. These Indians would have either become inbred or extinct had they not accepted whites and blacks as husbands and wives. But, whatever the color of their skin, or whether their blood quantum tilts more to Indian or black, they, like the Lumbees and others, continued to ethnically and culturally identify as American Indian, and so they should be regarded today. An Indian with one-half Indian ancestry

---

[25]To see a marriage license changed from "Indian" to "mixed" by the Virginia State Registrar's office in 1940, see "Battles in Red, Black, and White: Virginia's Racial Integrity Law of 1924," at <http://xroads.virginia.edu/~CAP/POCA/POC_law.html>.

[26]Rountree, *Pocahontas's People: The Powhatan Indians of Virginia through Four Centuries*.

[27]Rountree, *Pocahontas's People*.

who mocks an Indian with 1/32 Indian ancestry as a "wannabe" perpetuates a flawed racial standard, though few have dared to say so.

Around 1700 the Rappahannocks lost their reservation. The Chickahominies were dispossessed of their lands before 1720 and the Nansemonds sold their land in 1792. Only a handful of tribes, including the Mattaponis, Pamunkeys, and Gingaskin, stubbornly held on to ancestral lands against state efforts to dispossess them.[28] In the twentieth century, Plecker dismissed Indians as "colored," which by the state's one-drop definition meant "Negro." Records show employees during his administration altering documents to show ethnicity in accordance with Plecker's definition. Between 1920 and 1945, people who were listed for centuries as "Indian" became "Negro" with the stroke of a pen.

J. David Smith describes the extent of Plecker's historic revisions:

> The Pamunkeys he discounted as "heavily mixed with negro and white (with) a faint trace of Indian." He described the Rappahannocks as a "group of similar origin [that] have about the same claim to being Indians." [Plecker said] "The Amherst-Rockbridge group of about 800 similar people, are giving us the most trouble, through actual numbers and persistent claims of being Indians." Plecker claimed of the Chickahominy Indians that "their existence as a tribe was a political trick, to enable the white people to maintain control of the county government, Indians not being voters."[29]

Contrary to the state of Virginia's wishes, the U.S. Census Department continued to identify Virginia's tribal people as "Indian." So Plecker began pressuring federal administrators to change the official classification from Indian to "colored." He was partially successful. In 1930 the federal census reported that 779 American Indians lived in Virginia. But, as a result of Plecker's insistence, the U.S. Census reported only 198 Indians in the state in 1940. Virginia's practice of "paper genocide" effectively reduced Indians in real numbers. The Racial Integrity Act of 1924 reclassified some Indians as "colored." Those identified by the state as "colored" were not even allowed to marry those who were still officially identified by the federal government as Indian.[30]

---

[28]Rountree, *Pocahontas's People*.

[29]J. David Smith, *The Eugenic Assault on America: Scenes in Red, White, and Black* (Fairfax VA: George Mason University Press, 1993).

[30]Rountree, *Pocahontas's People*. And see "An Act to Preserve Racial Integrity"

Helen Rountree reported the tragic consequences that resulted. At least one Indian committed suicide after the state annulled his marriage. According to Rountree, Dr. Plecker,

> continued actively and more or less successfully to place Indian people where he thought they belonged. County clerks had the right, according to the Racial Integrity law, to deny marriage licenses to couples who could not prove upon demand that they were of the same race. By his own account, Plecker also "furnished information upon which to base annulments of interracial marriages, and perhaps prevented other similar marriages by giving out the facts to inquiring young people whose suspicions were aroused." I know of one Indian-white marriage thus broken up; the Indian man involved killed himself in despair as a result.[31]

When Indian midwives filled out birth certificates stating that the infant was "Indian" the state threatened prison:

> In January 1942, for instance, [Plecker] sent a crushing letter to a Chickahominy midwife, informing her that she had violated a state law by "falsifying" a baby's race, thus making her liable to criminal prosecution. He went on at some length, knowing that the woman would take the letter to her chief: "This 'Indian' stuff has gone far enough, but I am not prepared just at present to say what will be done to make examples of some people. . . . " [Three Rappahannock men had been sentenced to (two years in) prison the day before for refusing to serve in the Army with blacks.] It did not take the Judge long to decide what they were. We expect a correct copy of this [birth] certificate to come in at once. [Other "Indian" certificates would be returned to her, and] Each case is a separate offense should it come into court."[32]

Plecker struck in as many areas as he could. Virginia forced Indian schools to close and sent Indian children to black schools to reinforce the state's claim that they were black. At Plecker's urging, some state game wardens were pressured to end the traditional fishing and hunting rights exercised by Indians on reservation land. Indians frequently appealed to various state offices and sometimes won and sometimes lost.[33]

<http://www.vcdh.virginia.edu/lewisandclark/students/projects/monocans/Contemporary_Monacans/racial.html>.

[31]Rountree, *Pocahontas's People*.

[32]Rountree, *Pocahontas's People*.

[33]Rountree, *Pocahontas's People*.

Even though the racial purity laws would remain in force decades after, in 1945, after Plecker's retirement, the state's most intensive efforts to enforce began to subside somewhat. The Virginia tribes of Rappahannock, Mattapony, Pamunkey, Nansemond, Monacan, and Chickahominy emerged from Plecker's reign, bruised but intact, and eventually regained state recognition in the 1980s. And yet some of the tribes, such as the Gingaskins have ceased from being a distinct people.[34] One year after Plecker retired, he was run over by a truck while crossing a street without looking. That very year, 1946, scientists convicted of Nazi war crimes, his old allies, went to the gallows.

Today, belatedly, Virginia and North Carolina are attempting to gain federal recognition for their surviving Indians.[35] Recently, Senator Elizabeth Dole of North Carolina has also filed a bill for federal recognition of Lumbee Indians. Federal recognition of the Lumbees is opposed by the Cherokees of the Eastern Band in North Carolina on the grounds of blood purity.[36]

Confrontation

As their ancestors before them, America's historic mixed communities did not passively accept twentieth-century persecution. Some fought with guns. Others turned to the courts as they had been doing for the past three centuries. During Plecker's administration, a county clerk in Rockbridge County denied a marriage license to Dorothy Johns, a woman of mixed white, Indian, and colonial African-American ancestry who intended to marry a white man. The basis of the denial was Virginia's Racial Integrity Act. Dorothy Johns was a descendant of William Johns, born about 1700, who married a "mulatto" woman whom he had refused to list as a tithable. This early family had produced grandsons who fought as free mulattos in the American Revolution. Philip Johns had led an early colonial insurrection and the Johns had married into the Morris families of the Melungeons and the Monacan Indians of Amherst and Rockbridge counties, and they had grown to a sizable community with their own origin traditions. Plecker

---

[34]Rountree, *Pocahontas's People*.

[35]For example, testimony of Congresswoman Jo Ann Davis before the House Resources Committee, re H.R. 2345, to extend Federal recognition to Virginia Indian tribes, 25 September 2002.

[36]"Dole Favors Full Recognition for Lumbees," Lumberton NC (AP), 20 February 2003.

would complain bitterly, "The Amherst-Rockbridge group of about 800 similar people, are giving us the most trouble, through actual numbers and persistent claims of being Indians."

Dorothy Johns demanded she be given the marriage license on the grounds that she was Indian and therefore exempt from the Racial Integrity law. Arthur H. Estabrook of the Eugenics Record Office in Cold Spring Harbor had investigated the genealogies of the Johns and the Melungeon Branhams, which he presented. Plecker showed up in court as an expert witness arguing at the trial that the Johns were not Indian but "Negro." Circuit County Judge Henry Hold denied the license to Dorothy Johns.[37]

The Act was challenged again by a cousin of Dorothy Johns named Atha Sorrels. The Sorrels were also of early free lineage. Atha's ancestress Judith Serell, a white woman, bore a "Molato" son, Thomas Serell, in 1738. The Sorrels also married into the Lucas family of the Melungeons. During the American Revolution, Judith's grandson James Sorrell had "served as a gunner's mate aboard the *Hero* and the *Larter*."[38] Although Virginians rightfully take great pride in honoring their ancestors from the American Revolution, Virginia did not hesitate to trouble the twentieth-century descendants of the patriotic Johns and Sorrels Revolutionary veterans. Atha Sorrels applied for a marriage license to marry a white man but was denied by the same clerk who had refused to issue a license to her cousin Dorothy Johns. The case went to court but,

> Unlike the case of Dorothy Johns, no witness appeared to testify that Atha Sorrels had a black race mixture in her genealogy. Judge Holt decided in favor of Atha Sorrels. He declared that there was no evidence that she was of mixed heritage according to the parameters of the law and that a license should be issued to Atha Sorrels and the man who wished to marry her.[39]

An infuriated Plecker stormed, "For any person to claim to be an Indian so as to be elegible for intermarriage with whites, it is necessary for him to show that there has never been any introduction of negro blood into his family."[40]

---

[37]Smith, *The Eugenic Assault on America*.

[38]Heinegg, *Free African Americans of North Carolina, North Carolina, and South Carolina*.

[39]Smith, *The Eugenic Assault on America*.

[40]Smith, *The Eugenic Assault on America*. See also "9-0 Decision Rules Out Virginia Law—15 Other States Are Affected," *New York Times*, 13 June 1967.

How could anyone, even Plecker himself, meet such a burden of proof? The whole Act was unenforceable as written. Without a demagogue like Plecker to carry out the law's covert function, it would have lain unused, gathering cobwebs. And when his reign ended, within a year of Hitler's, fortunately there was no one willing to carry on, at least not as aggressively as had he, Powell, and Cox. For more than two decades, from 1924 to 1948, during an era that included the Great Depression, the state of Virginia and states with similar laws made the lives of America's smallest, poorest, and most vulnerable communities even more miserable. But, the children of the seventeenth-century Virginia *malungu* survived to see W. A. Plecker buried like their enemies before him. They also saw his law buried when the U.S. Supreme Court overturned it in the case of *Loving vs. Virginia* in 1967.

Back-to-Africa Schemes

Parallel to Nazi Germany in the 1930s and 1940s, powerful forces were moving steadily to send not only blacks, but whites and American Indians with "one drop" of African blood to Africa. The plan reached the U.S. Senate and had strong black and white support.

Eugenics-based pure-race laws were said by their supporters to protect "all" races from alleged mixed degeneration. Was this true? In a national speech in 1924 Plecker said of the Racial Integrity law he helped write:

> This is working no hardship and no injustice upon the other races; for the same effort tends at the same time to maintain the purity of their races as well. That the mongrel races are liable to perpetuate the undesirable qualities of both their constituent stocks is abundantly demonstrated by a study of the larger and older of the mongrel groups in Virginia, as well as upon a study on a far larger scale in various other parts of the world. The colored races therefore should be equally zealous in preventing both the legal and illegal admixture of the races.[41]

Plecker lied. The wording of the Act and its enforcement shows that though people with one drop of African blood could not marry "pure" white

---

[41]Walter Ashby Plecker, "Virginia's Attempt to Adjust the Color Problem," read before the 53rd annual meeting of the Public Health Administration and Vital Statistics Section of the American Public Health Association, Detroit, Michigan, 23 October 1924, as published in *Eugenics in Relation to the New Family and the Law on Racial Integrity, Including a Paper Read before the American Public Health Association*, 12-28 (Richmond: D. Bottom, supt. public printing, 1924) and in *The American Journal of Public Health* (1925).

people, nothing prevented white people with one drop of African blood from marrying black people.[42]

Plecker, Earnest Cox, John Powell, and other powerful white segregationists were working with black segregationist Marcus Garvey when they passed the Racial Integrity Act in 1924. These strange bedfellows jointly planned to raise both white and black support to literally remove all people with as little as one drop of black blood to Africa to make America "pure" white.[43] Garvey corresponded extensively with Cox and his partner Plecker, and shared with them his plan for the return to Africa. In 1925 Garvey wrote several letters to Earnest Cox, to tell him, for example:

Dear Mr. Cox, . . .

[25 June 1925] [F]or seven years we have successfully fought against the entire Negro press, churches, organizations, and leaders and have held our own and won millions of converts, against their vilest opposition. . . .

[8 August 1925] I promise you all the support I can give to carry out the general plan. . . .
     Convey my best wishes to Mr. Powell and Dr. Plecker and assure them of my cooperation and support for the cause.

With best wishes,
Yours Sincerely,
Marcus Garvey[44]

Two years later Garvey was in prison for fraud, and facing extradition. Cox and Plecker appealed to President Calvin Coolidge to pardon him. Cox wrote Coolidge,

---

[42]Racial Integrity Act of 1924, State of Virginia. See "An Act to Preserve Racial Integrity" online at <http://www.vcdh.virginia.edu/lewisandclark/students/projects/monacans/Contemporary_Monacans/racial.html>.

[43]Peter Hardin, "Signs of the Times, Eugenics in Virginia," *Richmond Times-Dispatch*, 26 November 2000. See also Paul Lee, "Strange Bedfellows: The Curious Courtship of Black Nationalists and White Supremacists," *The Michigan Citizen* (Highland Park), 24 Feb 24, 2002: Garvey letter to Cox, Atlanta, 25 July 1925; Garvey letter to Cox, Atlanta, 8 August 1925; Cox letter to Pres. Coolidge, 901 West Grace St., Richmond, 23 March 1927. And also see Plecker letter to Coolidge, 19 March 1927.

[44]See "Marcus Garvey to Earnest S. Cox — 25/6/25" at <http://www.marcusgarvey.com/wmview.php?ArtID=150> and "Marcus Garvey to Earnest S. Cox — 8/8/25" at <http://www.marcusgarvey.com/wmview.php?ArtID=154&page=2> (both accessed 14 Dec. 2005).

Sir:

Because of my sympathy for the Negro Marcus Garvey, now in a federal prison, I beg to be allowed to join with those who express to you a hope that his application for a pardon may meet with your approval. . . . He teaches his people to value their blood integrity and not seek to mate with the whites. . . .

. . . His opposition to miscegenation seems to have strengthened his cause among the blacks but to have aroused the enmity of the mulatto leaders of the race.

I have had considerable correspondence with Garvey, sent a personal representative to him in prison, and have received representatives from him on two occasions. . . .

It has been my privilege to publish a small volume in support of Garvey's ideal of race integrity and of his desire to lessen the Negro problem in America by reviving the movement of American Negroes to Liberia. More than 20,000 copies of the work have been ordered by Negroes in this and alien countries and numerous expressions of appreciation cause me to believe that Garvey is held in high esteem by Negroes who do not wish to solve the Negro problem by mixing the blood of the Negro with that of the white.

. . . I, for one, will be greatly pleased . . . if executive clemency may, at this time, effect his liberation in terms which will not cause his deportation from our nation.

Respt.,
Earnest S. Cox[45]

According to the state of Virginia, Indians and Melungeons with one drop of black blood were African, and, in the view of Cox, Powell, Plecker, and others, they should be first on the ship to Africa. Virginia was gathering records to determine, among other things, which American citizens were to be sent into exile from these shores. As Plecker wrote of the Melungeons, "The law of Virginia says that any one with any ascertainable degree of negro is to be classified as colored and we are endeavoring to so classify those who apply for birth, death, and marriage registrations."[46] To affect their removal, twentieth-century segregationists may

---

[45]"Earnest S. Cox to President Calvin Coolidge — March 23, 1927" as online at <http://www.marcusgarvey.com/wmview.php?ArtID=198>.

[46]Plecker letter to the Tennessee Secretary of State, Nashville, 5 August 1942.

have contemplated the same coersion urged by Northampton County Virginians a century earlier to force free people of color to Liberia—refusal to sell to or trade with people of color, but on a national scale.

The African repatriation movement in the twentieth century was treated with all seriousness. After all, thousands of American Jews voluntarily repatriated to the newly formed state of Israel at this same time. Cox, according to William H. Tucker, considered African repatriation to be,

in his own words, "a holy cause." Although Cox complained of white "negrophilists"—neurotic apostles of miscegenation—his much greater fear was the "touchy mixbreed," who had been transformed into "the bitterest enemy" because [they were] denied "full and unrestricted access to the white man's homes and daughters." And everywhere he looked Cox saw "a cancer that will eat deeper and deeper into the white race: aggressive negroids," bent on revenge for their enslavement, attempting to "inject the blood of Africa into Caucasian circles." Obsessed by the thought of such contamination, Cox described the prospect of a dusky future in what he clearly considered to be horrifying detail: "Imagine the mulattoes and the nearer whites of the United States to be greatly augmented in numbers. Suppose they constitute two-thirds of the population. They possess the ballot. . . . Caucasian ideals would assert a dwindling influence in politics, economics, and social aims. No white could hold high office without mongrel support, and the prospective office holder could not obtain such support without special concessions to the mixbreed element. White politicians would vie with each other in making promises which sooner or later would have to be fulfilled. Eventually the nation would cease to reflect Caucasian ideals and cease to represent Caucasian culture. The pall of Africanism would settle upon the land. Mulatto senators! Revolutions! Creative ingenuity gone, the arts and sciences would decay, sky-scrapers would crumble, plantations would be weedgrown. . . . The halls of the national capitol, once familiar to the noblest of the Saxons, would echo to the tread of mulattoes, and a mixbreed would sit as President."[47]

---

[47]William H. Tucker, *The Funding of Scientific Racism: Wickliffe Draper and the Pioneer Fund* (Urbana: University of Illinois Press, 2002) citing Ernest Sevier Cox, *White America: The American Racial Problem as Seen in a Worldwide Perspective* (Richmond: White America Society, 1923; rev. ed., 1937). Tucker's extensive quotation of Cox is from chap. 8 of *White America*, "Civilizations That Are Imperiled through Contact with Colored Races: Latin America." The complete text of *White America*, 2nd ed., is now available online at <http://www.churchoftrueisrael.com/cox>.

Influential whites in power shared Cox's paranoia and he

> found a hospitable home in Richmond for his supremacist and eugenic
> ideas. He moved there and published in 1923 the book *White America*,
> warning against destruction of the white civilization from racial intermar-
> riage. As cofounder with Plecker of the Anglo-Saxon Clubs of America,
> Cox provided much of the ideological firepower behind the Racial
> Integrity Act. Cox also teamed up with racist Theodore Bilbo, U.S. senator
> from Mississippi between 1935 and 1947, to promote bills for returning
> blacks to Africa. (Sen. Bilbo introduced the Greater Liberia Act into the
> U. S. Senate in April 1939.) Cox's book became a textbook for many
> university professors and was distributed, with funding from Wickliffe
> Draper, to members of Congress. The Virginian enjoyed support in high
> ranks of the national eugenics movement and was invited to address the
> Eugenics Research Association, a mainline group, in New York in 1936.
> Plecker went along. They visited the homes of national leaders, including
> Draper and Laughlin. Later Cox made contact with two Nazi racial
> theorists. One was Wilhelm Frick, the Nazi secretary of the interior, to
> whom he mailed a copy of *White America*. In a 1938 letter to Frick, Cox
> spoke of the "common Teutonic heritage" of Southern whites and
> Germans, and added, "Personally, I hold a high admiration for your
> country and an affection for your people." For Frick's activities as a Nazi
> administrator during the Holocaust, he was convicted during the Nurem-
> berg trials and executed in 1946.[48]

Cox also got the support of Harvard, the university that a century
earlier had taught polygenetics:

> William McDougall, the prominent professor of psychology and chair
> of the department at Harvard, endorsed Cox's work, calling a separate
> territory for blacks, preferably in Africa, "the only sound" policy. E. A.
> Ross, a well-known sociologist at the University of Wisconsin and one-
> time president of the American Sociological Association, also provided a
> statement of support for the book; a year later, after a lengthy trip through
> Africa, Ross wrote to Cox, agreeing that "African territory to which
> American negroes might be deported should be governed not by the
> inhabitants but from this country." And the *Eugenical News*, in its review
> of the book, declared that Cox "will be a greater savior of his country than
> George Washington" if he could save America "for the white race" by
> bringing about the expatriation of blacks—the only real solution to what

---

[48]Peter Hardin, *Richmond Times Dispatch*, 26 November 2000.

the *News* called "the worst thing that ever happened to the . . . United States, . . . the bringing of large numbers of the Negroes, nearly the lowest of races, to our shores.

With such enthusiastic endorsements, Cox was soon accepted as a fellow expert by those who sought a "scientific" solution to racial issues, someone to whom they could turn for advice on translating science into policy; indeed, his stature among eugenicists increased significantly in the 1930s as many respectable scientists, who had earlier been attracted to eugenics, abandoned the movement, leaving it primarily in the hands of scientific racists and Klan sympathizers. Cox provided expert assistance to Dr. W. A. Plecker, Virginia's state registrar, in crafting an amendment to the state's Racial Integrity Act that would prevent "near-white negroids" from passing as white or claiming to be "Indian" in order "to marry into the white race." When Plecker was invited to read a paper before the International Eugenic Conference in 1932, he merely restated *White America*'s argument that separation was the only alternative to eventual intermarriage, embellished by some details of Virginia's local effort to prevent "amalgamation." Cox's work also came to the attention of foreign experts interested in race. Madison Grant requested that Cox send a copy of *White America* to Professor Hans Günther, "one of the most distin-guished anthropologists of Germany," who "is in accord with all our views"; appointed by the Nazis to a major professorship over the local faculty"s opposition, Günther provided the theoretical foundation for the regime's racial theory and was regarded as its official ideological spokesperson on race.

The recognition of Cox's expertise produced an opportunity to speak to the Eugenics Research Association at its annual conference in New York in 1936, where he met, for the first time, with a benefactor who would solve the financial problems that had hindered his campaign. In early March, Cox received a letter from the association's president, Clarence G. Campbell, agreeing that "repatriation is the only true solution of the Negro problem," and within weeks an invitation to speak on that topic arrived from biologist Harry H. Laughlin, a long-time activist in the eugenics movement; as editor of the association's official organ, the *Eugenical News*, Laughlin had earlier written its highly favorable review of *White America*. Cox quickly sent Laughlin a copy of the talk he intended to give: the usual diatribe against the presence of blacks in the United States, which noted that the "white man's" meager support for repatriation was being interpreted in some quarters as an indication of his "assent to a final solution of the race problem by amalgamation."

However, one particular white man saw Cox's words and vowed not to assent to such an odious prospect. In the week before leaving for the conference, Cox learned from a number of sources that a wealthy New York was looking forward to meeting him. "One of our colleagues, Colonel W. P. Draper, is particularly interested in your work," wrote Laughlin. As editor of *Eugenical News* and someone who knew of Draper's interest in the evils of miscegenation and his willingness to provide resources to oppose it, Laughlin had informed him of Cox's imminent appearance in New York and the substance of his speech, recommending that the two colonels "meet personally." A biology professor at the University of Virginia, who had been offered financial assistance by Draper, also notified Cox that "Draper is seriously interested in the probable solution of the negro problem. He believes that repatriation is the only satisfactory solution and I believe will be able to support you in your work." Draper did indeed share Cox's obsession with repatriation, but more important he would provide the resources Cox lacked, making it possible for him to reach a much broader audience and acquire some influential political support. Cox's holy cause was about to become Draper's holy cause as well.[49]

The segregationists did not stop Marcus Garvey's deportation, but their scheme did not end:

> Garvey continued to associate with white supremacists during his exile in Jamaica and London, including John Powell of the Anglo-Saxon Clubs and propagandist Earnest Sevier Cox . . . [and] Sen. Theodore G. Bilbo, one of America's most notorious segregationists, who introduced the Greater Liberia Act into the U. S. Senate in April 1939. . . . [Bilbo], too, received the strong backing of Garvey.[50]

Whatever agreement Marcus Garvey thought he had with Virginia's white racists, it is clear they meant to betray him and retain control in Africa:

> Even after their removal to Africa, blacks would remain subordinate to whites in Cox's scheme: "The United States, as sovereign power over the repatriated negro will be possessed of executive . . . status" and "may enforce beneficial measures." "It is to the negro's advantage," Cox

---

[49]William H. Tucker, "Our Northern Friend: A Tale of Two Colonels," chap. 1 of his *The Funding of Scientific Racism: Wickliffe Draper and the Pioneer Fund* (Urbana: University of Illinois Press, 2002).

[50]Paul Lee, "Strange Bedfellows: The Curious Courtship [of] Black Nationalists and White Supremacists," *The Michigan Citizen* (Highland Park MI), 24 February–2 March 2002, as posted, "in slightly different form," at <http://afgen.com/bedfellows.html>.

maintained, "that the white extend influence over the negro, whether the latter dwell in America or Africa."[51]

Sterilization and prison were just parts of Virginia's final solution for the Melungeons. The state's segregationists, with help from New York industrialists and Marcus Garvey, meant to quarantine Melungeons in Liberia. As Garvey wrote to Ernest Cox on August 8: "The mongrel in our midst is a danger to both races and it is equally dutiful to black and white to stem the tide."[52]

In the Garvey Papers is preserved Dr. Plecker's letter of March 19, 1927, to President Coolidge.

Sir:

> I learn that the application of Marcus Garvey for pardon, and release from the Federal Prison at Atlanta, is to be presented to you shortly by the Department of Justice. I am one of a considerable number of white people of Virginia who have given his case thought. . . . I plead in his behalf that he may be pardoned, and permitted to continue his work with his race in this country. One of Garvey's chief aims is to inspire his people with the desire to preserve their racial purity, and to teach them abhorrence of mongrelization as it is progressing in the South in spite of restrictions as to intermarriage, and in other sections at a more rapid rate, because of the lack of such restrictions.[53]

Mixed Americans faced two foes—white and black. Plecker said: "The mongrels . . . lack the creative power of the higher race, and cannot sustain a lasting civilization that will rank with the best of the world."[54] Garvey responded, "The mongrel in our midst is a danger to both races and it is equally dutiful to black and white to stem the tide."[55]

---

[51]Tucker, *The Funding of Scientific Racism*, chap. 1, n. 8, quoting Cox's *White America* (353, 354).

[52]"Marcus Garvey to Earnest S. Cox — 8/8/25" online at <http://www.marcusgarvey.com/wmview.php?ArtID=154>.

[53]"W. A. Plecker to President Calvin Coolidge," 19 March 1927, as at <http://www.marcusgarvey.com/wmview.php?ArtID=196>.

[54]Plecker, "Virginia's Attempt to Adjust the Color Problem," in *The American Journal of Public Health* (1925) and now online at <http://www.webcom.com/~intvoice/powell5.html>.

[55]"Marcus Garvey to Earnest S. Cox — 8/8/25" at <http://www.marcusgarvey.com/wmview.php?ArtID=154>.

Senator Bilbo's World War II bill to deport U.S. citizens of color to Africa was outlined in his book, *Take Your Choice, Separation or Mongrelization.* In the introduction to Bilbo's book, Earnest Sevier Cox, named after the old Welsh myth-making, land-stealing governor of Tennessee, described more than a century of failures to send blacks to Africa:

> The Virginia General Assembly had memorialized the Congress to grant aid to Negroes who desire to continue the colonization of Liberia. . . .
>
> . . . Senator Bilbo, in a speech of more than two hours duration ably set forth the efforts made by Jefferson and Lincoln, and by other eminent Americans, to effect the colonization of the Negro.
>
> . . . Jefferson and Lincoln knew that a race problem is a biological one that cannot be solved save by separating the races, or by their blood amalgamation.

Cox lamented that mixed Americans opposed African repatriation: "This agitation is led almost wholly by certain mixbreeds, the products of race mixing and the advocates of it."[56]

By the outbreak of World War II, the U.S. Liberia Act was taken off the front burner.

---

[56]Earnest Sevier Cox, introduction to Theodore Gilmore Bilbo, *Take Your Choice: Separation or Mongrelization* (Poplarville MS: Dream House Pub. Co., 1947; repr.: Decature GA: Historical Review Press U.S.A., 1980). The complete text of *Take Your Choice,* including of course the introduction, may be accessed online at <http://www. churchoftrueisrael.com/tyc/tyc_toc.html>.

Chapter 11

Complexities of Complexions

During 400 years of British migration to North America, mixed marriages have occurred legally during only two generations. The first generation began with the church wedding of John Rolfe and Pocahontas in Jamestown in 1614. Mixed marriage remained legal until 1691 when the Virginia legislature forbade whites marrying blacks or Indians. This ban lasted almost 300 years, until the landmark 1967 U.S. Supreme Court case of *Loving v. Virginia.*

In 1958, Richard Loving, a white man, and Mildred Jeter, a black woman, were married in Washington D.C. Their home state of Virginia was one of sixteen states opposing mixed marriage. The Lovings moved to Caroline County, Virginia, where in 1959, deputy sheriffs entered their home at night and arrested the couple in bed for violating state law. Tried and convicted, each was sentenced to a year in prison. The judge offered to suspend the sentence if they left Virginia for twenty-five years. The Lovings moved and then sued over the constitutionality of banning mixed marriage. The Virginia Supreme Court of Appeals upheld the law in 1966, but the following year, the U.S. Supreme Court unanimously ruled the law unconstitutional.[1] *Loving v. Virginia* launched English-speaking America's second legal mixed generation of today.

In recent decades, a so-called "positive" racism—still the quest for ethnic pride—has emerged in the U.S. Children as early as grade school receive institutionalized indoctrination on the "importance of knowing

---

[1]"Loving v. Virginia," in *The Guide to American Law: Everyone's Legal Encyclopedia*, 12 vols. (St. Paul MN: West Publishing Co., 1983–1985). Supreme Court of the United States, "Loving v. Virginia," no. 395, argued April 10, 1967. Decided June 12, 1967. 388 U.S. 1. See online: <www.brownat50.org/PostBrownCases/LovingvVirginia1967.html>.

where you came from."[2] However, this "diversity training" pressures mixed children to pick one parent's ethnicity over the other.

Mixed families responded to positive racism by demanding a legal identity in the legislatures and courts.[3] Susan Graham of ProjectRace and others went to Congress and got the 2000 U.S. Census changed to let people choose more than one ethnic category. Seven million Americans responded.[4] Next, mixed Americans pointed out that they lack civil rights enjoyed by whites and minorities. For example, an employer may have no bias against whites, blacks, American Indians, and Asians. But suppose the employer disapproves of mixed marriage and discriminates against someone of mixed ancestry? The multiethnic employee cannot file a complaint with the EEOC unless that employee files as a single-minority category. Federal law protects an employee of one race who is married to a person of another race, but does not protect a mixed-race employee.[5]

The law protects employees described as "light-skinned African Americans."[6] Mixed people regard the term "light-skinned African American" as perpetuating the old "one drop" law of segregation.[7] "One

---

[2]Dianne Sawyer and Robin Roberts, Racial relations interview with groups of Mobile, Alabama children about race, "Good Morning America," ABC Television, 20 January 2003.

[3]W. S. C. Poston, "The Biracial Identity Development Model: A Needed Addition," *Journal of Counseling and Development* 69/2 (November-December 1990): 152-55.

[4]"CensusScope. Census 2000 Data Charts, Maps, and Rankings," analyzed by the Social Science Data Analysis Network (SSDAN), Population Studies Center, University of Michigan. An online resource at <http://www.censusscope.org>.

[5]"Tetro v. Elliott, Popham Pontiac, Oldsmobile, Buick, and GMC Trucks, Inc., 173 F.3d 988, 994-95 (6th Cir. 1999)." EEOC Directives Transmittal no. 915.003 to EEOC Compliance Manual holders. Online: <http://www.eeoc.gov/policy/docs/threshold.html>.

[6]"Walker v. Secretary of the Treasury, 713 F. Supp. 403, 405-08 (N.D. Ga. 1989)." EEOC Directives Transmittal no. 915.003 to EEOC Compliance Manual holders. Online: <http://www.eeoc.gov/policy/docs/threshold.html>.

[7]Susan Graham, the mother of a multiracial child, was influential in arguing for census changes enabling respondents the chance to check more than one box in the list of racial categories in the 2000 U.S. Census. In an e-mail message, Graham wrote to me: "In reality, the EEOC does not recognize multiracial persons, and therefore, a multiracial person cannot file a claim for discrimination. The EEOC still uses a method of racial classification that we call 'eyeballing.' EEOC form 100 instructs employers to classify employees by race by looking at them, and not to ASK an employee their race. So, in reality, a person in HR looks at an employee upon employment and 'guesses' their race (not races). Even if they 'guessed' that a person was multiracial, under the U.S. government counting scheme, the person would be tabulated back into the five main racial and ethnic categories. A multiracial person could sue if they were discriminated against because someone thought they were black, white,

drop" meant that anyone with as little as "one drop" of African ancestry was black.

Why is a *light-skinned black* not regarded as a *dark-skinned white*? . . . Today, the United States still uses "one drop" for African ethnicity.

As mixed activists pressed the government to reform "one-drop" enforcement, they met opposition, but not from whites. Seeking support and inclusion with minority advocacy groups they were rebuffed.[8] Fearful of a mixed category, "the NAACP, the National Council of La Raza, and a number of Native American advocacy groups opposed a multiracial category, concerned that it could negatively affect voting rights enforcement and allocations for social and school programs based on minority participation."[9]

But, with an estimated 100,000 mixed American children born each year, the pressure to acknowledge mixed Americans is building and people are speaking out.[10]

Tiger Woods, the son of a father who is one-half black, one-quarter American Indian, and one-quarter white, and a mother who is one-half Thai and one-half Chinese, is bothered *only* by being called black and describes himself with a word he made up, "Cablinasian," that is, Caucasian-Black-Indian-Asian.[11]

Self-definition bothers African American activists who fear minority-voting strength will suffer from redistricting. During congressional hearings

---

Asian, Hispanic, or American Indian, but NOT multiracial. It's completely unjust." E-mail: Subject: "Multiracial EEOC." Date: 3/31/03 7:26:35 AM Central Standard Time. From: Susan Graham, President, Project RACE, Inc.

   [8]Jane Ayers Chiong, *Racial Categorization of Multiracial Children in Schools* (Westport CT: Bergin & Garvey, 1998).

   [9]Wendy Schwartz, "The Identity Development of Multiracial Youth," *ERIC/CUE Digest* no. 137 (New York, November 1998) 9 pages. (ERIC = Education Resources Information Center, U.S. Dept. of Education; CUE = Clearinghouse on Urban Education.) Full text at <http://www.eric.ed.gov/ERICDocs/data/ericdocs2/content_storage_01/0000000b/80/2a/2c/90.pdf>; unofficial version of text at <http://www.ericdigests.org/1999-3/identity.htm>.

   [10]Maria P. P. Root, *The Multiracial Experience: Racial Borders as the New Frontier* (Thousand Oaks CA: Sage Publications, 1996).

   [11]Tiger Woods: "Growing up, I came up with this name: I'm a 'Cablinasian.' . . . I'm just who I am, . . . whoever you see in front of you." As interviewed by Oprah Winfrey (29 April 1997). And see "Cablinasian like Me: Tiger Woods's Rejection of Orthodox Racial Classification Points the Way to a Future Where Race Will No Longer Define Us," by Gary Kamiya, online at <http://www.salon.com/april97/tiger970430.html>.

on allowing "Multiracial" as a category in the 2010 U.S. census, Representative Carrie Meek (D-NY), opposed:

> I understand how Tiger Woods and the rest of them feel. But no matter how they feel from a personal standpoint, we're thinking about the census and reporting accuracy. . . . The multiracial category would cloud the count of [the] discrete minorities who are assigned to a lower track in public schools, . . . kept out of certain occupations, and whose progress toward seniority or promotion has been skewered. . . . Lastly, . . . multiracial categories will reduce the level of political representation for minorities.[12]

Unless legally recognized, mixed Americans have little recourse against hate crimes, when, for example, mainstream moviemaker Spike Lee whose movies present negative portrayals of mixing, says, "I give interracial couples a look. Daggers. They get uncomfortable when they see me on the street."[13] Lee's hostility is traditional in a society where bias against mixed couples and mixed people is centuries old.[14]

Despite legislative apathy, mixed topics are being treated more evenly in some recent movies[15] and by mixed actors.[16] Today, the face of America on magazine covers is Jennifer Lopez, Jessica Alba, Vin Diesal, and Christina Aguilera. *Teen People* magazine editor Amy Barnett says "We're seeing more of a desire for the exotic, left-of-center beauty that transcends race or class."[17]

According to Ruth La Ferla of the *New York Times*, some are even beginning to question the reality of race: "Such a transition—from racial

---

[12]Carrie Meek, Congressional hearings testimony, Census 2000, 106th Congress, 1st session, 23 April 1997, reported, e.g., by Amitai Etzioni, "A New American Race?" *The Responsive Community* 10/2 (Spring 2000); see online at <http://www.gwu.edu/~ccps/rcq/rcq_newrace_etzioni.html>.

[13]Barbara Grizzuti Harrison,"Spike Hates Your Cracker Ass," *Esquire Magazine* (October 1992): 132.

[14]For example, Thomas Branagan in 1805 Philadelphia, cited by Lerone Bennett, *Before the Mayflower*, 7th ed. (Chicago: Johnson Pub., 2003).

[15]See "Race Relations Guide on About.com." ("Kimberly Hohman is the guide for this About.com expert guide on race relations. The guide examines political and social issues related to race.") <www.racerelations.about.com>.

[16]Best Actress category, Halle Berry. See "The 2002 Oscars" at <filmcritic.com>.

[17]Quoted by Ruth La Ferla, "Generation E.A.: Ethnically Ambiguous," *New York Times*, 28 December 2003. Archived online at <http://forums.yellowworld.org/archive/index.php/t-11986.html>.

diversity portrayed as a beautiful mosaic to a melting pot—is in line with the currently fashionable argument that race itself is a fiction." La Ferla quotes Harvard professor Evelyn Hammond who describes race as "a concept we invented to categorize the perceived biological, social, and cultural differences between human groups."[18]

But while American culture is waking up to the new "Generation MiX," the U.S. Congress slumbers. The Commonwealth of Virginia still refuses to reveal the surnames of the victims of eugenical sterilization, surnames that Melungeons wished Virginia had not revealed to Walter Plecker sixty years ago.

The Return of Eugenics

Disgraced by German atrocities, eugenics faded after World War II, but today neo-Galtonion eugenics is again pervading scientific and legislative circles. Col. Draper's Pioneer Fund continues to this present day to push U.N. population-control policies in underdeveloped nations and to support radical eugenical scientists. James D. Watson, the celebrated codiscoverer of human DNA is now the director of Cold Spring Harbor Labs, started by Hitler's old pal Harry Laughlin. In 1989, Dr. Watson was appointed to direct his pet project—the National Center for Human Genome Research, which is part of the international aim to map the human genome in the world's different ethnic populations.[19] Dr. Watson, an unapologetic eugenicist, defends radical eugenics policies: "People say we are playing God. My answer is, if we don't play God, who will?"[20]

More than two decades after World War II, Watson's codiscoverer and fellow eugenicist, Francis Crick, shocked an audience of scientists with a lecture on future scientific approaches:

> [Francis Crick] inferred that "[W]e cannot continue to regard all human life as sacred." The idea that every person has a soul and that his life must be saved at all costs should not be allowed; instead the status of life and death should be reconsidered. If, for example, a child were to be

---

[18]La Ferla, "Generation E.A.: Ethnically Ambiguous."

[19]Cold Spring Harbor Laboratory <http://www.cshl.edu>.

[20]As quoted in *Predictions: 30 Great Minds on the Future*, ed. Sian Griffiths, and with an introduction by Jonathan Weiner (New York: Oxford University Press, 1999). See also "The Stuff of Life," *Observer Magazine* (Sunday, 6 April 2003): " 'If scientists don't play God,' [Watson] wonders, eyes bright, 'who else is going to?' "

considered legally born when two days old, it could be examined to see whether it was an "acceptable member of human society." It might also be desirable to define a person as legally dead when he was past the age of 80 or 85, and then expensive medical equipment should be forbidden to him.
. . .

If new biological advances demand a continuous readjustment of ethical ideas, how are people to be persuaded to adapt to the situation? Clearly by education, and [Crick] did not think it right that religious instruction should be given to young children. Instead they should be taught the modern scientific view of man's place in the universe, in the world, and in society, and the nature of scientific truth. Not only traditional religious values must be reexamined, but also what might be called liberal views about society. It is obvious that not all men are born equal and it is by no means clear that all races are equally gifted.[21]

Racism is not inherent in the underclass. American racism began 300 years ago when monarchs, gentlemen, and scholars ruled. Within such racism is a denial of conscience and morality either by the scholar, such as that by social Darwinists Crick and Watson, or ascribed by scholars to the targets of loathing, as by Virginia lawmakers who in 1732 claimed the *malungu* generation of the *White Lion* were

people of such base and corrupt natures, that the credit of their testimony cannot be certainly depended upon. . . . That no negro, Mulatto, or Indian, either a slave or free, shall hereafter be admitted in any court of this colony, to be sworn as a witness, or give evidence in any cause whatsoever, except upon the trial of a slave, for a capital offence. . . . [22]

Examine the silenced testimony of the *malungu*. Were they tricksters, children of perdition? Perhaps. Seeking equality, some claimed to descend from a Cherokee princess, or to be Portuguese, Phoenician, Welsh, Black Dutch, or Black Irish.

-----

[21]From a review of Crick's Rickman Godlee Lecture, "The Social Impact of Biology" (24 October 1968) in *Nature Magazine* (2 November 1968), as quoted by Daniel Eisenberg, "Why Medical Ethics?" online at <http://www.aish.com/society/Work/sciencenature/Why_Medical_Ethics$.asp>.

[22]William W. Hening, ed., *The Statutes at Large; Being a Collection of All the Laws of Virginia, from the First Session of the Legislature in the Year 1619*, 13 vols. (1819–1823; facsimile repr.: Charlottesville VA: University Press of Virginia, 1969) 4:327: "Negros, Mulattoes, and Indians disabled to be witnesses, except on the trial of a Slave" (sidebar).

But weigh their myths against the deadlier myths of fools who claim to be gods and supermen, who deny conscience and morality either in themselves or in the "inferiors" they victimize.

The "children of perdition" aspired not to be supermen but to be equal.

Selected Bibliography

Berry, Brewton. *Almost White*. New York: Macmillan Co., 1963.

Block, W. T. "Meanest Town on the Coast." *Old West* (Winter 1979).

DeMarce, Virginia Easley. "The Melungeons." *National Genealogy Society Quarterly* 84/2 (June 1996).

_____. "Very Slightly Mixt: Tri-Racial Isolate Families of the Upper South—A Genealogical Study." *National Genealogical Society Quarterly* (March 1992).

Deal, Douglas. *Race and Class in Colonial Virginia: Indians, Englishmen, and Africans on the Eastern Shore during the Seventeenth Century*. (Revision of the author's dissertation.) New York: Garland, 1993.

Draper, Lyman C. *The Life of Daniel Boone*. Edited with an introduction by Ted Franklin Belue. Mechanicsburg PA: Stackpole Books, 1998.

Evans, Raymond. "The Graysville Melungeons; A Triracial People in Lower East Tennessee." *Tennessee Anthropologist* 4/1 (1979).

Gallagher, Nancy L. *Breeding Better Vermonters: The Eugenics Project in the Green Mountain State*. Hanover NH: University Press of New England, 1999.

Gregg, Alexander. *History of the Old Cheraws: Containing an Account of the Aborigines of the Pedee, the First White Settlements, Their Subsequent Progress, Civil Changes, the Struggle of the Revolution, and Growth of the Country Afterward; Extending from about A.D. 1730 to 1810, with Notices of Families and Sketches of Individuals*. New York: Richardson and Co., 1867. Repr.: Baltimore: Genealogical Publishing Co., 1967.

Hashaw, Tim. "Malungu: African Origin of American Melungeons," *Appalachian Quarterly* 6/3 (September 2001) and 6/4 (December 2001).

_____. "Malungu: The Mbundu-African Origin of the American Melungeons," at <http://freepages.genealogy.rootsweb.com/~gowenrf/malangu.htm> (no date).

_____. "Malungu: The African Origin of the American Melungeons," at <http://www.eclecta.org/v5n3/hashaw.html> (no date).

_____. See also links to a series of my articles on the Gowen Research Foundation's "Melungia" page: <http://freepages.genealogy.rootsweb.com/~gowenrf/melun.htm> (modified and accessed on 7 November 2005).

Haun, Mildred. *The Hawk's Done Gone and Other Stories*. Edited by Herschel Gower. Nashville: Vanderbilt University Press, 1968.

Heinegg, Paul. *Free African Americans of North Carolina, Virginia, and South Carolina from the Colonial Period to about 1820*. Fourth and revised edition. Baltimore: Genealogical Publishing Co. and Clearfield Company, 2001.

Hening, William Walter, editor. *The Statutes at Large. Being a Collection of All the Laws of Virginia, from the First Session of the Legislature in the Year 1619*. Thirteen volumes. Facsimile reprint: Charlottesville: University Press of Virginia for the

Jamestown Foundation of the Commonwealth of Virginia, 1969. Originally published 1819–1823 pursuant to an act (5 February 1808) of the General Assembly of Virginia. (Most of Hening has been transcribed and posted on the internet and may be accessed at <http://www.vagenweb.org/hening/>.)

Ivey, Saundra Keys. "Oral, Printed, and Popular Culture Traditions Related to the Melungeons of Hancock County, Tennessee." Thesis, Indiana University, 1976.

Jordan, Winthrop D. *White over Black: American Attitudes toward the Negro, 1550–1812.* Chapel Hill: University of North Carolina Press for the Institute of Early American History and Culture at Williamsburg VA, 1968.

Jordan-Bychkov, Terry G. *Trails to Texas: Southern Roots of Western Cattle Ranching.* Lincoln: University of Nebraska Press, 1981.

Kingsbury, Susan Myra, editor. *The Records of the Virginia Company of London, 1607–1626.* Four volumes. Edited with an introduction and bibliography by Susan M. Kingsbury. (From the Thomas Jefferson Papers, series 8: Virginia Records Manuscripts, 1606–1737.) Washington DC: Government Printing Office, 1906–1935.

Kühl, Stefan. *The Nazi Connection: Eugenics, American Racism, and German National Socialism.* New York: Oxford University Press, 1994.

Lapon, Lenny. *Mass Murderers in White Coats.* Springfield MA: Psychiatric Genocide Research Institute, 1986.

Lombardo, Paul A. "Eugenic Laws against Race Mixing. Image Archive on the American Eugenics Movement." Dolan DNA Learning Center, Cold Spring Harbor Laboratory. <eugenicsarchive.org>.

Malchow, Howard L. *Gothic Images of Race in Nineteenth Century Britain.* Stanford CA: Stanford University Press, 1996.

Marler, Don C. *Red Bones of Louisiana.* Hemphill TX: Dogwood Press, 2003.

Morton, Samuel George. *Crania Americana; or, A Comparative View of the Skulls of Various Aboriginal Nations of North and South America: To Which Is Prefixed an Essay on the Varieties of the Human Species.* Philadelphia: Dobson, 1839.

_____. *Crania Americana; or, A Comparative View of the Skulls of Various Aboriginal Nations of North and South America; Crania Ægyptica: From Transactions of the American Philosophical Society, volume 9 (1844).* Facsimile edition, with an introduction and editor's notes by Robert Bernasconi. American Theories of Polygenesis 1. Bristol VA: Thoemmes, 2002 (1839).

_____. *Crania Ægyptica; or, Observations on Egyptian Ethnography, Derived from Anatomy, History, and the Monuments.* ("From the Transactions of the American Philosophical Society, volume 9 [1844].") Philadelphia: J. Pennington, 1844.

Price, Edward T. "The Melungeons: A Mixed-Blood Strain of the Southern Appalachians." *Geographical Review* (April 1951).

Reilly, P. R. "The Virginia Racial Integrity Act Revisited: The Plecker-Laughlin Correspondence: 1928–1930." *American Journal of Medical Genetics* 16 (1983): 483-92.

Rountree, Helen C. *Pocahontas's People: The Powhatan Indians of Virginia through Four Centuries.* The Civilization of the American Indian series 196. Norman: University of Oklahoma Press, 1990.

Sluiter, Engel. "New Light on the '20 and Odd Negroes' Arriving in Virginia in 1619." *William & Mary Quarterly* 54/2 (1997).

Smith, J. David. *The Eugenic Assault on America*. Fairfax VA: George Mason University Press, 1993.

Sovine, Melanie Lou. "The Mysterious Melungeons: A Critique of Mythical Image." Thesis, University of Kentucky, 1982.

Thornton, John. "The African Experience of The '20 and Odd Negroes' Arriving in Virginia in 1619." *William & Mary Quarterly* 55/3 (1998).

Tucker, William H. *The Funding of Scientific Racism: Wickliffe Draper and the Pioneer Fund*. Urbana: University of Illinois Press, 2002.

William and Mary Quarterly. A Magazine of Early American History and Culture. Continues *William and Mary College Quarterly Historical Magazine* (1892–1918/1919, 1921–1943). Publisher: Omohundro Institute of Early American History and Culture.

Woodson, Carter Godwin. *Free Negro Heads of Families in the United States in 1830, together with a Brief Treatment of the Free Negro*. "Second of a series of documentary studies of the free Negro provided for by a grant . . . from the Laura Spelman Rockefeller Memorial in 1921." Washington DC: Association for the Study of Negro Life and History, 1925.

Index